On

Being

and

Having

a

Case

Manager

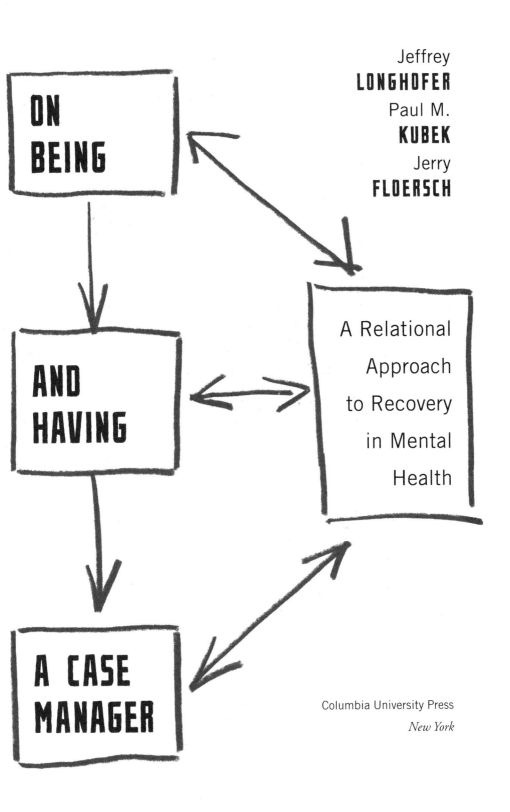

ON BEING

AND HAVING

A CASE MANAGER

A Relational Approach to Recovery in Mental Health

Jeffrey **LONGHOFER**
Paul M. **KUBEK**
Jerry **FLOERSCH**

Columbia University Press
New York

Columbia University Press

Publishers Since 1893

New York   Chichester, West Sussex

Copyright © 2010 Columbia University Press

Library of Congress Cataloging-in-Publication Data

Longhofer, Jeffrey L. (Jeffrey Lee)

On being and having a case manager : a relational approach to recovery in mental
health / Jeffrey Longhofer, Paul M. Kubek, and Jerry Floersch.

p. ; cm.

Includes bibliographical references and index.

ISBN 978-0-231-13265-7 (cloth : alk. paper) — ISBN 978-0-231-13266-4 (pbk. : alk. paper)
— ISBN 978-0-231-52553-4 (ebook)

1. Psychiatric social work—Case studies.   2. Mental health personnel and patient.
I. Kubek, Paul M.   II. Floersch, Jerry.   III. Title.

[DNLM: 1. Professional-Patient Relations—Case Reports.   2. Social Work, Psychiatric—
methods—Case Reports.   3. Case Management—organization & administration—Case
Reports.   4. Mental Disorders—rehabilitation—Case Reports.   WM 30.5 L8540 2010]

HV689.L56 2010

362.2′0425—dc22

2009041205

Columbia University Press books are printed on permanent and durable acid-free paper.

This book is printed on paper with recycled content.

Printed in the United States of America

c 10 9 8 7 6 5 4 3 2 1

p 10 9 8 7 6 5 4 3 2 1

References to Internet Web sites (URLs) were accurate at the time of writing. Neither
the author nor Columbia University Press is responsible for URLs that may have expired or
changed since the manuscript was prepared.

In memory of John Michel

Contents

Acknowledgments

We have many people to thank. This study involved case managers and consumers who were more than willing to let us into their daily lives over many months. They welcomed us. They were eager to tell their stories. And it is through our working with and listening to managers and consumers that this book developed. Many of the ideas developed here come directly from our work with them. Many, many thanks for your patience and guidance. It has been a great pleasure to have you as our teachers. At Columbia University Press, we owe the late John Michel special gratitude. He invited and encouraged this project and offered advice along the way, and it is to his memory that the book is dedicated. Thanks, too, to the Ohio Department of Mental Health, specifically Dr. Michael Hogan (now head of the New York State Department of Mental Health) and Dr. Dee Roth for supporting the work with a generous grant. We owe a special thanks to Lisa Oswald. Lisa, a graduate student at the Mandel School of Applied Social Sciences at the time the research was conducted, collected data and produced volumes of detailed and thoughtful and feelingful notes that led to these rich narratives. It is to Dr. Anna Janicki that we owe our understanding of shame and its dynamics in the delivery of mental health services. She helped us know what shame feels like and how it differs from other human emotions. And it may well be the one emotion that makes the difference. Finally, we'd like to thank Dr. Richard Edwards, dean of the Rutgers University School of Social Work, for offering a new opportunity.

On

Being

and

Having

a

Case

Manager

Introduction

The
Relational
Method
for
Recovery

There is something about the scent of a freshly lit cigarette. It is simple and sweet. Maybe it has something to do with the initial moment when fire touches tobacco and sets free the secrets of the earth contained within the leaf. There is something about the glow, too, the way it signals the presence of that first breath, which draws the sweetness of tobacco down into the secrets of the soul. Maybe this is why Marilyn is so deliberate about lighting her cigarette. Maybe this is why she stares, as if watching a dream, as she pushes the smoke past her lips in a steady stream toward the sky.

She is twenty-three. Her face is round and heavy and white. She seems older. Marilyn is sitting at a picnic table across from Lisa, a social work researcher, who has been helping Marilyn prepare for a move to a new apartment. They are revising a to-do list; and Marilyn is telling her that she needs to save money. She needs to buy appliances and furnishings. She must arrange for a truck and for people to carry moving boxes. She needs to learn how to use a checkbook. She reminds Lisa that she is working with the social service agency to complete the paperwork to get control of finances. Her mother, now managing her money, wants this to end.

The picnic table where they sit is in a park on a hill overlooking Lake Erie, the shallowest of the Great Lakes. The shoreline, seventy feet below, stretches to the northeast and to the northwest as far as the eye can see, in one big arching smile that curves toward Canada, which no one can see. Out there is nothing but water: It fills the smile with its mood.

It is a perfect summer day. The sky is a deep, comforting blue, spotted with billowy white clouds. It is warm but not hot, and a gentle breeze pushes the water lightly against the large rocks along the shore. From the hilltop where the women sit, there is no sound, just the view of water and sky. It seems just the right setting for their conversation today.

For years Marilyn has dreamed of moving to an apartment of her own. And for the first time it seems close to reality. The social service agency has placed her on a list for the next available unit. It is exciting; and although she feels the prospect of change, she is calm. She changes the topic with the stutter-start of a question she is not quite sure she should ask. With this question, she invites Lisa to a church festival in the neighborhood where she grew up. Her mother, sister, and two nieces will be there. She looks to the lake before saying to Lisa, "It would be a good time for you to meet them."

In this moment, Lisa cannot decide whether her attendance will fit into the guidelines of the research study. She is supposed to be observing the interactions between Marilyn and the people helping her recover from symptoms of mental illness, including family members, friends, and health and human service workers; a church festival may not qualify as an observable event.[1] Lisa does not want to cross the line that separates the professional from the personal, a line that gets fuzzy with questions like this. Before directing the conversation back to the list of things for the pending move, she tells Marilyn that she will check her schedule.

Marilyn responds with the stutter-start of another question. She is hesitant to ask. Again she is staring out over the lake, at that long thin line of nothingness where the sky and water converge. "What happens to me when the study is over?" she asks. "Do I ever get to see you again?"

* * *

This book is written for everyone like Lisa and Marilyn who wonders about the role of human relationships in mental health recovery. We argue for the importance of relationship by closely examining its process, that is, the back-and-forth exchange of attention and information that occurs between people. We will explain how case managers can use the process of sharing attention and information intentionally to help clients develop or enhance abilities to achieve their greatest potential for living independently in the community with hope, satisfaction, and success.

We focus on case managers and clients with symptoms of severe mental illness because these are the main characters in the story that unfolds on the following pages. The research project that inspired this book and provided the rich data and case studies for the telling of Marilyn's story is described in appendix 1.[2] Lisa is a social work researcher in Cleveland, Ohio, who is a participant–observer case manager. Marilyn, a client in the public mental health system, is navigating relationships with others in the community, including family members, friends, and health and human service providers such as psychiatrists, physicians, nurses, housing specialists, and employment specialists. The story you are about to read unfolds in a linear time sequence. Each chapter and reported event has two parts: a scene titled "Observe," which describes the interaction between Marilyn and Lisa, and a reflection on the scene, titled "Reflect," which explores the work of the case manager and how she used the relationship to draw attention to her client's strengths, namely, her own feelings, thoughts, and actions.

The story is told in a third-person narrative voice that acts as a movie camera in each scene. Sometimes it hovers close to the client. Sometimes it hovers close to the case manager. Sometimes it drifts up and out of the scene in a panorama to report on larger issues. In moments like these, we draw on what we know about the social, historical, and intellectual context of what the narrator reports. In many scenes, the narrative voice hovers close to the case manager because she is the one who conducted the research and observed, not only Marilyn but also herself. This is why the book is written for case managers. However, it is not written exclusively for them but for everyone with whom they interact in everyday relationships, including consumers, family members of consumers, and other service providers.[3] In short, this is a book about being and having a case manager.[4]

Keep It Simple

This book describes a practical method for engaging in supportive recovery relationships. Because the method uses ordinary everyday language, everybody involved in mental health care, including service providers, clients, and family members and close friends, can share it. It is important to emphasize that we are not proposing here a new service model for mental health treatment. This is not meant to be a substitute for the many, varied, and important case management models: recovery, assertive community treatment, or strengths.[5] Rather, we offer a method of relating that is down-to-earth and intentionally collaborative. The method functions like a common user interface for and a complement to existing models. This is why the ordinary everyday language in this book is built on clinical theories that have been developed from close observations of human relationships, including therapeutic relationships, but it keeps most of that language in the background.

Do not let the words *clinical theories* and *therapeutic relationships* intimidate you. We use them here simply to distinguish between relationships that are arranged to help people understand and navigate their intrapersonal (internal) and interpersonal worlds and those that are not. For example, relationships between psychotherapists and their clients are therapeutic. However, relationships between employers and employees are not, nor are those between teachers and students and between parents and children. Relationships between case managers and clients are often not as clearly delineated. Sometimes the relationships are therapeutic. Sometimes they are not. It depends on the philosophy and mission of the organization that employs and trains managers and provides mental health services. However, as you will discover from the story that unfolds in the following chapters, it is helpful for case management relationships to lean toward the therapeutic, especially because those relationships are intended to help people live with and recover from disruptive and debilitating symptoms of mental illness. Of course, the case manager cannot substitute for the psychotherapist or psychiatrist. And although it is not the role of the case manager to provide therapy, case managers trained to use a more clinical approach and the method proposed here will not only complement the work of psychiatry and psychotherapy. It will also prepare managers for ways of relating with others in the community: family members, psychiatrists and nurses, and co-workers. And perhaps most important, understanding how to relate, using this method, can enhance all models of case management, in many settings and with many populations.

Before we outline the relationship method and language explored in this book, we first need to clarify a few ideas about mental illness, mental health, and recovery. One of the simplest and most effective ways to understand human experience is to think about the relationship between our internal (intrapsychic) and external worlds (interpersonal or intersubjective). Throughout life—from birth to old age—each of us uses internal resources (feelings and thoughts) to acquire external resources, such as food, clothing, housing, medicine, education, employment, income, and supportive relationships and services. In short, we strive to meet our needs and desires. The internal and external worlds constantly interact, each influencing the other (figure I.1).

SELF AND SOCIETY

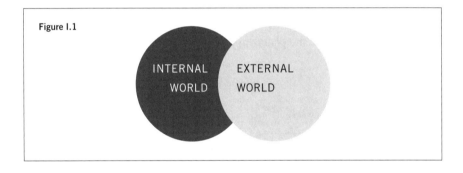

Figure I.1

INTERNAL WORLD

EXTERNAL WORLD

Like the world around us (our social surround or environment), our internal world is in a constant state of flux. It is always changing. Sometimes we feel vibrant and alive. Sometimes we feel quiet and still. At times, the shifts are manageable: We find a way to manage the tension between the two to achieve our goals with success and satisfaction. In other words, we maintain our mental health. However, sometimes the shifts are difficult to manage. We experience unbearable, disruptive, or debilitating feelings and thoughts, which inhibit our abilities to take care of ourselves, to interact with others, and to feel satisfied. In other words, we experience mental illness.

Mental health and mental illness are complex topics, and there are limitations to these simple definitions. However, we want to inspire you to think about both in the context of ordinary everyday life. Mental health and mental illness—like physical health and illness—are a part of our collective human experience. The potential for both coexists in each of us continuously. Mental illness is not something that happens only to "others," like Marilyn. We must be cautious, always, not to treat those with symptoms as "others," so different from us that we lose contact. And if we lose contact, we're likely to treat "others" as cases, as objects to be managed.

Symptoms

The technical or clinical term for mental illness is *mental disorder*. All disorders have symptoms, which are internal experiences (feelings, thoughts, self-perceptions) and external expressions (behaviors or actions). There are many symptoms—too numerous to list here.

In an attempt to understand symptoms and their impact, the American Psychiatric Association publishes the *Diagnostic and Statistical Manual of Mental Disorders* (*DSM*), which most mental health and human service providers use to assess clients, diagnose mental disorders, and plan their work with clients (table I.1).

TABLE I.1

SYMPTOM CHECKLIST

Examples of Symptoms	Type of Mental Disorder
Depressed mood Loss of interest in life Changes in sleep Changes in appetite Feelings of worthlessness Suicidal thoughts	Depressive mood disorders
Panic attacks Phobias (unreasonable fears) Chronic worrying Obsessions (intrusive thoughts)	Anxiety disorders

Compulsions (rituals that must be performed to decrease obsessions)	
Hallucinations (hearing voices or seeing things that others do not) Disorganized speech Disorganized behavior Delusions (fixed false beliefs)	Schizophrenia and psychotic disorders

Continuum of Symptom Severity

The severity of symptoms occurs along a continuum from mild to severe. Mild symptoms do not always disrupt or debilitate. With mild symptoms, we do not lose our ability to take care of ourselves, to maintain relationships with others, and to achieve personal goals with success and satisfaction. Severe symptoms almost always do.

The relationship method described in this book can be used with anybody who experiences symptoms at any point on the continuum. However, it is particularly relevant for those with severe symptoms, because we are more likely to experience negative life outcomes, including the following:

- Broken relationships with family members, friends, and co-workers
- Underemployment and unemployment
- Poverty
- Arrest, incarceration, and re-incarceration (recidivism)
- Homelessness
- Inadequate health care
- Poor nutrition
- Hospitalization and emergency room visits
- Complications resulting from chronic illnesses such as diabetes and cancer
- Witnessing and being victims of violence, including physical assault, sexual assault, and death
- Suicide

In this book, we will assume that symptoms are always meaningful. What does this suggest? Keep four things in mind as you think about symptoms. First, although we may have and occasionally use a checklist meant to be applied to all people, symptoms always mean something different; in short, our symptoms are unique, individual, specific, and particular. For example, you may get a headache because your sinuses swell easily when you are exposed to allergens. Someone else will get a headache when they are under stress. When they are not under stress, the headache goes away. Both share the same symptom, a headache, but the symptom means something very different for each. And they may even relieve the symptom by taking the same drug, aspirin. Second, because symptoms are always meaningful, the meanings will change through time, even during the course of the day: We may be incredibly stressed when we're with strangers at work but quite comfortable with family and friends. Third, it is best to discover how a person experiences symptoms over time. Sometimes our symptoms have been with us for a lifetime. Sometimes they are brought on by an identifiable event or exposure (e.g., dust or pollen, stress, or traumatic events). Sometimes symptoms worsen incrementally; they appear slowly over time. At other times, symptoms appear suddenly and surprisingly. Fourth, we are often not aware of our symptoms. Some can live quite happily with their symptoms. Perhaps there are times we'd rather not trade our symptoms; for example, some people would rather be sad than angry. In short, using the relational method of case management, we take symptoms seriously. It is our job to know and be familiar with symptoms so that we can offer a relationship to someone appropriately.[6]

Recovery

The concept of recovery is somewhat new in mental health services. However, many people (advocates, policymakers, researchers, service providers, family caregivers, and people with mental illness)[7] have come to agree that recovery is a personal journey toward independence with many paths that may last a lifetime. Moreover, it does not proceed in a straight line toward a single destination. It occurs in forward and backward loops and cycles; and therefore every person has a different experience of recovery. For example, there is no one optimum level of independence.

In its guidebook *Emerging Best Practices in Mental Health Recovery*, the Ohio Department of Mental Health defines recovery as "a personal process of overcoming the negative impact of a psychiatric disability despite its continued presence" (Townsend et al., 2000:7). Clinical psychologist Patricia Deegan adds that recovery is not just about finding a new way of surviving in the external world but also about finding a new way of understanding the internal world:

> Disabled persons are not passive recipients of rehabilitation services. Rather, they experience themselves as recovering a *new sense of self* and purpose within and beyond the limits of the disability. . . . Recovery refers to the lived or real life experience of persons as they accept and overcome the challenge of the disability. (Deegan, 1988:11–12)

In other words, recovery is a process of understanding and managing symptoms in the context of everyday life and taking care of the self by engaging in daily activities, such as finding employment, seeking and maintaining friendships, using money, and finding safe and affordable places to live.

Human Relationships

The activities of daily life require each of us to continuously engage in relationships with others. And our success in navigating the external world of goods, services, and support depends on the nature and quality of our relationships. Likewise, our success in navigating the internal world of feelings and thoughts depends on relationships. In other words, it is in our relationships that we maintain and recover mental health (Stanhope and Solomon, 2008).

In the most supportive service environments, the human relationship is the primary tool of mental health intervention and treatment. Of course, it is enhanced by other tools, such as psychotropic medications, which are especially helpful in minimizing the negative effects of symptoms.[8] To be effective, case management relationships must be specific and intentional about the work they do. Simply getting together for a cup of coffee, a cigarette, or small talk about recovery goals and medication regimens will not make symptoms more manageable; this may help fulfill a basic human need for social interaction, but it will not help those with difficult symptoms work toward recovery. In addition, the relationship cannot be one-sided. The person giving help must not take control. He or she must not simply assert authority and power over the client, even with the best intentions (Berlin, 2005; Borden, 2000; Reid, 2002).

The Mind

As described earlier, there are three basic domains of our mental lives: feelings, thoughts, and actions (behaviors). All three are in constant interaction (figure I.2). In addition, these domains influence and are influenced by our social environments: family culture, ethnicity, neighborhoods, work, school, gender, and much more. In the dynamic interaction between us and others, the human mind emerges and continuously develops throughout life (Allen and Fonagy, 2006; Bateman and Fonagy 2006; Damasio, 1994; Fonagy, 2002; Kandel, 2005; Siegel, 1999). Alone our brains and bodies do not produce a mind. The mind results from complex and dynamic interactions between the person and his or her environment—the exchange of attention and information about feelings, thoughts, and actions.

THE WORKING TRIANGLE

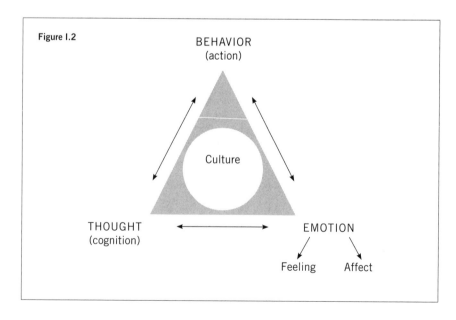

Figure I.2

BEHAVIOR
(action)

Culture

THOUGHT
(cognition)

EMOTION

Feeling   Affect

Self-Reflection

Some part of the mind reacts automatically to its environment, without reflection. As a result, we often do not know or understand why we feel, think, or act as we do. Another part of the mind observes, evaluates, and responds, after reflection. Some have called this the observing self. Others have called it the observing ego. Still others have described this as the mindful self. Self-reflection is sort of like slowing your internal video, watching it proceed frame by frame, pausing it from time to time, and peeling away layers of thought, feeling, and behavior—from the present and past—to understand how they help or hinder.

Self-reflection is not easy. Nor does it emerge spontaneously. Rather, it develops over time in relationship with others as we notice them noticing us—what we feel and think, what we say and how we say it, and what we do and how we do it. Self-reflection is continuously refined throughout our lives. For example, in childhood we learn to count by having someone watch us, encourage us, and point out paths toward success. In adolescence, we learn additional math with the same technique, especially with peers and teachers. And throughout adulthood, if we remain open to feedback from others (e.g., supervisors, instructors, and consultants), we refine our skills for more sophisticated purposes. A similar process occurs not just with thinking but also with feelings and actions. For instance, young children learn to understand their emotions with adults who observe changes in facial expressions, tone of voice, and behavior and to name the feelings that inspire those changes. Similarly, in adolescence, and if we stay open to this process throughout adulthood, we learn from others (e.g., from our supervisors, case managers, teachers, and psychotherapists) how our feelings, thoughts, and actions interact and facilitate or inhibit success and satisfaction.

This dynamic and complex process (bringing the outside world inside as we notice others who notice our feelings, thoughts, and actions) has been called mentalizing (Allen et al., 2008).[9] There is much more to be said about this very important concept, but a discussion of it here would detract from the central purpose of this book (see "Suggested Readings" at the end of this chapter if you want to explore these ideas further). We use this idea to give emphasis to the simultaneous action between two or more people in reflective case management: noticing, evaluating, and exchanging attention and information about feelings, thoughts, and actions. Self-reflection thus is always an interpersonal activity. So it is that reflective case management is also an interpersonal process.

Reflective Case Management

Throughout life, symptoms of mental illness influence the process of self-reflection, often inhibiting it. However, the consistent presence of another person who is committed to helping us notice when and how we shift away from then back toward an awareness of our feelings, thoughts, and actions—and those of others—can help us develop or recover our self-reflective skills. This can be accomplished in part because the symptoms of mental illness are included in the process. In other words, the person who supports us during recovery notices our symptoms and talks about them in a way that promotes, with empathic understanding, our awareness of and mastery of them.

Case managers are in a perfect position to help those of us with problematic symptoms enhance our self-reflective capacities because they spend so much time in the community helping us from day to day. It is the most logical and practical context in which to begin this work. This book is an exploration of how to do this work. Here is a brief overview of the method.

Honesty and Openness

Case managers can encourage and support trust in relationships with clients by being scrupulously truthful and by maintaining professional boundaries. One way to accomplish both is to continuously discuss and clarify the purpose of your relationship. In the engagement stage (discussed in greater detail in chapter 1) of case management, some clients might not be ready. They might need time to decide whether the relationship with you will be safe—that you will address their needs and not shame or take advantage of them. However, once you establish trust and help them identify their goals—that is, their needs, hopes, and dreams for daily living—you might say something like this to explain your work together:

You have told me that your goal is to find a quiet and safe place to live. My job is to help you through the process of achieving that goal for yourself. It is also my job to help you through the process of maintaining that goal. Sometimes you will need me to do things for you. Sometimes you will need me to do things with you. Sometimes you will just need me to stand by and be there for support. And, finally, sometimes you will do things for yourself. It is important for us to talk about your experiences. This is the purpose of our relationship: We help each other understand when and why you need me to do for you or do with you, and we help each other understand when and why you need me to stand by for support and when you need to do things for yourself. Our job is to keep talking about this.

Of course, it is important to let the conversation occur naturally, in your own words, and to stay open to your client's response. It is also important not to overwhelm your client with too much information or too many questions, especially in the early stages of your relationship. However, it is important that you discuss, openly, all the terms of the relationship. Here are other thoughts that might be conveyed. Remember, you will need to find your own words to express these ideas, and they should come when the time is right:

A big part of my job is to help you notice that your feelings, your thoughts, and your actions influence each other. They can help you achieve and maintain your goals. They can also disrupt you and prevent you from achieving what you want. So we have to keep talking about your feelings, your thoughts, and your actions, especially when we are working together. You are going to feel things and think things and do things when I am working with you, and it is important for us to talk about this. The more we do this in our work together, the more you will learn to do this for yourself, especially when you are with other people. We will work together to help you use feelings, thoughts, and actions to achieve goals. Sometimes you might not know what you are feeling, thinking, or doing. Or perhaps you won't have words for them. So when this happens, I might have to do *for* you: I might observe what I think you are feeling, thinking, and doing. And I might be wrong. The only way we will know is if we keep talking and reflecting together. If you think I am wrong, you have to tell me, and we will explore it together. When we explore together, I will be doing *with* you. Eventually you will do *for yourself.* This is how we are going to work together. Sometimes I will do for you, sometimes I will do with you; sometimes I will stand by for support; sometimes I will let go and you will do for yourself.

As a reflective case manager, you talk with your clients about their feelings, thoughts, and actions in the context of your relationship. And you are constantly talking to yourself and with your supervisors in a similar way.

The Relationship Matrix

The relationship matrix combines all the elements of the reflective relationship discussed earlier (table I.2). The matrix may be used to track and thereby focus your relationship with clients for most activities of daily living. With this approach you can more clearly see the ongoing and changing nature of your relationship.[10]

TABLE I.2

ELEMENTS OF REFLECTIVE CASE MANAGEMENT

Reflective Relationship		*Three Primary Domains*		
Person Who Supports Recovery	*Person Who Engages in Recovery*	*Feeling*	*Thinking*	*Acting*
• *Do for you* • *Do with you* • *Stand by for support* • *Let go or do for oneself*	• *Do for me* • *Do with me* • *Support me* • *Do for myself*			

Independence

In this book, the words *independence* and *living independently* have very specific meanings. First, there is no such thing as a self-made man or woman; no person stands alone in the world. Second, because human beings are in constant relationship, we are influenced by and reliant on others; in short, we are always in and products of relationships. Third, *independence* for us refers to specific kinds of relationships and ways of relating, ones in which both (or all) people strive for independence in seeking needs and wants, setting goals, and asserting ourselves in interactions and negotiations with others to obtain, to achieve, and to live with success and satisfaction.

Here is another point of clarification. Although independence may often be the goal in helping relationships, it is not always attainable or sustainable. Marilyn's story in the chapters that follow represents a noticeable pattern in human experience that is reflected in the relationship matrix. Although each of us may strive for independence, there is for everyone an ebb and flow between independence (i.e., doing for oneself), interdependence (i.e., doing with and standing by to support), and dependence (i.e., doing for). Anyone who has ever experienced disruptive or debilitating episodes of physical illness, mental illness, or even economic hardship knows that the fluctuations between dependence, interdependence, and independence occur every day and are often quite troubling. If we pay close enough attention, we will discover that we often cycle, recursively (back and forth), through doing for, doing with, standing by for support, and doing for oneself many times, even during the course of a day. In figure 1.3, you get a visual sense of how your relationship to others may change, even rapidly, throughout life. In sum, the goal of recovery relationships should be to help each client maintain a level of feeling, thinking, and acting necessary to achieve his or her greatest potential for recovery and independent living. And the potential for independence is different for everyone. Some will need more support than others. Some will never seek independence. Others will face daily, moment-to-moment barriers to independent living. And it is especially important to recognize that mental health professionals and interventions may not be needed as one reaches for recovery. As we will show in this book, they may even interfere. Some have argued, as we will show in this book, that our clients often use self-help models or deploy personal support systems. Sells et al. (2004:96) argue that when services are used, we should endeavor not to intervene and minimize symptoms; instead, our purpose is to act as "a facilitator of self-definition."

THE RELATIONAL CYCLE

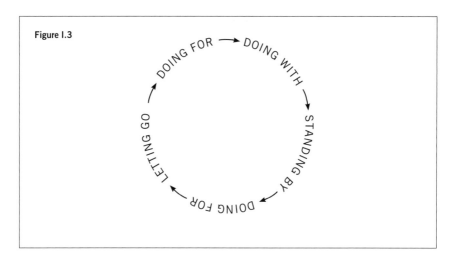

Figure I.3

Professional Use of Self

In your work as a case manager, you may be required to observe and conform to the codes of ethics set forth by your profession (e.g., social work, counseling, psychology, family and marriage counseling), your organization, or the laws of the state in which you practice. Ethics are codes of conduct that describe acceptable standards for your behavior.[11] However, to be most effective in supporting consumers in recovery, managers must also reflect on their own feelings, thoughts, and actions in the context of their relationships with others. We call this the professional use of self.[12] Managers may develop and enhance this capacity in their relationship with their supervisors. For example, as you work with clients to make sense of their internal experiences and behavior, your supervisor may help you make sense of your experience with your clients. This, in turn, deepens the supervisory relationship and the professional use of self. Reflecting in this way helps you become more aware of how your feelings, thoughts, and actions support or inhibit clients on their recovery journeys.[13]

One way to increase self-reflection is to use the relationship matrix after visits with clients and supervisors. It will help you evaluate progress toward doing for oneself in the primary domains—feeling, thinking, and acting—while engaging in the activities of daily living. It will also help you evaluate whether you encourage or discourage progress by doing too much for. The research produced for this book suggests that managers often get stuck in doing-for modes of relating. Indeed, this may be one of the factors contributing most to burnout and thus staff turnover. We'll have more to say about this in the pages that follow. Whereas some with severe and persistent symptoms may need other people to do for them with great frequency, others like Marilyn may not; they may need more doing with and standing by to encourage them to internalize confidence in their own abilities. One solution for decreasing burnout and staff turnover might be found by carefully monitoring and reducing the number of doing-for activities.

By using the matrix to track interactions with clients, you will be collecting data for agency planning and supervision. For instance, you might find that you are, in fact, engaging in too much doing-for activity because of your own anxiety and fear of failure, or you might be engaging in doing-for activity because your clients need it. Knowing these differences is crucial to your own professional development, success, and satisfaction. And in supervision you will learn to balance caseloads by assigning a mix of clients, not just those who need doing-for activity.

Personal Narratives: The Importance of Stories

Recovery is a personal journey in which each person defines a new sense of self and purpose within and beyond the limits of his or her symptoms. It is a process of personal change that involves a transformation of self-perception. It is a process of creating a new story about the self that acknowledges limitations (or deficits) but focuses primarily on personal strengths and positive attributes. Yet creating this new narrative of the self can be quite challenging, especially in the present state of mental health service systems.

Unfortunately, for those of us who turn to systems of care for help, our personal stories do not begin with our strengths and positive attributes; instead, they begin with our deficits. After all, we seek or are referred to treatment because of a particular problem or set of problems. In addition, after an initial assessment, our mental health provider will probably assign one or more diagnoses from the *DSM*. Therefore, our story in treatment typically begins with the official language of deficit and pathology. Although the *DSM* is valuable for helping service providers make sense of symptoms and in planning interventions, it also conveys a negative message to us and to all those within view or earshot of our diagnosis. In short, it produces stigma (Corrigan, 2007). A narrative of a client that begins with a diagnosis reads like this: "You have a disorder. You have problems. You are ill." The client's internalized version of this story might go something like this: "I have a disorder. I have problems. I am different from other people. I am ill."

Here is another way to look at this situation. By maintaining an emphasis on diagnosis and assigning a *DSM* identity, the mental health system is doing for us in the domains of feeling and thinking. It makes us dependent on their interpretations—their story—of us as flawed human beings (Stanhope and Solomon, 2008). Unfortunately, it is not easy to avoid a diagnostic identity and diagnostic narrative because the diagnosis is often required by public and private insurance organizations, and both consumers and mental health providers depend on this financial support.

Although the diagnostic narrative is unavoidable, the reflective case manager refrains from doing for in this way. The reflective case manager does not impose a diagnostic disorder story. Rather, we help clients construct their own stories about strengths and positive attributes within and beyond the limits of their symptoms through the process of self-reflection, using the relationship method and language outlined in the matrix in table I.2. In other words, the reflective case manager helps clients notice strengths and accomplishments by calling those strengths and accomplishments to attention.

As human beings, all of us are storytellers; it is in our nature. Through the art of storytelling, we learn to understand ourselves, the world around us, and our relationships to others. Storytelling is one of the primary technologies available to us. It is there. It is free. And you don't need a prescription.

How to Read This Book

The story that unfolds in the next three chapters may appear, at first glance, to be one story: Marilyn's struggle for recovery and independence. Yet we invite you to consider that several narratives are at work simultaneously. There is Marilyn's story, of course, as observed and told by Lisa. Then there are glimpses of Marilyn's story as observed and told by family members, friends, and other service providers such as the housing specialist, work supervisor, nurse, psychiatrist, and physician. Then there is the narrator's story of Marilyn as the hypothetical client, Lisa as the de facto case manager, and you as the hypothetical case manager. You may be wondering why we have included you in the narrative. We will explain in a moment.

First, we call to your attention the multilayered narrative reality of this book to point out that this is how narrative occurs in daily life, out there in the community. There is never just one story about you and the people you know. Think about your own family and your own circle of friends. Each person in your social network has a different perspective—a different take on the details. Each perspective contributes a piece to the puzzle. And each narrative perspective says as much about the storyteller as it does about the main character. Therefore, in the story that unfolds in the next three chapters we include you, the reader, because we are inviting you to begin the process of reflection that is necessary to become a reflective case manager, a reflective supervisor, and a reflective supporter of recovery.

It is our intention with this book not to present an authoritative view on the value of self-reflection and reflective case management. Rather, we want to inspire you to use this book to create your own narrative about self-reflection, about reflective case management, and about the value of reflective relationships in the context of everyday life. If you are a seasoned case manager or a case manager in training, we invite you to use this book not only to reflect on Marilyn's story. We hope that you will also reflect on your stories and those of your clients. Use this book with your clinical supervisor at your service organization, with professors and instructors at the college or university you attend, and with the trainers and consultants from technical-assistance organizations that are providing you with continuing education. Collaboration with others is the key to lifelong learning and discovery. Try applying this method to the model of management used at your agency. It is an opportunity to notice the beauty in the complexity of feelings, thoughts, and actions as they emerge in the context of human relationships.

You will notice that throughout this text we observe the powerful effect of shame in the case management relationship. We've done this because we found substantial evidence in the ethnographic data collected for this book. And it is our hope that you will gain from our understanding of how shame is an ever-present dynamic in the daily lives of those we work with.

Finally, there are two ways to read this book. If you are interested in the historical and cultural background of case management, you might consider starting with chapter 4. If not, we advise that you read the chapters in order.

On Being and Having a Case Manager Online

Please see our Web site (http://relationalcasemanager.com) for podcasts and additional resources on topics covered in this chapter:

SUGGESTED READING

Arnd-Caddigan, M. and R. Pozzuto. 2008. Use of self in relational clinical social work. *Clinical Social Work Journal* 36:235–243.

Fonagy, P. and J. G. Allen. 2006. *Handbook of mentalization-based treatment.* Chichester: Wiley.

Fonagy, P., J. G. Allen, and A. W. Bateman. 2008. *Mentalizing in clinical practice.* Arlington, Va.: American Psychiatric Publishing.

Fonagy, P., M. Target, G. Gergeley, and E. J. Jurist. 2002. *Affect regulation, mentalization and the development of the self.* New York: Other Press.

Topics for Discussion

1. For one week, keep a personal journal. Each day observe how, what, when, where, and who you depend on to do for you (e.g., partners, parents, teachers, supervisors, peers); also observe when you do for others. Describe these in detail, each day, and note how they differ. Also, observe when you are doing with someone and when someone is

doing with you. Note in your journal the differences between the doing-for and doing-with activity. Finally, observe the things you do on your own. How do they differ from activities that you do for others or have done for you? Note your feelings as you think about each of these activities.

2. You will find on the World Wide Web numerous examples of codes of ethics for case managers. For example, the state of New Mexico has a very strong code of ethics for case management. Find several, read them, and then consider the following. Joe is a case manager at the Hope Mental Health, Inc. After work he meets a client at a local coffee shop and shares with him the details of a recent struggle and conflict with his supervisor at the agency. Is this a possible ethical conflict? If so, why? See these sites for codes of ethics:

    http://www.health.state.nm.us/ddsd/regulationsandstandards/Operations/
    documents/CODEOFETHICSv3.pdf
    http://www.yournacm.com/guidelines.html
    http://www.Johnson-county.com/mhdd/pdf/TCMPolicy.pdf

3. This book can be used to complement comprehensive texts in qualitative research methods. It is an in-depth example of an ethnographic project from beginning to end, from question formulation to the writing phase. Students will see how qualitative and ethnographic data are collected in a natural setting and how grounded theory techniques are used for coding. If you use this book in teaching research methods, we suggest that you begin with appendix 1. Then read chapter 4. The remaining chapters should be read in order. Students will see how problems are identified and how data are collected. They will see how an analytic strategy is developed and how research is written up for a broad audience. First, we identify the research question in everyday provider–client interactions and show how relationships were used to facilitate recovery from severe mental illness. Second, we show how ethnography and participation–observation are used for data collection. Third, we show how grounded theory coding techniques are used for comparison of everyday problem-solving activities. Fourth, we compare the relational activities of all observed instances and identify the constructs: doing for, doing with, letting go, and doing for oneself.

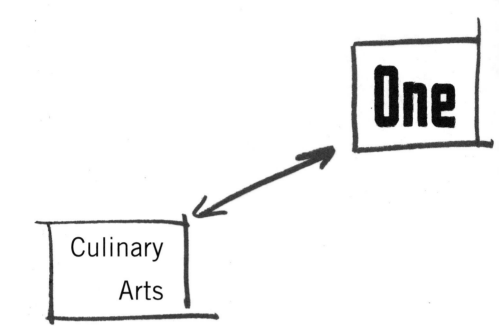

Observe

The first experience is always the most difficult because there is nothing to compare it with. It's like walking into a room filled with unfamiliar people. There is no connection with anything. There is you, your environment, and the awareness of your separateness pushing against you.

Inside, the rooms feel large and empty, but there is evidence that many people live here. In the living room, there are several old couches and upholstered chairs set around a television. In the kitchen, there is a huge sink and appliances big enough to service a restaurant. The walls are bare. And in the dining room, there is a table long enough to accommodate a party of twelve. Two researchers, Lisa and Jerry, sit at one end with three women: the group home supervisor and two residents, Marilyn and Sophie, who have expressed interest in the project. As Jerry and Lisa explain the purpose of their work, the supervisor encourages the residents to participate. She tells them that they might learn something from the experience. She tells them that the staff will support them and assures them that they do not have to participate. The decision is theirs to make.

The first resident, Sophie, is short and quite heavy. Her face, round and wrinkled, conceals her eyes through the shadows of deep sockets. She appears forty, but she is twenty-nine. She listens to Jerry and Lisa. She is silent and somewhat intimidating. When she speaks, though, she radiates playfulness. She instructs her guests to call her "Hope." Eager to sign the consent forms, she tells them she can meet again tomorrow because she does not work.

The other resident, Marilyn, a friend of Sophie, is quite unlike her: She is younger, twenty-three, and not as heavy. Her skin is smooth. She's neither intimidating nor playful. She's nervous. She takes refuge in the smoke of cigarettes, which the residents are allowed in common areas on the first floor. Nearly everyone smokes here. Smoking is part of the culture; the walls have a thick patina of tobacco. By the end of the conversation, Marilyn agrees to participate in the study because Sophie has. Marilyn trusts her friend.

Reflect

Case management is challenging and creative work that offers many opportunities to experience the healing power of human relationships in real-world environments. In traditional psychotherapy, it is the client who walks through the office door into the unfamiliar. In case management, you cross that threshold. It is likely that both you and your client will experience strong emotions as you enter: fear, shame, disappointment, anger, and many others.

In beginning a relationship (some call this the engagement phase), it is especially important to start where the client is, which means that you acknowledge and respect the client's current reality, his or her present situation, and what the client brings to you in each moment of your interaction. The alternative, starting with where you are (i.e., with your agenda, your feelings, your thoughts, or with a checklist of things to get done), rarely works to support the beginning engagement. Take a few minutes to imagine a time in your own life when you wanted, badly, someone to listen to your story or worry and the listener wasn't fully present. Instead, the listener was focused on his or her own problems or on the future or yesterday, looking out the window, were watching the television or listening to music, answering cell phones or fiddling with a text message, or distracted by another interaction. It's like listening to the melody without hearing the lyrics. In our everyday interactions with clients, we try to stay in the moment.[1] Listen. Remain attentive to what you, along with your client, are feeling, thinking, or doing. Second, avoid becoming active; if you feel the impulse to act, not only are you likely to step out of the present, you are also taking control. Third, you must know where you are. That means that you must be aware of what you are feeling, thinking, and doing. Fourth, when we are not mindful of our present feelings, especially uncomfortable ones, we are more likely to pass them along to others.[2] Often we offload that which does not make us feel good. Imagine a time in your own life when you felt someone's anger at you, but somehow things got all turned around. They said to you, instead, "Why are you so angry?" This was anger they couldn't bear to feel, so they turned it into an angry feeling in you. In short, "I'm not angry, you are." At these moments it's not easy to stay in the present. It takes patience and practice. Practice this in your own relationships, every day, and in your supervision. Listen and observe. You will not only learn about your client. You will learn something about how you relate to others and how others make you feel.

As you enter your client's physical and psychological space, notice your body, notice your movements, the tone of your voice, and the choice and timing of your words. What does all this say about what you are feeling and thinking? Talk to your supervisor about it. While you are noticing, also notice your client—her posture, her tone of voice, her word choice, and her movements. These details provide clues about what she might be feeling. As these clues begin to reveal themselves over time, you will recognize a pattern: yours and theirs. With this knowledge, you will be equipped to help your clients recognize their own behaviors and feelings. This self-reflective skill is essential for recovery.

When you meet your client for the first time, your first goal is to be respectful. You may accomplish this by accepting the table your client sets for you. For example, you may not smoke cigarettes and may find a smoke-filled room uncomfortable or repulsive. Yet by accepting this environment you not only show respect; you also adopt a nonjudgmental attitude. In the engagement process, it is important to use gentle observation. In this way each encounter with your client will present new and potentially useful information. It is important to let information reveal itself naturally and in its own time; if you ask a question, you will get an answer. Imagine a time in your life when someone threw questions at you like darts at a board, continuously. How did it feel, especially when answers did not come easily? In the scene described earlier, observations reveal subtle and important information. Marilyn and Sophie need encouragement to explore. It is the supervisor who encourages them to participate. We also learn that Marilyn is more hesitant. Her friend Sophie is more eager for a trusting relationship, less protective of her inner self, or both. Finally, we learn that Marilyn may be using tobacco to manage intense feeling. This is an important detail to observe. It may offer future opportunities to help her notice feelings that motivate her to reach for the comfort of fire and smoke.

In sum, as you begin work with a client, keeps these things in mind:

- Acknowledge and respect the client's current situation. Stay in the present. This is sometimes called starting where your client is.
- Avoid the tendency to become active, to take control. Listen and observe.
- Know where you are, that is, monitor your own feelings, thoughts, and actions.
- Don't pass your feelings along to others. And beware when others offload their feelings onto you.

Observe

June 29

The television room is not always the best place for conversation, but that's where Marilyn is sitting, and that's where she is staying until she decides differently. She does not say this. But she does not have to: Her arms are folded defiantly and protectively. Lisa, sitting nearby on an old upholstered chair, is trying to keep her attention from being sucked into the black hole of the rapidly changing images flashing across the television screen. Lisa feels the motion ripping a hole in the fabric of time and space but gathers the strength to keep her mind right where it is, in this room at this time. She then gives way to questions about Marilyn's social network: "Do you have family?" and "Who are the people most likely to give you help when you need it?"

and "Tell me a little bit about each person." Marilyn responds with a list of facts that are easy to record:

- Her mother is still alive and living in the same house.
- Her older sister has two young daughters. They all live with her mother.
- She has a twin brother, but they are not close.
- Her father died when she was seven from an illness related to alcoholism. Her sister was ten or eleven.
- She and her twin brother were adopted.
- Her sister was also adopted but not from the same biological family.

An appetite is a compelling distraction, and Marilyn's need for food takes her into the commercial-sized kitchen, where she mixes leftover Johnny Marzetti elbow noodles and chili in a ceramic bowl. She tops it off with a clump of mayonnaise. As Marilyn mixes the ingredients and begins to eat, Lisa feels nausea, so she suggests they sit at the dining table. There, with the mix of mayo and chili out of sight, Lisa continues to record Marilyn's many answers to questions about her social networks (family and friends), her work history, her interests and hobbies, and her goals. Marilyn has two friends at the group home, both of whom are older. She has a boyfriend. She worked at Cedar Point amusement park in Sandusky for two summers after high school, which she enjoyed, but she could not save money because she spent it at shopping malls near the park, mostly on food, knick knacks, and "stuff" from dollar stores. She has always had trouble saving money, so her mother is her legal payee; she pays all of the bills. Marilyn's interests include the following:

- Listening to music
- Hanging out with friends
- Going to movies
- Playing video games
- Riding roller coasters
- Being fascinated with castles, haunted buildings, and witchcraft (the good kind)

- Watching science fiction and alien-horror-type television shows (her favorites include *Roswell*, *Buffy the Vampire Slayer*, and *Charmed*)
- Sleeping
- Sitting
- Smoking
- Cooking traditional meals such as chicken paprikash
- Experimenting with odd food combinations, such as peanut butter and baloney sandwiches and stew that is made with noodles, chili, and mayonnaise

Lisa leaves with three things on her mind. Marilyn has a boyfriend whom she has known for almost a year. He lives by himself in Lakewood, a nearby suburb, and does not own a car. She wants to get a better job and save enough money to buy a PlayStation II. She hopes to start culinary school at a local community college in the fall.

Reflect

Our external and internal worlds are in constant relationship. Each affects the other. Your clients exist in your outside world, yet they influence your emotions and thoughts even when you are not with them. Likewise, you exist in the external worlds of your clients and influence their internal lives even when you are not with them. This is the nature of relationships. Imagine for a moment how you exist in a web of relationships, past and present, each with significant feeling, good and bad (figure 1.1).[3]

In this scene, we do not know why Marilyn ignores Lisa in the living room. She may be feeling self-conscious. She may be feeling ashamed. She may simply be protecting her privacy. We do not know. However, from our observations we do know that she finds refuge in watching television and that she apparently likes to share this safe space with others; she does not ask Lisa to leave. We also know that Marilyn seeks comfort in preparing food. Did you notice what happened just before Marilyn went into the kitchen? Before reading on, try to recall. Revisit this scene. She was talking about relationships with family members. It is possible that her move to the kitchen was away from feelings stirred by the conversation. Imagine for a moment the things

THE HELPING NETWORK

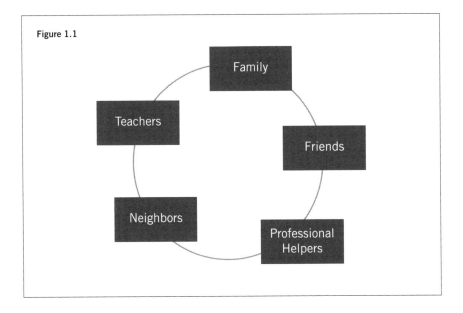

Figure 1.1

you do to avoid strong feelings. Before you finish readings this book, start a journal. Make a note of the things you do to avoid strong feelings. This will help you relate (feel with) to the ways others avoid them.

During the engagement process, it is very important to notice details such as these but not to call attention to them. Many of your clients will not be ready for this. And some will never want you to notice their feelings. Others may tolerate your noticing their behaviors, but they will not be comfortable when you notice their feeling states. Still others may be comfortable only when you notice unclear thinking. For some, calling attention to behavior may provoke uncomfortable feelings.

Imagine a time in your life when someone called attention to your behavior.[4] How did it make you feel? It can feel intrusive. Were you embarrassed? Did you want to hide? Often it can feel shameful ("Are you seeing something about me that I have not noticed? What special observing powers do you have that I lack?"). And for some who feel paranoid, it may feel as if others can read their minds. However, after you have established trust and your clients feel comfortable with you, it might be productive to help them notice the connections between their behaviors and their feelings. It might be helpful to say to Marilyn, "I noticed something, and I am wondering if you noticed it, too. You are eating food that you have prepared for yourself and that you obviously enjoy. I noticed that you felt the need to do something nice for yourself as soon as we finished talking about your family. What were you feeling when we were talking?"

Keep this in mind: You cannot wonder about your actions or feelings unless you have first noticed them. Notice first. Wonder later. We must first develop our observing skills. In short, we cannot wonder about what we cannot notice. We might even say that wondering without seeing is like being out of sync.

It would also be helpful to inquire about Marilyn's feelings toward you. A follow-up question might be, "What do you feel and think about revealing this information about your past to me?"

A home visit in the community provides a lot of information about your clients, yourself, and your emerging collaboration. As you prepare for a home visit, expect to be surprised by what you witness and what you feel. At times, the flood of information and sensation may be overwhelming. Like Lisa, you may feel uncomfortable about being ignored by your client or afraid that you are not doing enough to help the client establish and achieve recovery goals. In moments like these, it is natural to want to unload uncomfortable feelings by doing something, such as making lists. The impulse to do for your client is often automatic. It is important to sit tight, though, to stay with your feelings and their feelings and to do with them. This will help build a trusting alliance. If they choose to watch television, watch television. There may be something in the activity they want you to notice and to eventually understand.

It is highly probable that your clients are experiencing the same desire to unload uncomfortable feelings. Over time, you will learn when and how they do this. A pattern will emerge. These events will provide unique opportunities for you to help them understand how their relationship with you (and with others) produces these feelings. As a professional case manager, you have the privilege to be present with them in these moments and to help them transform uncomfortable internal experiences. Perhaps most important, you have the unique opportunity to do this with them in places where they live their lives: communities, neighborhoods, group homes, apartments, coffee shops, with family and friends, and with doctors and nurses. As you might suspect, this takes time, patience, and gentle persistence—from both of you.

In your interactions with clients, remain focused on both the process and the content of your relationship. Public and private health insurance requires you and your agency to focus on content, such as client goals and activities of daily living. Although you must always do this, be aware that success at completing tasks and achieving goals depends on the ability to regulate emotions, thoughts, and behaviors (the process). Success in the community depends on one's ability to relate to others. Keep in mind that relating to others is not limited to outward appearances, such as clean and pressed clothes, sustained eye contact, a confident voice, and a firm handshake. Relating to others includes being aware of and using feelings and thoughts, the process of the relationship as it unfolds.

You should not assume that your client feels most comfortable with you in his or her home. In our current mental health system, case managers regularly visit homes. Every day mental health centers arrange for thousands of visits. In preparing yourself, imagine a guest visiting your home. In preparation for the visit, how do you feel? What do you do to prepare? How do you feel after they've arrived? Are you eager for the visit to end? You must get to know how your client feels about your visits, for their benefit and personal safety and for yours. Negotiating the private space of a client's home is like a guest visiting yours.

The home visit is a product of the late-twentieth-century policy to empty and close hospitals. The movement of patients out of hospitals and into communities meant that the caregiver also left the institutional space. Some of the consequences of emptying hospitals were unintended. For example, no one thought about the influence home visits would have on the caregiving relationship. The community and home context now produces a specific kind of question that is found throughout our experience with Marilyn: In a client's home, how active or passive should a caregiver be? Who should take the lead? Is the caregiver an investigator or police enforcer, monitoring to see whether everything in the client's home is properly ordered? Or is the caregiver a guest, meaning that the client feels in control? Recall that it was Marilyn's home that Lisa was invited into.

Observe

July 3

The office of a lumberyard is no place for a woman who wants to cook for a living, but this is the job that social services has found for Marilyn, and somehow she makes the best of it. Marilyn is sitting at a desk in a small reception area. There is a desk, a phone, a typewriter, and a two-drawer filing cabinet. She is answering calls, typing new orders, and stamping, stapling, and filing receipts of ones that have already been filled. Lisa sits and waits for Marilyn's next break. Time is moved silently by gears that nobody can see.

A customer calls with a question that Marilyn does not know how to answer. She asks the caller to wait, puts him on hold, and then hollers for a supervisor. It is a question about price. The supervisor explains the policy and assures Marilyn that she has made the right choice to ask for help. Marilyn returns to the caller and ends the conversation, demonstrating finely tuned customer service skills. She returns to filing.

The lumberyard collaborates with a social service agency located a few miles from the group home. The manager, familiar with Lisa and the study, has allowed her to visit during lunch break, which arrives. Lisa and Marilyn talk in the lunchroom, which is big enough to accommodate a round table and four chairs. Lisa asks Marilyn more questions about her social support network—about the people who give her help with everyday problems—but Marilyn draws a blank. Lisa suggests that her work supervisor and group home supervisor might qualify. Marilyn agrees. She makes no effort to engage in conversation.

Lisa remembers that the group home supervisor has been encouraging residents to swim at the local YMCA for exercise. She thinks that swimming might be a good opportunity to get to know Marilyn. She asks about this, hoping it might lead to conversation. Marilyn acknowledges that it is good exercise and that she likes swimming. She says, "Maybe next year I'll be able to fit into some nicer clothes."

"If you want to go swimming, give me a call, and I will go with you." Lisa writes her cell phone number on a piece of paper and pushes it across the table. She encourages Marilyn to call the YMCA about its open swim hours and to call her with the news. As Lisa stands to leave, Marilyn adds an important detail to the conversation they had a few days ago at the group home: Her two favorite PlayStation video games are "Mortal Combat III" and "Road Rage."

Some topics of conversation make more of a connection between people than others. At 8 P.M. Marilyn calls Lisa to report that open swim is scheduled for Wednesday from 11 A.M. to 2 P.M. However, she wants to know whether Lisa would like to play video games instead. Lisa agrees.

Reflect

Visiting clients in the community presents clients, case managers, and supervisors with many difficult challenges. Imagine this. With many thousands of home visits, you may wonder about your safety.[5] You may be shocked by what you experience. You may be overwhelmed with not knowing what to say or do. It is important to be aware of the many feelings you encounter as you venture out into the community. You should also look at how your thoughts and feelings motivate your own behavior. For example, take a moment to imagine how you respond to crisis. Keep notes on how you react. Do you become active and take control? Or do you lose control? To whom do you turn for support? Because we all respond to crisis in different ways, it is useful to become aware of how we respond and how our colleagues respond. It is also important to pay attention to your internal danger detector, that is, feelings that alert you to keep yourself or your client safe.[6] Sometimes, for a case manager it is difficult to measure the severity of mental health symptoms and determine whether those symptoms are impairing your client's ability to relate to people and their external environment. Therefore, it is good practice to develop conversational techniques to test clients' awareness of themselves and their external reality. What you are striving to learn is something about what is often called reality testing.[7] A break from reality, both internal and external, may be dangerous for you, your client, and other people. Prepare a plan for crisis intervention. Ask your supervisor to explain your agency's crisis protocol. Also, find out whether your agency has a collaborative relationship with other professionals in your community who interact with your clients, such as people in your local police department, hospital emergency room, and inpatient mental health facility.

Visiting clients in community locations presents other challenges. Whenever you meet with clients, regardless of location, it is your responsibility to protect their privacy. This is especially true and especially difficult in public spaces. Imagine a time in your life when your privacy was violated, when you felt exposed and vulnerable. *Violation* is an appropriate word here. It is violent not to respect another's privacy. There is a line that separates our private from our public lives, and when we work in public spaces with our clients we must remain especially vigilant about respecting and protecting those lines. For clients who do not want others to know about their mental illness, do as Lisa does above. Be a quiet and respectful observer.

Because much case management takes place in public spaces, you need to work closely with your client about such visits. And always show your respect by asking for permission. Know that your presence may raise the curiosity of others, which may, in turn, reveal information about your client that she does not want others to know. It is also important to talk in advance about how you will relate to her around others and to prepare her for possible surprises. For example, how does your client want others, friends or family, to know you and to be introduced to you? Tell your client that it is your job to protect her privacy, and remind her from time to time that you always keep this in mind. Here's a little exercise to consider. Each time you enter a public space with your client, check to see whether you and your client are comfortable. Consider that there might be times when meeting in a public space—depending on the nature of your work and expectations, or your client's mental health—might be especially inappropriate. This is yet another way that you learn to do with your client. It is also in this way that you will earn and show respect.

As a case manager, it is your job to observe. It is also your job to know that clients are observing you. They are on the lookout for many things, including evidence of trust and mistrust. One of the simplest and most effective ways to develop and maintain trust is to allow each client to express her motivations for recovery, her personal goals, and her understandings of quality of life. Simple statements and questions can accomplish a lot. For instance, if you say, "I've noticed that you keep appointments with me. What keeps you coming back?," her answer may reveal her motivation, her goals, and her desires. In addition, help her observe discrepancies between her wishes and thoughts and actions that sabotage success. This is an example of doing with your clients in the domain of reflective thinking because you are directing her attention to herself. As time goes by, doing-with activity will transform to standing by to admire as your client begins to do this work more and more for herself. Be alert. The shift may be subtle. Be prepared to help her notice the movement toward independence.

Lisa observes Marilyn as she constructively responds to a phone call from a customer with questions she cannot answer. She also observes the supervisor express approval. In a situation like this, it might be appropriate for a case manager to help her client notice the supervisor's admiring comment. You may begin by doing for your client in the domain of thinking and shift to doing with. This can be accomplished in a few short statements. Imagine saying something like, "I noticed your supervisor was noticing how well you handled yourself when the customer asked a question. You have told me how important it is to find another job that you really enjoy. You demonstrated a skill that all supervisors would like. It is problem solving. Your supervisor noticed that you have that skill. Did you see that?"

By observing your client in this way, you are staying in tune with the process of your relationship—the process of observing. In addition, you encourage your client to stay in tune with her own behavior, her own thoughts, and her own feelings. This is called empowerment.[8] It is Marilyn who uses her thoughts to process the question from the customer, to realize that she does not have the answer, and to decide she needs help from a supervisor. It is Marilyn who translates her thoughts into positive action—without realizing it. In this situation, the case manager helps Marilyn use reflective thinking.

Behind Marilyn's thoughts and positive actions are feelings about which we know nothing. At this point, it is not necessary to know. Whatever those feelings are, they apparently inspire thoughts that result in positive action. This seemingly insignificant episode in Marilyn's daily routine is evidence that she acts independently. Let's call it Exhibit A, which Marilyn can use for her own defense when in the future she attempts to prosecute herself as a bad or incapable woman. Help her remember this evidence. Help her notice her good feeling and her ability to do.

In this scene, there is an important lesson: Avoid doing for. Here, one can easily see how to avoid doing for Marilyn in the domain of feeling. You may feel the impulse to say something like, "Don't you feel good about your supervisor noticing you?" Or you might be tempted to say, "You should feel proud of that." Remember, these are your feelings and your words. These are not her feelings. Therefore the words have little meaning. Meaning is created when a feeling inside a person can be expressed to you. Imagine times in your life when someone tried to name a feeling for you and was terribly wrong. What did it feel like? When internal feelings attach to or identify with external objects—such as places and faces and things—personal meaning is created. You cannot impose meaning from the outside because that's not where your client's feelings and thoughts exist. You client's feelings and thoughts exist inside.

* * *

There is another quality of the reflective relationship found in this scene. It is called setting boundaries. Marilyn and Lisa are figuring out how to draw the line between the private and the public. Lisa offers to go swimming with Marilyn because the group home supervisor thinks Marilyn will feel safe in the informal activity. However, Marilyn does not respond with a simple "yes" or "no" to the offer. Rather, she talks about the value of swimming as a form of exercise and says, "Maybe next year I'll be able to fit into some nicer clothes." Note the choice and timing of the words. It is quite possible that the message behind this message is that Marilyn is self-conscious about her body and that swimming is too intimate an activity—too private. Imagine her message being, "I do not want to be seen up close like that. I do not want to be that exposed." In other words, Marilyn sets a boundary by saying "no" to swimming without actually using the words. Notice that she makes a counteroffer: to play video games. Lisa intuitively lets Marilyn take power back by accepting the offer. This is a good example of how a case manager can make a subtle yet significant shift from doing for in the domain of thinking to doing with. The negotiation is a success. The next step in the process is to let your client know that you have observed the shift so that she, too, will notice how important it is for her to have control of her decisions and her boundaries.

In your work, you're not likely to offer to swim with clients. However, you might suggest going for a walk or getting a cup of coffee. At other times, in making these or other suggestions, you may be feeling anxious about the relationship or the possibility of failure. If you find yourself making suggestions, take note. It is *your* suggestion, not your client's. And you may be using your feeling to do for in the domains of thinking and action. If this occurs, don't sweat it. This will happen. The best corrective action you can take is to notice the slip, sit tight, and wait quietly. And it might be appropriate to admit that the suggestion to get coffee or go for a walk was yours, not hers. You might say something like, "I noticed something important: I made the suggestion that we go for a walk. I think it is important for you to choose what is comfortable. What do you think? What is important to you?"

At some point, your clients will ask you to participate in an activity that might feel like an invitation to cross the line that separates your professional from your personal life. Be prepared. It is likely to occur. When it does, you might feel shock. The feeling is probably your internal privacy protector telling you that an invitation has been made to cross the line. It is important to protect yourself. Do not cross the line. However, it is also important to use the feeling to help your client reflect on her own feeling. You might say something like, "You would like to get to know me more. That's natural. Tell me about your curiosity." The answer may reveal information about how your client is accustomed to forming relationships with others. This may offer important information for future relationship-building episodes in your client's life, such as when he or she applies for a job and begins to interact with supervisors, co-workers, and customers. Or when they struggle to form friendships and meaningful relationships.

Observe

July 5

Sophie's smile is contagious, especially when she recognizes a friendly face. It is this smile, and a loud half-sung baritone "Hi," that greets Lisa at the door. "Come in quick," Sophie says. "Don't let Sparky out."

Lisa steps into the house, scanning the floor for the quickstep motion of a curious cat anxious for the freedom of the street. The door shuts behind her. It is 1:15 P.M. There is no evidence of the cat.

Lisa finds her host, Marilyn, sitting on a sofa in front of the television, engrossed in a movie. She does not look up from the screen but says, "Hello." Lisa sits in a chair near the TV. She inquires about the plot.

Marilyn doesn't flinch. She says, "It's a good action movie."

Lisa asks about the video games that Marilyn had invited her to play and is told that the system is not working.

Lisa stares blankly into space while she waits for inspiration about what to do next. The movie plays a bit before Marilyn asks whether Lisa would like some Pepsi. Lisa declines, and Marilyn returns with a two-liter bottle and glass. She sits in silence, sipping soda for the duration of the movie.

Fortunately, the television screen goes blank when the VCR stops and enters the rewind mode. This leaves a few precious seconds for conversation to begin or to pick up where it left off. Lisa takes advantage of the moment. She says, "So what brought you here to live at this house?"

Marilyn begins to talk. It is as if the Pepsi were medicine—a truth syrup. "It was a consensus," she says, "between my mother, my sister, and me." Here begins a short history of her early life.

Stories are easier to understand when they're told in chronological order, but this is not how Marilyn tells her story. Lisa has to arrange the information in order to make sense of it. This is what she comes up with.

Marilyn grew up in a small three-bedroom, one-bath bungalow in a working-class neighborhood. She and her twin brother had been adopted at age one. Earlier, her older sister had been adopted from a different family. She describes her sister as "daddy's girl" and herself as "mommy's girl." She was close to her mother, she said. "I liked to hang out with her." She did not know her father well. He died when she was seven, from a disease related to alcoholism, and as a result her mother had to work full- and part-time jobs, which forced her sister to do much of the parenting. She cooked for, fed, and supervised Marilyn and her brother. "She really didn't let me do much, or help much. She kind of took over the role of mom, I guess."

As the siblings got older, the mood in the house changed. There was increasing tension. Marilyn, in her words, became "very angry and difficult to manage." Her brother, too, struggled with his feelings. He became violent and repeatedly threatened his mother and small children in the neighborhood. At twenty, her sister got pregnant, and it was decided that the child would be safer if her brother was not in the home. Marilyn was especially relieved when they sought foster care for him.

At the birth of her sister's baby, Marilyn, now age eighteen, was in high school. Her mother had not yet turned forty. Because of an illness (which she could not describe) Marilyn missed much of her senior year. She repeated her final year. And after finishing school at age nineteen, she worked at the Cedar Point amusement park in Sandusky. These two summers, she said with exuberance, were her "first chance to live away from home." She stayed in a dorm with co-workers; there were dollar stores near the amusement park, and every dime earned she spent on junk and food.

At some point during these two summers, her sister and niece moved out of her mother's home. Then, her mother suffered a stroke and heart attack. Marilyn moved back to take care of her and found work at a nearby Wendy's and Pizza Hut. Soon, because Marilyn was unable to keep up with the demands of caring for her mother, her sister moved back. Now she had two children.

"I was not really getting along with anybody," Marilyn reports. "I was not used to being around small children all the time; they had certain needs that had to be attended to."

To decrease tension at home, Marilyn moved into the group home voluntarily.

"It was a chance for me to learn to live on my own," she said. "I wanted to live on my own."

With a wave of her arm, Marilyn invites Lisa to the front porch, where she lights a cigarette and continues to weave her story into the present. Friends and family, she says, have noticed change for the better since her move into the group home. "They said that I had more control over my temper and got along fine with the group of people and personalities." She smiles before letting Lisa know how pleased she is with her improved relationships with her mom, sister, and nieces.

Staring at the smoke of her cigarette, she pushes it toward the street with her breath, and after a long, deep exhalation she tells Lisa that she is going to spend the weekend with her mother and that she is supposed to have lunch with her twin brother on Saturday. She's not seen him in two months. She's hesitant and silent, and she thinks a long while about the upcoming visit.

Reflect

Every encounter with your client is an opportunity to learn more about his or her personal story. Personal narratives are important because they help us organize thoughts about ourselves, about others, and about how we initiate and maintain interpersonal relationships. Imagine how you tell a story or stories about yourself. Where do you begin your story? And why do you tell the story? When do you tell stories about yourself? As you see in Marilyn's story, your client might not have her personal narrative organized chronologically, and she might not understand the significance of some events. However, you will have opportunities to do with her in the domain of thinking about her history. You will have the opportunity to co-create a personal narrative with her. First, though, your client needs to feel safe enough with you to tell her story.

Prepare for the unexpected. You'll need to find a way of being comfortable with surprise. In this scene, Marilyn ignores Lisa. Lisa is surprised and uncomfortable. Marilyn does not greet her at the door and makes no effort to follow through on her invitation to play video games. Instead, she keeps her attention sharply focused on the movie. Lisa feels it. There will be many occasions when you will feel ignored or unnoticed. Don't be discouraged, though. These uncomfortable feelings provide an opportunity to explore the process of your relationship as it is occurring in the moment. How might you use your feelings to understand your client's present feeling state? Do you think she is ashamed or frightened or exposed by having you in her home? Does she perceive you as a threat to her privacy, or is she ignoring you to protect herself from an intrusion into her psychological and physical space?

Before you can begin to explore the meaning of your discomfort, you must first learn to notice it. It is useful to think about this as a two-stage process, for you and your client: First notice and observe, then wonder. Think about it. You can't wonder about something unless you have first observed or noticed it. Uncomfortable feelings, for example, often arise as physical sensations. Do you feel a tightening in your chest, a quivering in your legs, or a flush feeling in your face? Does your face turn red? Do you sweat? It is different for everyone. Yet it is natural and should be expected. When it occurs, make a note of it. Observe. Rest with it. Before you act or wonder about it, make sure you've used all your observational skill. This technique of nonaction will interrupt the impulse to dispel uncomfortable feelings through action. And it will interrupt your impulse to do for (or to impose on) your client. Let us summarize this important sequence of activities, noticing and wondering, by asking you to imagine a moment in your life when someone asked you to wonder (question, inquire, imagine, probe, ponder) about something that you'd not yet noticed or observed. Did you feel shame? One way we respond when someone else sees something that we've missed is embarrassment. You might say to yourself, "How did I miss that? It's so obvious." If this happens repeatedly, we might feel even more shame and embarrassment. In short, be cautious in noticing and wondering and be especially alert to wondering about something before others share the observing moments.

When you feel ignored by your client, you have the opportunity to align with her feeling and experience. Think of it this way. All of your clients are typically required to interact with many different service providers to get what they need: psychiatrists, nurses, case managers, counselors, employment specialists, housing specialists, probation officers, credit counselors, and a variety of people at agencies such as Social Security and Medicaid. To each, your clients are asked to tell their story over and over and over. Maybe they feel like an object, processed and passed from one part of the service factory to the next without any sense of recognition as a human being—as a person who feels, thinks, dreams, and struggles to achieve her goals with success and satisfaction. Imagine a time in your own life when you've had to tell your own story, repeatedly, and it seemed like no one was really there, listening or recognizing you. Some have argued that we have a need for recognition.[9] Here's how this need might be met in your day-to-day interactions with clients. Remember and acknowledge them, in and outside the office. By conveying warmth and familiarity, especially during crises, you will help bridge the gap between the past and the present, between good and bad times. Remember their struggles and how they have responded to crises.

In the engagement phase of your relationship with your client, you may be eager to get her story to demonstrate your willingness to understand. Don't be tempted. Getting a personal history may feel intrusive and aggressive, and it is likely that your client will experience it as too much, too soon. Although there are times when you need a history quickly (e.g., during crises), be cautious even then; get only what you need to get. The evidence is in the language. To get a personal history from someone is to take it from her. To get a personal history is to do for your client in the domain of thinking. By asking her to answer your questions about her experiences, you are sending a message that might feel like this: "It is important for you to understand who you were in the past, who you are now, and who you want to be in the future." How would that feel? This message may be in direct conflict with her thoughts and feelings. Maybe she does not want to know. Maybe it is too painful to know. Let your client bring her history to you in her own way, in her own time. And be prepared to sort out the details later, as Lisa does here.

* * *

When managers visit with clients, they are required to listen for some specific content: recovery goals, adherence to medication regimens, and success with the activities of daily living. They must also listen for various risks: suicide, overdose, harm to self. They must listen for emotional states also. All of this is important. However, a reflective case manager does not just listen *for* information; she will also carefully listen *to* what the client is saying, how he is saying it, and when. For instance, what words, tone of voice, and body language does your client use in response to what you have said or not said? This information will reveal how your client is reacting to you. This will also help your client feel more accurately how she reacts to others. Sometimes, when we listen for something, we will hear it. If, for example, we're listening for goals, we will probably hear something about goals and not about what is at the moment most important to our client (Arlow, 1995).

In this scene, the content and process of Marilyn's answer to the question "What brought you [to the group home]?" raise another issue to think about. What messages do your clients communicate through silence or omission? Marilyn gives a brief history of her family—her mother, her father, her sister, and her brother—but she does not talk about the details of her emerging mental illness in the history or context of her family. She focuses on her sister's out-of-wedlock pregnancy, her brother's delinquency and violent behavior, and the effects of both on her living arrangements. She says very little about the effects of these events on her feelings, thoughts, and self-esteem. However, on the front porch, in a more private space, away from other residents, Marilyn reveals her feelings about the coming weekend. She is anxious about being with her mother and brother, and her worry says as much, if not more, about her past and her present mental health. Her relationship with her mother, an authority figure, produces uncomfortable feelings. In addition, her relationship with a peer, her brother, produces the same. Think of the implications of this for her current recovery goal: developing a career in the culinary arts. What feelings might arise in her encounters with authority figures (supervisors) and peers (co-workers)? How will she manage the feelings? How will she manage the thoughts and actions inspired by those feelings? How will she manage her relationships?

Observe

August 3

Lisa reflects on her interactions with Marilyn thus far and does not think she is developing much of a relationship. Their conversations seem strained, almost forced, so she asks the group home supervisor for help. The supervisor recommends that Lisa take Marilyn to the community college she wants to attend and help acquaint her with the campus. The personal time, she says, might help her feel comfortable.

Lisa calls Marilyn and offers to take her on a tour of the campus. Marilyn thinks it's a great idea and asks Lisa to accompany her on registration day as well.

August 5

Marilyn calls Lisa to cancel their campus tour. She is not feeling well. She says, "My favorite friend came to visit." This is a code phrase for her period. She gets terrible cramps.

Reflect

In this scene, Lisa does not know where she stands in her relationship with Marilyn. She asks for help. The group home supervisor suggests that she take action as a way to connect. Without knowing it, the supervisor suggests that Lisa do for her client in the domains of thinking and action. Marilyn appears excited by the idea to tour the campus. Later she cancels. Thus, we see the client and the case manager in a dance of approach and avoidance. It is quite possible that Marilyn is accustomed to having things done for her, so she agrees to the idea at first. Yet it is also possible that she does not like it when people actually do for her. She may intuitively experience the doing-for activities as an intrusion into her desire to do for herself. However, at this point we do not know for sure what her feelings are.

Not knowing is not a bad thing.[10] The engagement process is filled with uncertainty, and managers and clients must feel their way through it. Always respect your client's ambivalence and your own discomfort with the emerging relationship. Both are useful and very real feelings. If your intuition tells you that being active will present opportunities to build trust and advance your relationship, find a way to transform your impulse to do for into a doing-with activity. State your ideas as questions. Your client may be thinking about these same ideas but has been unwilling to share them. For instance, in this scene, the supervisor could say, "Ask Marilyn if she's interested in going to the college and walking around to get acquainted. If so, ask her if she would like company. Ask her if she would like you to tag along."

Notice that the language is subtly different from the original, but the change in meaning and feeling is significant. It focuses on Marilyn's interest. It puts her out front and the case manager at her side. In other words, it sets up a doing-with relationship in the domain of action. If your client wants to explore the college campus, then you are interested in exploring it with her. If your client wants to explore the college campus but does not want your company, then you have at least validated her thoughts about visiting the campus. Some argue that we have a need for validation or affirmation (Akhtar, 1999). To be affirmed is to feel understood. We all need to feel that our psychological experience is valid; imagine what it would be like to circulate through our mental health system, without this occurring, every single day.

The need for affirmation also means that as a case manager you are available. Validation might also motivate your client to do the activity for herself. By validating her thoughts, you demonstrate respect for her ideas and desires. Respect enables the client to lead the dance of approach and withdraw in which you are engaged and to adjust to changes in her direction and tempo. By staying flexible and knowing when to be active and when to be passive, you will communicate your willingness to tolerate shifts in ideas and moods. This is the foundation for building trust.

There are times when your interactions with clients will be fleeting, as in the two short scenes here. These moments do not have to be understood immediately, but they may have some significance in your client's emerging personal narrative and the story of your developing relationship. Respect the dynamics of these fleeting moments. In particular, respect the experience of not knowing. The human mind is always at work processing information. The significance of seemingly minor events like these will present themselves to you and to your client when each of you is ready.

Observe

August 8

In the 1960s, cinderblocks and concrete rose out of the ruins of tenement houses to form Cuyahoga Community College. It was a boom era for higher education in Ohio. Government officials financed the construction of universities and colleges throughout the state. It was their response to industrial decline. Unemployed factory workers and their children needed something to do, so slums were demolished, buildings were built, faculty members were hired, and the doors swung open for those with little or no money to pay for a private college education or with test scores low enough to be overlooked by admissions counselors. Over the last forty years, as the smoke in the factory districts has thinned and the wires on the electrical poles have thickened, enrollment at the community and state colleges has steadily increased. To thousands of people and their families, these institutions have been a godsend.

Marilyn has an appointment in the department of the college that helps people with physical, emotional, and intellectual disabilities. It is called the PASSWAY office. Lisa watches Marilyn shake hands nervously with the advisor, Ms. A, who has initiated the greeting. Marilyn stands stiff as a board and forgets to introduce Lisa, who introduces herself and explains why she is with her. The three women sit at a private table as Ms. A reviews Marilyn's file, which indicates that she has been diagnosed with dysthymia, a chronic form of depression, and is taking twenty milligrams of fluoxetine for the symptoms. Ms. A explains that the college is still waiting for Marilyn's high school records, including her SAT and ACT scores. Ms. A then explains that people with disabilities are entitled to assistive services from her department. Marilyn is eligible to

- Take tests with a proctor in a private room in the PASSWAY office that minimizes noise and other distractions.

- Use an hour and a half for a test that typically allows for one hour.
- Have a staff person read her the math and English placement exam and take an hour and fifteen minutes to complete it (the typical time is forty-five minutes).
- Receive free tutoring; however, she should sign up now because the sessions get filled quickly.

Ms. A reminds Marilyn that she must take the placement exams before she can enroll in classes, and with that, she begins an individual education plan (IEP). She recommends that Marilyn complete her required math, English, and lab science courses before she takes courses in her major field of study. She shows her the IEP; with part-time study it will take her five years to complete the degree, an associate of applied business in culinary arts.

* * *

Lisa's pickup truck is set high off the road by sixteen-inch wheels and heavy-duty springs, affording driver and passenger a view over the side rails of the bridge into the valley below. Down there, the Cuyahoga River flows northward on a bed of glacial till that has lifted the water more than 600 feet closer to the road than its Pleistocene predecessor. The river is a vein that feeds Lake Erie—the descendant of Glacial Lake Maumee—with an assortment of rural, suburban, and urban toxins: pesticides, herbicides, motor oil, road salt, and raw sewage from drain pipes that have been connected to storm sewers.

Halfway over the bridge, Marilyn complains about her IEP. She cannot believe it will take her five years to complete a two-year program. She sounds embarrassed and a little depressed, so Lisa assures her that many people experience a prolonged course of study, especially if they are working part time as they attend classes. She uses herself as an example.

Marilyn finds no comfort in this reassurance. There's a long silence before she changes the subject and asks Lisa to take her to a convenience store and then to the lumberyard so she can say "hello" to her boyfriend. Lisa obliges.

On the way back to the group home, Marilyn asks what it will be like to live on her own. "You know," she says, "I lived in a dorm at Cedar Point, but that doesn't count for living on my own."

Lisa is surprised by the spontaneity and the personal nature of the question but is encouraged by the possibility that Marilyn may be feeling more comfortable to share her thoughts and feelings—her truth. "Actually," Lisa says, "it's probably a lot like your experience at Cedar Point, but you are responsible for everything. You cook. You clean. You shop. And you have to pay the bills or the electricity gets shut off."

Marilyn listens intently until the truck makes its turn into the driveway. Then, her attention darts to the back door, the one that leads into the kitchen. She begins to talk rapidly. She tells Lisa that it is her turn to cook, and she doesn't want to be late because everyone is counting on her. She cooked last night, too, though it wasn't her turn. She likes to help out. The other residents like her meals, especially her chicken paprikash. It's authentic. To her, cooking is not a chore. It's a pleasure.

Marilyn struggles to hold the admission papers from the college and the two two-liter bottles of Pepsi and cigarettes she bought at the convenience store. As Lisa watches her fumble for the door handle, she notes that Marilyn is demonstrating an awareness of her responsibility to others. She cares about them. She doesn't want to disappoint. "Do you need help getting into the house?" Lisa asks.

"That would be great. I need one hand free so I can open the door and shut it quickly, in case the cat tries to get out."

At the back door, Lisa holds the bottles of Pepsi as Marilyn unlocks the door and barely breaks its seal with the jamb. She has her back to the door and motions for a hand-off. Lisa gives Marilyn the bottles and watches her fall back against the door and spin into the kitchen like a fullback who breaks a tackle for a lunge at an extra yard. Marilyn kicks the door shut. Behind the closed door, there is an ensemble of voices. "Don't let Sparky out!"

* * *

On the way home, Lisa thinks that Ms. A at the college did not ask Marilyn whether she might feel overwhelmed if she takes both math and English in her first semester and did not ask whether Marilyn would like help developing a plan to manage routine homework and reading assignments. In the few weeks she has known Marilyn, Lisa knows how important cooking is to her. An associate degree in culinary arts would be perfect. It would break Lisa's heart to see her fail.

Lisa also wonders why Marilyn did not ask her for help when she was struggling with her groceries and her papers at the back door. She thinks maybe that it was easier for her to ask about the details of living in an apartment of her own than it was to ask for help. Maybe she thinks they are not close enough to be asking for help. Maybe she is too embarrassed to ask. Maybe, at that moment, she felt a wave of vulnerability and was just trying to get out of the truck and into the house to make the feeling go away.

Reflect

Community case management is a world saturated with the possibility for shame, because so much work is done with clients in public. The spotlight of attention from people in the community often makes clients feel on stage, under interrogation or surveillance. In this scene, Marilyn walks into an unfamiliar setting to reveal to a complete stranger that she has a mental illness and that she takes medication. Community settings offer little or no anonymity, and, unfortunately, your presence will contribute to this lack of privacy. At the very least, your presence will raise the curiosity of others. As a result, attention will be directed toward and focused on your clients as people who need help. And you too may feel the same attention.

When you accompany your client in the community, it is important to do with her in the domain of feeling. To accomplish this, you must allow yourself to feel what she is feeling. Notice how Marilyn feels shame at the community college. She stands stiff as a board. She forgets that Lisa is with her. If this happens to you, notice your own feelings. Do you feel ashamed of being ignored even though you are standing next to her? Or do you simply feel bad for her? No matter how you feel shame, it is important to allow and notice it. Resist the impulse to dispel your feeling and your client's by stepping in and doing for her in the domains of thinking or acting. Encourage your client to answer questions posed to her. Later, in private, help her notice the connection between her stiff posture, her forgetting you, and her feeling shame. You might let her know that it is natural for people to feel ashamed in strange settings and that there are ways to use the feeling in a positive way. Ask her what she would like to say or do when she feels ashamed. This will help her develop a self-directed response that is personal and therefore meaningful. In this moment, you will do with her in the domains of feeling and thinking. You will have many opportunities to stand by and admire her as she uses her response in future situations. Look forward to a day when she will do this work spontaneously for herself. It happens.

* * *

There is a difference between shame and stigma, but they are related. Stigma is the social process of marking the body. Shame is an individual emotional reaction to it. Stigma occurs in the external world; shame occurs in the internal world. Shame is the flipside of pride. Shame is felt in the body as a falling-in feeling, like gravity. Pride is felt as a flying-out feeling, like radiant light.

The relationships between stigma, shame, and pride are complex. Let's take an example from American literature. This might help you feel shame. In Nathaniel Hawthorne's novel *The Scarlet Letter,* written in 1850, Hester Prynne is marked by people in her community as an adulteress. They force her to wear a red letter "A" on her gown for conceiving a child out of wedlock. She is stigmatized with the letter "A." Although they do not banish Hester from town, they attempt to banish her in every other way; they banish her emotionally. They shame her.

Today, people in local communities, at least in most places around the world, do not physically mark the bodies of those with mental illness. In other ways, however, we mark as we acquire information and label others. In fact, this is one way that we imagine and create "others." A diagnosis or the names of medications are among the ways that people with mental illness are easily recognized. In short, information always presents the possibility of producing stigma. And by categorizing and labeling, we create "others" who are recognizably different from us. In short, we create an "us" and "them." Think of times in your own life when someone shared personal information about some aspect of your life that you would have preferred remain private. Imagine in this scene how Marilyn is marked as mentally ill. At the community college a woman reads aloud her diagnosis and medication. How would this feel? And although she does not physically mark "M" for medication or "D" for diagnosis, it does leave a social and psychological mark. Imagine that the woman now has the ability to project a red letter "M" (for *mental*) from one eye and a red letter "I" (for *illness*) from the other like the laser-guided aim of a gun; the stigma information follows Marilyn wherever she moves. She can feel it on her back as she walks toward the door. Imagine that all of your clients experience this each time a service provider or any other person in the community acquires information about them. It is important for you to help minimize stigma by protecting the privacy and confidentiality of your clients. You must also remain sensitive to what it means to feel exposed in public places and to be publicly scrutinized by being placed in a box or category: ADHD, bipolar, schizophrenic, medicated, on Ritalin, or on antipsychotics.

Marilyn's experience of shame is deepened in this scene by two additional facts. First, she is enrolling not in a "normal" four-year college but in a two-year college at the bottom of the ladder. She also learns that it will take five years to complete a two-year degree. She is ashamed of not proceeding at the "normal" two-year pace, and she is anxious about the possibility of academic failure. This appears to provoke another anxiety about failure. Will she have the capacity to live successfully in an apartment of her own? Notice that Marilyn's unnamed feelings grow in mass and force as she travels away from the community college toward her perceived future. Shame in the here and now inspires the fear of future shame.

Marilyn's request to see her boyfriend is evidence of an effort to do something about her bad feeling—maybe to ignore or abandon it. We do not know her motivation; however, it might be useful to help her notice her feeling and her response to it, namely, her desire to connect to someone. Marilyn makes a second effort, and this one is obviously positive, but she is unaware of its significance. It is the kind of event that presents a case manager with a wonderful opportunity to help her client notice her own strength.

As Marilyn gets closer to the group home, she suddenly remembers that it is her turn to cook for her fellow residents. At the back door, she transforms shame and anxiety into pride and positive action as she hurries into the kitchen and into her role as culinary artist. From the perspective of reflective case management and mental health recovery, cooking is an important practical therapeutic tool for Marilyn. However, it is not a tool that the manager uses to fix her; rather, it is a tool she uses to transform herself. Some people might call it a therapeutic activity. Others might simply call it a meaningful activity. Whatever you call it, here's how the mechanics of the activity support and promote recovery. For Marilyn, cooking is a specific behavior that enables her to relate to other people in a positive way. Note that the act of cooking is inspired by her feelings and her thoughts—no one else's. Marilyn's fellow residents acknowledge, accept, and appreciate her actions, feelings, and thoughts and serve them back to her with gratitude. In the act of cooking for others, Marilyn is not stigmatized as mentally ill or incapable. She does not feel the gravity of shame. Instead, she is affirmed and celebrated for being useful and, as a result, feels pride. You will recall that some, like Salman Akhtar (1999), argue that affirmation and recognition are human needs. What do Marilyn's fellow residents do to fulfill these needs?

Something else contributes to Marilyn's good feeling, and it is worth noting here. Inside the group home, Marilyn does not feel stigma. Why? Everyone there shares with her a diagnosis. In short, her "difference" (her otherness) is not felt in the same way. As a result, the frequency, intensity, and duration of shame are minimized. Inside the home, it is okay to be as you are. Indeed, as a case manager, you are the outsider. Although your client may trust and feel comfortable with you, you still represent the outside world—the one that creates the "other" through stigma (Corrigan, 2007). Finally, be prepared to respect your client's choice to leave you, even abruptly, when she has returned to a safe and familiar place.

A reflective case manager helps her client notice her own intuitive ability to recover pride in shameful moments. Remember that pride and shame are private, internal experiences. They are feeling states. You cannot convince someone to feel pride. It has to come from inside. Avoid telling your client, "You should be proud of yourself" or "I am proud of you." These statements are your thoughts, not her feelings. Instead, ask your client how it feels when other people appreciate and acknowledge her hard work. If she says, "It feels good," affirm that feeling. Noticing pride is essential for independence—for being able to do for oneself. You can say, "I can tell that you feel good about your accomplishment." Think for minute how different this kind of statement is from, "I'm proud of you."

Observe

August 9

Clean clothes can be made to appear dirty if they've been stuck at the bottom of a two-foot pile of clothes. It's the wrinkles. They distort the texture of the fabric. Marilyn's clothes are usually messy in this way, but today, they are not. Fresh from the laundry, they seem pressed. She is wearing a short-sleeved shirt and new jeans. Her hair is combed; she is wearing makeup. Lisa is pleasantly surprised. "You look nice," she says, with the upswing pitch of genuine admiration.

"I was going to wear a dress, but it's sleeveless. It would have looked stupid with my tattoo." Marilyn raises her sleeve. There is a delicate little flower.

Lisa decides to do some thinking for Marilyn, to make sure she has everything she needs. "Did you find your W2 form?"

"Yes. We have to complete one section."

As Lisa looks at the form, Marilyn tells her that she found the form in a shoebox the group home manager provided for important papers. Lisa notes that Marilyn may have difficulty with managing information, especially about herself.

One of the other residents enters the kitchen. Dolores, a woman in her late forties, says, "I'm ready to go," which surprises Lisa.

"She'd like to come with us," Marilyn says. "I told her it was okay." She looks for Lisa's approval and gets it.

* * *

Backseat drivers are just that: backseat drivers. They have no business telling anyone what to do. They have no steering wheel, no brake pedal, no gas pedal, no keys. They are not in control but try to be; this is what makes them annoying. No matter how hard you try to ignore them, you cannot make them go away. There they are, forever lurking in the letterbox frame of the rearview mirror. Each sentence they speak is like a slap on the back of the head: "Do this. Do that. Turn up the air conditioner. Turn down the radio."

However, when the backseat driver is a charming person, somehow, she isn't really a backseat driver at all. She becomes a part of the experience. Traffic is light, but it is still making Dolores nervous. Lisa can tell she hasn't been in a car in a while. She is tense. She sits in the backseat of the extended cab with the posture of a hawk on the hunt. She says, "Watch this car on your left," and "Don't go too fast," and "Don't trust that guy up there." Lisa has noticed that, of all the residents in the group home, Dolores is most like the mother of the group. She's also noticed that the psychiatrist seems to be getting the right mix of medication for Dolores. She appears less lethargic, more animated. Lisa looks into the rearview mirror and teases Dolores good-naturedly. She calls her "our tour guide."

Dolores smiles. "I used to be a driver. You know I drove."

Marilyn says, "At least you had a chance to drive. I never have."

"I used to go to college, too," Dolores says. "Marilyn is inspiring me. I'm thinking about going to college again."

This exchange seems to encourage Marilyn to talk more, and she wonders out loud whether college will be too difficult. She says that her family is not encouraging her. However, people at the group home and the lumberyard support her; they told her about the community college and the office that helps people with disabilities.

The financial aid office, like most on campus, is a large, cavernous cinderblock room. It's cold. Dim light passes through the narrow windows, giving the place a dark and depressing feel. From outside it looks like a prison. The furniture is orange and brown and shoddy. The carpet is worn. The first thing you see is a sign on the wall: "All visitors sign in." If you were anxious, like Marilyn, the experience could be intimidating, especially if you were alone. There is nothing familiar or warm here. There is nothing to latch onto emotionally, and the currents of the impersonal could quickly drag you down into the undertow. If you sought the refuge of a chair against the wall to make the anxious feeling go away, you might forget to sign in and sit there all day, with nobody calling your name.

Marilyn signs the sheet and quickly finds a seat. She moves about anxiously. She hands her financial aid and tax forms to Lisa, who, without thinking about this moment as a moment for learning, begins to ask Marilyn questions and fill out the forms for her. When Marilyn's name is called, she and Lisa go to the clerk's window. The worker behind the desk seems tired and unapproachable. You can feel his eagerness to end the day. And you are a reminder that it's hours away. Mumbling, almost inaudibly, he says, "Are you a student here? Been here before?"

"Not yet," Marilyn says. "I am applying and have orientation today. I need to turn this in and get a purchase agreement form."

"Is your high school transcript on file in the admissions office?"

"Not yet. I've requested it."

Brusquely, he says, "You can't turn anything in until we have your transcripts." He takes a phone call and after several minutes returns with two forms. Nothing is said about the long wait. Curtly, he says, "These need to be filled out, and you didn't mark the aid form correctly, so you're gonna have to fill it out the right way and white out any stray marks. I'll have staff check the computers for your grade. Fill out the forms and bring them back here. You have to fill these out. You don't have to sign in again. You just have to come to the desk." One can feel his desire to be somewhere else and to be doing something different with his life, much as Marilyn feels.

Soon Marilyn returns with forms in hand; the clerk, still exuding annoyance, instructs her to hold them, "all of them," and to return them to the financial aid office after the high school transcripts have been delivered to admissions.

With Lisa's cell phone Marilyn calls the board of education in her old neighborhood. She's relieved: Her transcripts can be picked up, today. The day's not yet over. In Lisa's truck they're off to retrieve the records. First, however, they drop Dolores at the group home; and as they pass through Marilyn's old neighborhood, she voices her frustration about the financial aid and admissions paperwork. She tells Lisa that she gets headaches if she reads a lot or watches a lot of television.

Lisa wonders whether she has ever had an eye exam. "Do you think you might need glasses?"

"I had them before, but the doctor said they wouldn't help me see better."

"How long since you've had your eyes checked?"

"Since the doctor said they wouldn't help me."

Lisa tries to figure out when that might have been—grade school or high school—but Marilyn does not remember. Lisa notes that the PASSWAY office did not ask about her eyes. It appears that the office is looking for the big disabilities and is overlooking the small ones. "You might want to consider getting an eye exam before school starts," Lisa says, "because the headaches will make you miserable when you start going to school. You'll have a lot of reading to do."

Marilyn agrees. She says, "I hope there's a one-stop place to get it done."

* * *

You can tell that back on her home turf Marilyn is at ease. She approaches, without hesitation, a woman at the end of a long hall, a woman she does not know. Not the least bit anxious, she says, "Maybe you can help me with this. I called earlier about my transcript and was told it would be ready."

With transcripts in hand, Marilyn returns with Lisa to the college. First to the admissions office, as they had been instructed, then to financial aid, where she is referred to Mrs. F, who instructs her to set another appointment to complete even more paperwork. By now Lisa and Marilyn are exhausted from the several trips and the many detours. Lisa cannot tell whether Marilyn feels disappointed. She senses that Marilyn is pushing the feeling away.

Reflect

Marilyn is dressed and ready to go. She is eager to achieve her goal for the day, that is, to register for classes. She carries with her positive words of encouragement from the staff at the group home, and her good friend, Dolores, accompanies her for support.

If you want to stop the momentum of self-confidence in its tracks, throw an institution into its path. In this scene, Marilyn collides with the college bureaucracy. The result: frustration and disappointment. Yet Lisa cautiously avoids advocacy. She knows that Marilyn must experience the rules, the regulations, and the procedures of the organization. When you accompany your clients to institutions, stand back, observe, and curb your impulse to become active or to advocate unless absolutely necessary. Instead, help your clients notice their frustration and verbalize their own ideas for remedying troublesome situations. Stand by to admire as they test out ideas and discover ones that work and ones that do not.

Goals are important. But don't overestimate their significance. Goals provide a context or purpose for the relationship between you and your clients. What transpires in that context is most important: your client's ability to notice her feelings, thoughts, and actions in her relationship with you and in relationships with people in the community, toward achieving goals. Goals are milestones or markers along the way toward recovery. And in reflective case management, we must be cautious not to get distracted by disappointment when clients fail to achieve goals. Instead, stay focused on the here and now; help your client, and others, notice when emotional reactions are too big, too small, or just right.

Stay focused on the process. How does your client fall apart? Remember, we all have moments when we become disorganized. How do you manage? How does she recover her good feeling and carry on? Notice something important about Marilyn's frustration in this scene. How does she feel in the unfamiliar setting of the college campus? Notice that she rebounds at the board of education in her old neighborhood. There, she assertively seeks help. How does she reconnect with her assertive side? Explore this with her. If she tells you that she feels more comfortable here because it is familiar, ask her whether she has ideas for making the college feel more familiar—more like home. Would getting a job on campus, maybe in the PASSWAY office, help her connect with the people at the college? Would this help make the place feel more familiar?

As things fall apart for our clients, we tend to become active. We become active to keep things together. This is often unavoidable. One way to become active is to resort to goal setting, a form of doing for your client in the domain of thinking. This can easily become a backward move. The more you revert to goal setting, the less likely you are to engage your client's capacity to observe what's going on. In a way, goal setting can trump the process and thereby inhibit our capacity for self-observation. When you review your work for the day, talk to your supervisor about your reactions to client goals. Staying in touch with your internal world will make you more effective at helping your client stay in touch with hers.

Observe

August 15

Marilyn is coughing terribly. Inside Lisa's truck, the cough is amplified. It makes Lisa uncomfortable. Today, Marilyn is scheduled to take her placement exams for English and math. First she has an appointment at the financial aid office. Lisa tries to help Marilyn with her anxiety. She says, "How are you feeling?"

Marilyn does not answer the question. She starts talking instead about her upcoming trip to Six Flags amusement park. "I've been saving my own money," she says, "and my mom is giving me some, too."

"How are you feeling about the tests?"

"Okay. A little nervous. Mostly, I feel real congested and tired from this cold."

"Do you have a pencil?"

"Yes. It's in my purse."

Marilyn arrives at the financial aid office with an hour and a half to spare before the entrance exam. She meets Mrs. F, the financial aid counselor, who signs a purchase agreement and tells her to go to Registration to enroll for classes. There, they wait in line for half an hour. At the window, the clerk tells Marilyn that her purchase agreement is useless until she is registered and has her student identification card, which she cannot get until she takes the entrance exam. After a deep sigh and long, frustrated silence, Marilyn begins to explain everything she has been told by the financial aid counselor and the PASSWAY office. The clerk, dismissive and defensive, produces in Marilyn one response: She abandons her assertive side. She stands silent and stiff as a board. Lisa steps in to advocate, with matter-of-fact determination. "Excuse me. I need to know the proper sequence and steps for getting registered." The clerk outlines the process:

1. High school transcripts
2. Financial aid forms
3. Purchase agreement
4. Entrance exams
5. Student ID
6. Registration for classes

Lisa repeats what the clerk said, then compares the new information with the old information Marilyn received from financial aid. Finally the clerk drops her defensive posture, apologizes, and says, "They were wrong."

On the way to the testing center, Lisa thinks that the college should do better with communicating how to navigate its bureaucracy and that the PASSWAY office should employ students to do this work with new students so they don't get overwhelmed by the complexities and quit. Marilyn might have given up had she been alone, she suspects.

There is a half hour before the test. Lisa asks, "What would be the most valuable use of your time? Would you like to be alone so you can eat your lunch and prepare? Or would you prefer company to distract you and keep you from getting too nervous?"

Marilyn has not taken a test since high school. She has never performed well. Staring into space, she considers her answer. "I think the second option is best."

In the cafeteria, Lisa buys Marilyn a Pepsi and wishes her luck. Marilyn eats the sandwich and chips she packed and talks again about her upcoming trip to Six Flags. She reminisces about the park and the changes it's undergone since her youth. There's a long silence before she takes a cigarette from her purse. It's one of those silences that feels like you've lost contact. She draws deeply from the cigarette while she tells Lisa. "I've been smoking since I was fifteen." She'd like to cut back, she says. She continues, "I didn't smoke much at home. I was afraid my mother would smell it." She now smokes a half to a full pack a day. "I need to calm my nerves," she says. Lisa secretly hopes that the cigarette will do the work that Marilyn intends. But she knows it will not.

* * *

The PASSWAY office is exactly as Marilyn and Lisa had left it: large, cold, impersonal. However, Ms. A recognizes Marilyn. She invites her to her office. There, she asks, "Do you have a pencil?"

Marilyn says, "It's in my purse."

For the first time, Ms. A informs Marilyn that she does not have to take both the math and English placement exams today. She may take one and postpone the other until next Tuesday or even next semester.

Marilyn smiles. Marilyn laughs and sighs with relief. "I'll take math next semester." Jubilantly, she says, "Next Tuesday won't work. I'm going to Six Flags."

In the test room, Ms. A introduces Marilyn to the proctor, who asks to see Marilyn's identification. The proctor invites her to sit and says, "Do you have a pencil?"

Marilyn responds to the question with a matter-of-fact consistency of the well rehearsed. "It's in my purse."

Reflect

Nobody wants to fail. Nobody wants to see those they care for fail. But how do you stop nervousness from gaining momentum and making that leap into a full-blown falling apart? As a case manager, you cannot stop your client from feeling what she feels and how she feels. However, you can help her notice the process. It is in the act of noticing (thinking) that we regain control. Noticing will acquaint her with her internal world. She will discover strengths and weaknesses and develop strategies for using her internal world to navigate the complex web of social relationships in the community.

* * *

On this day in Cleveland, Ohio, where the story of Marilyn takes place, calm northwesterly winds bring cool, dry air and cobalt blue skies down from Canada, over Lake Erie, and into town. As the dog days of summer approach, these winds remind us of how that same lake can turn terrifyingly severe. Today, however, the lake gives one the sense and assurance that no matter what happens, life is good, it has been good, and it will continue to be good. Eventually, there comes a subtle shift; if you don't notice, if you don't consider its significance, you will not be prepared.

A solitary breath of warm, moist air from the southwest marks the subtle shift. It passes as quickly and insignificantly as a car on the street, but it foreshadows the disappearance of the cool northwest breeze, the stillness, then the quiet, then the nervous rustling of leaves, the whirling of dust and debris, the thick gray clouds, the rolling thunder, the roaring wind, and the pulverizing rain.

There is a moment of caution before any big event, like an English or math exam, that inspires each of us to get motivated. Yet if that restless feeling goes unnoticed, it may gain momentum as one gets closer to the event and transform into hesitancy, doubt, depression, anxiety, the harsh clamorous voice of the internal self-critic, the feeling that you have failed and that there is evidence, once again, that you are no good. There are a couple of possible external expressions for this kind of internal event, and they are much like the responses you might have to one of those foreboding storms that roars out of the south during August in Cleveland. You will either stop dead in your tracks and watch in awe, incapable of uttering a single thought or word, or you will turn and run like hell.

No compassionate case manager wants to see her client become overwhelmed by powerful feelings in the face of a stressful event and fail to achieve a goal. Therefore, you might feel the impulse to help your client prepare by reviewing mental checklists that focus on the content of the task at hand. You might ask her some questions: "Do you have your forms? Do you have your prescriptions? Do you have your bus fare? Do you have a pencil?" Notice that these thoughts are yours. Notice, too, that your thoughts have feelings behind them. Maybe your client is not alone in feeling anxious. Maybe you are feeling anxious. If so, your anxiety will not help; rather, it will add to hers. She will intuitively feel the burden not only of her anxiety but also yours. The best way to help prepare for a stressful event is to help her notice her internal reaction to it. Help her notice the natural nervousness, the healthy anxiety, and her ideas for actions that help maintain a positive outlook. Help her notice, too, what has worked in the past. Remind her that there have been times when she's not felt overwhelmed.

When preparing for a trip to an institution such as a college, a welfare office, or a service agency, it is helpful to remind your client that she may encounter unhelpful or aggressive people and to remind her of your observations of her reactions to these kinds of people. It may be helpful to role-play and prepare responses.

In this scene, we do not know exactly what Marilyn is feeling in the registration office with the dismissive clerk. However, we do know that she responds with a silent and stiff posture. It is safe to assume that her internal storm (her fear of failure) is strong and that, as a result, she is unable to organize her thoughts, formulate words, and speak the billowing truth about the situation: She is spending a lot of time in the wrong lines, not getting what she needs, and people are not accurately communicating the registration process. This is not her fault. This is their fault. And nobody is taking responsibility for poor customer service.

When you find yourself in a situation where you have to advocate for your client, know that you are doing with her in the domain of feeling and doing for her in the domains of thinking and acting.[11] Take the time afterward to explore this so she can become aware of it. Consider saying something like, "I was feeling very frustrated because they were not treating you fairly. They were not giving you information you needed. I could tell that you were also feeling very frustrated and overwhelmed. Did you notice that you were quiet? Did you notice that you were unable to respond to the clerk when she got snippy with you?"

Wait for your client's response and work with it, then find a way to talk further about it. You might consider saying, "We spent a lot of time in those lines, and they were the wrong lines. We listened to the advice, and it was the wrong advice. So it wasn't our fault. Did you notice that I asked the clerk to give us a step-by-step outline of what we needed to do? In a way I was doing for you. But I am doing with you now. I am *thinking with you so* that you will have a way of taking care of yourself when I am not here."

Sometimes you will not have the luxury to talk with your client after the event. Sometimes you will act immediately to help her observe in the moment of crisis. Imagine saying, "I see that you do not know how to respond right now. I am not sure if this will help, but I have a thought. Let's try this and see if it works." It might feel awkward or a bit artificial to help your client observe herself in these moments, but it may also be a constructive activity; it invites her into the advocacy. She notices herself being stuck and notices that there is always a way out.

* * *

One final note: When you meet people involved in your client's life, notice who and how many are accustomed to doing for your client in the domains of thinking and acting; notice, too, what they are inclined to do. You could make a list; study the list, and over time you will see patterns. Perhaps you do for Marilyn in the domain of action. Perhaps a sibling does something else.

Observe

September 5 to 8

Marilyn receives a new financial aid form and calls Lisa to ask for her help in understanding and filling it out. Lisa meets her at the lumberyard and reviews the paperwork with her. Marilyn is taking an English class and physical education and likes them both. She asks to borrow Lisa's mini-cassette recorder, so she can tape lectures. Lisa lends the equipment.

Reflect

Marilyn takes initiative. She asks Lisa to help her with the new financial aid form. She does not expect Lisa to do the work for her. Marilyn, too, does some independent problem solving: She anticipates that a mini-cassette recorder will help in coursework and asks to borrow the equipment. In this brief encounter we see how clients move between all four forms of relationship in the matrix (see table 1.2). Marilyn may have needed Lisa to do for her a week before, but this week she is doing for herself. Help her notice this. Remember, we all have times in our lives, even during the course of the day, when we move back and forth between doing for, doing with, standing by, and letting go.

Observe

October 6

Lisa helps Marilyn acquire four things all in the same day: prescriptions, cigarettes, coffee, and conversation. Marilyn likes this coffee shop because she can smoke. Lisa likes it because there is a patio where Marilyn can smoke and she can breathe.

The patio of the coffee shop is on a sidewalk, adjacent to a brick street in a part of the city near downtown. It is a comeback neighborhood whose story has been told and retold in the local papers for twenty years. Revitalization in the rustbelt is slow.

The coffee shop, on a short street lined with a microbrewery, a wine bar, and a posh restaurant, caters to those whose tastes are calibrated for California wines and locally grown produce sold at a historic market a stone's throw away. By *local,* they mean Ohio. Actually, the emphasis on local is a good idea. It helps people find the value of what's in front of them and around them. The revitalization is also good. The neighborhood offers a vibrant public culture, and here at the coffee shop everyone seems welcome.

Lisa talks to Marilyn about her social network. She is trying to find out how much help she is getting from her case manager, the group home supervisor, and the staff at the community college. But Marilyn is more interested in discussing her favorite PlayStation games and horror films and what she and her friends do for fun and leisure. She smokes, drinks coffee, and watches people as they pass. She cannot wait for Halloween. It's her favorite holiday. She is not sure what costume she will wear. She wants to dye her hair.

"Do you think I'm too old to go trick-or-treating?" she asks.

Lisa tries to answer the question gracefully. "People are not accustomed to seeing grownups out trick-or-treating," she says, "and perhaps it's best to dress up for fun and take your nieces out in the neighborhood."

* * *

Lisa drives Marilyn to her mother's house, where she will spend the weekend. In Cleveland's postwar working-class neighborhoods, identical bungalows stand shoulder to shoulder as far as the eye can see. Marilyn shows little interest in having Lisa meet her family. She tells her to stop at the driveway, grabs her bag, jumps out, and says, "Thanks for the ride," then shuts the door and walks toward the house.

The monotonous scenery on the bungalow-lined backstreets makes Lisa think about her current dilemma. Marilyn, like a teenager who responds to adults with abbreviated answers to important questions, offers only curt responses: "Classes are good" and "I'm reading a book" and "People are okay." She wonders whether Marilyn understands her questions and, if not, why she does not ask for clarification. She wonders whether the questions feel intrusive and whether Marilyn remains silent for protection.

Reflect

In this scene, Marilyn is obviously not interested in talking about recovery-related topics. Social networks are not on her mind. She talks instead about fun stuff: video games and Halloween. Notice, too, that she is about to spend the weekend with family. The shift to reflecting on her youth, especially Halloween, may serve the same purpose as her discussion of the amusement park did just before the stressful event of her college entrance exams. Talking about Halloween may be an attempt to regulate or avoid anxious feelings about being with family. Help her observe the shift. If she is reluctant to talk about it, respect her wish, back off, but flag the incident in your mind. Pay attention to these shifts. There will be other opportunities to help her observe them. And by paying attention to them, you will learn more about what they mean to Marilyn.

There is clearly a moment in this scene for the work of reflexive case management. Marilyn asks whether she is too old for trick-or-treating. She is twenty-three. Of course she is too old. How can you help her observe this? Lisa decides to help by suggesting that she share her enthusiasm with her nieces. Marilyn reports that they like her because she can relate to them. Here is an opportunity for her to be a caregiver who is willing to connect with her nieces in an unorthodox way by getting into character for the ritual.

Observe

October 11

Marilyn needs support to talk to Ms. A, the advisor in the PASSWAY office at the community college, so Lisa goes with her. She is falling behind in English and wants to be transferred to a health education course. One option, physical education, is too strenuous, and she's not accustomed to that level of activity.

Ms. A suggests that Marilyn sign up for tutoring at the PASSWAY office, but there is a two-week wait, or she can go to the humanities office, where there is no wait. She also helps plan classes for next year. Marilyn understands "math,' "English," and "health education," but she does not understand "social sciences" and "humanities." Ms. A explains that these include art appreciation, foreign language, anthropology, sociology, and social work. Lisa observes that Marilyn is having a hard time understanding. To her, life is more concrete. There is cooking, dancing, reading, writing, painting, and counting things. Marilyn's eyes glaze over, fixed trance-like on the lips of the woman who delivers the complex jumble of words, as if she'd not heard a single one. Finally, she says to Ms. A, "Can I have access to a computer to look up my identification number for financial aid information?"

* * *

There seems to be something about the bridges over the Cuyahoga River that inspires reflection about the relationship between nature and the urban worlds we've constructed. In 1969, saturated with industrial pollutants, the river caught on fire, though not for the first time in Cleveland's history. *Time* magazine wrote of the incident,

> Some River! Chocolate-brown, oily, bubbling with subsurface gases, it oozes rather than flows. "Anyone who falls into the Cuyahoga does not drown," Cleveland's citizens joke grimly. "He decays." . . . The Federal Water Pollution Control Administration dryly notes: "The lower Cuyahoga has no visible signs of life, not even low forms such as leeches and sludge worms that usually thrive on wastes." It is also—literally—a fire hazard. ("The Cities," 1969:41–44)

On the bridge, Marilyn reveals that she recently went through a "nasty breakup" with her boyfriend that sent her into several days of increased panic, anxiety, and depression. She was unable to concentrate and to complete her basic activities of daily living: getting out of bed, taking a shower, fixing meals, and doing her daily chores around the group home. She missed a couple of classes and several days of work. Her ex-boyfriend works at the lumberyard, not too far from the bridge, and she panicked about the possibility of seeing him. He has since transferred to another place of employment, so she has returned to work. It is easier to concentrate without him there. She told her mom and sister about the breakup, and this made her feel stupid and self-conscious, like a failure, as if it were her fault. She says this is what usually happens when she has a breakup. She asks whether Lisa knows of any groups or social clubs where she might be able to meet somebody.

Reflect

If you focus on the content of this scene, there are two issues with which Marilyn struggles: the complexities of higher education and troubles with relationships. Yet if you focus on the process of her relationship to these events, you will discover a theme that connects them: an emotional resonance that vibrates below the surface. For Marilyn, these are feelings of inadequacy and shame.

The reflective case manager must help her client hear this resonance and understand its influence on her life. In a situation like that described here, you might consider saying something like, "You asked me to go with you to the PASSWAY office. You told me you needed moral support. Tell me about the feelings you were having when you asked for help. And what about the feelings while you were talking to Ms. A?"

Listen to your client, then bring her back to her boyfriend. "You told me how you felt after you talked to your mother and your sister about the breakup." Again, wait. If she has trouble, help her. Tell her that she reported feeling inadequate and ashamed. Then, help her make a deeper connection: "Although you told me about your response to your family, you did not tell me about feelings you had when your boyfriend broke up with you. Perhaps there's a way you can talk about these."

It is quite possible that your client will try to avoid these painful feelings. Resist the temptation to assure her that she'll be "okay." Assurance is a form of doing for your client in the domain of feeling. Instead, find a way to remind her that she is safe. Re-state what she has said about her feelings and let her know that you are feeling with her; one way to do this is by telling her, "I am sorry. It must have made you feel so hurt and unhappy that your relationship ended. Losing somebody you care for is very difficult." Feeling with can been described as empathy, as a shared feeling or emotional attune-ment. However, you should not assume that everyone is looking for you to share a feeling. In fact, some may be frightened or threatened by your empathic gestures or attempts at emotional attunement.[12] You may also find another's attempt at attune-ment equally offputting. And some of these differences may be cultural ones. It is im-portant to know that empathy is an emotional state that is relational, shared, negoti-ated, and potentially disruptive (Freedberg, 2007; Halpern, 2001; Hollan, 2008).

The next important step is to help your client connect her feelings about the loss of her boyfriend to difficulties with concentration. Here's one way to do it: "I no-ticed that when you recalled the hurtful feeling and the shame, you got very quiet. You drifted. You had a hard time concentrating and finding words. I know you can concentrate and think for yourself. I remember how you answered the phone at work and responded to customers. I remember how you listened to my questions about your past and how you recalled in such detail your summers at Cedar Point amusement park. And I also recall how you always remember to cook for the others at the group home and that you prepare meals with such pleasure and confidence."

By remembering with your client in this way, you may be fulfilling one of our most basic human needs: the need to remember a time when things were okay. This is a special kind of remembering. It is remembering that will help your client develop a sense of a remembering self: one who has remembered and can remember. It also offers continuity of self-experience: "I was this way yesterday, and I experience myself similarly today." You are simply helping her remember. When the time is right, help your client complete the work of remembering both the happy and the hurtful moments and the relationship between the two. Try saying something like, "When you get very embarrassed, you feel a lot of shame and forget that you can concentrate and do for yourself. I wonder if you've observed this, too? Do you see that your feelings of pride help you take care of yourself? Do you see that overwhelming shame makes you forget your pride and your ability to do for yourself?

* * *

There is another significant event in this scene. Marilyn asks Lisa whether she knows of any social clubs that she could attend to meet a new boyfriend. She is obviously interested in moving on, and you may feel the impulse to help her do it. After all, you do not want to see your client suffer. A reflective case manager resists the temptation to give her client a list of social clubs and instead helps her notice her own desire and ability to move on. Here is an example of a doing-for response that should be avoided: "I'll help you find those clubs. We got to get you out there, girl. For someone like you, there have to be a dozen guys out there."

In contrast, here is an example of a doing-with response: "I can hear in your voice your desire to move on and to find someone who is right for you. I know you can use this feeling to your advantage. How did you do it before? How did you find a boyfriend in the past? What qualities do you want your new boyfriend to have? Do you have any ideas about how or where you might find Mr. Right?"

Observe

October 13

Lisa takes Marilyn to a movie to get her mind off her old boyfriend. She purposely avoids asking Marilyn questions. She just lets the relationship happen. They talk about nothing but the movie. Marilyn thinks that Mel Gibson is cute.

November 1

Marilyn is receiving payment-due statements from the community college. They are making her nervous. There is apparently information still missing in her financial aid file. She asks Lisa for help. The letters are intimidating. They tell her that she signed a purchase agreement. She is responsible for all payments. They threaten to withhold her grades if the college does not receive the money. Marilyn feels bad. The feeling is pressing in on her. Her world seems heavy and gray. She is a bad because she got involved in a relationship that did not last. She is a bad because she missed work. She is behind in classes. She is a bad because she owes money she doesn't have. Everything is her fault, she says.

Lisa picks her up at the group home around 9:30 A.M. They arrive at the financial aid office by 9:50. Ms. F assures her that everything will work out.

Reflect

There are times when you must leave your client alone with her feelings, especially when they are overwhelming. Stay in tune with the feelings but resist the temptation to poke at them with the big stick of persistent questioning or to smother them with a warm quilt of reassurance. Here, again, you may be meeting one of our most basic human needs: to have our feelings acknowledged, not questioned. In short, it is a quiet listening presence.

If you listen carefully to Marilyn's story, you will hear that she is missing her boyfriend. She is missing work. She is missing her payment deadlines for school. She is missing classes. Yet if you listen for the emotional resonance that connects these incidents, you will hear a theme: Marilyn is experiencing the pain of separation. Two weeks ago, she felt shame for being cut off from her boyfriend. Now, she is feeling very alone and turning that pain inward, toward the self. She is adding to the weight of shame by shaming herself. In the internal eye of her self-perception, she's not done something bad, she *is* bad. That's the essential difference between the feeling of shame and the feeling of guilt. With shame, we feel damaged, flawed, rejected. With guilt, we feel like we've done something wrong. The difference is great. Try to remember it.

In situations that present your client with negative consequences, help her sort out what is realistic. This will establish a clear definition of what is within her control, what can be changed, and what can't be changed. You should know that her "I'm bad" attitude, language, and story get in the way of (or inhibit) her confident self. It is a language of dependency. It is as if she is saying, "I'm bad, so will you do these things for me?" Help her transform this dependent attitude into creative thinking and positive action. You might consider helping her name her current emotional state by saying something like, "It seems like these bad feelings come and go a lot, and you direct them toward yourself and make yourself feel worse. I know that you are capable of going to the financial aid office to take care of this overdue statement. I know you are asking for my help because you are feeling overwhelmed. However, I think this is an occasion when you need to tell me that you are feeling overwhelmed and that it would help to have my support, and this is why you are asking me to do this with you. It is so important for you to say this to me now, because it puts you in control. You are taking control by telling me you are overwhelmed and that you would like me to go with you." *Empowerment* is another useful way to describe the feeling one gets from being in control.

* * *

Your job as case manager is to respect your client's emotional state and to encourage her to assume as much responsibility as possible. Avoid slipping into the habit of focusing on goals. If you do, you're no longer paying attention to the process of your relationship. Consider this. It is possible that when we find ourselves reverting to routines, such as goal setting, we may be feeling burnout. Take a break. Ask your supervisor to do with you in the domain of thinking. Ask him or her to help you evaluate your interactions with clients. Maybe you're just doing for too much. One way to understand your unique experience of burnout is to keep a daily log of the hours you spend doing for, doing with, standing by, and letting go. At the end of the day or week, look at how your time is allocated. If you find yourself doing for much of the time, consider visiting with your supervisor about reallocation of the work so that activities are more evenly distributed. You many also find that you are doing for when you should be allocating more effort to doing with. At other times, you may find that your agency and social policy environment leaves few options but to do for. At the other extreme, we may find ourselves letting go before our clients are ready. Remember, we all move between these, even during the course of the day. And there may be times when you need to reevaluate your motivations for this kind of work. Are you a doing-for kind of person? We all have different motivations for entering the helping professions, and it's always a good idea to explore them. This might be something you take up with your supervisor, or in your own reflective moments you might want to ask, "Am I doing for someone because it is my habit to do so?"

Our tendency to do for often manifests in two ways: It may come from you or from your client. You may be acting on your own need to take care of someone, and, as a result, you may not be taking time to notice and reflect. On the other hand, your client may be acting on her desire to be taken care of. She may not voice her need for help. Either way, you should notice this silence when possible. You can reduce the burden of this kind of caregiving by breaking the pattern of doing for by noticing and talking about it. When you use your voice, you organize your thinking. And these thoughts function like a sorting bin for future action. The process works the same for your client. When she voices her ideas and hears her options, it is as if she is seeing the options. It gives her a chance to choose. Eventually, with practice, she will learn to do this for herself, with little thought, in her relationship with you and with others. She will not be afraid to think, to voice, to choose, to try, and to try again until she gets what she wants and needs—with success and satisfaction.

Observe

December 3

There are other people Lisa works with in the study of mental health services in Cuyahoga County, so she attends to those who call. Lisa has not heard from Marilyn for nearly a month. Today, suddenly, she calls. Lisa is on her way to work. She answers.

"It's me, Marilyn. I'm calling to get advice."

"Okay." Lisa does not know what to expect.

"Was it a mistake to go to college this semester? I've missed seven days of classes because of illness."

"Physical illness or because you're having a hard time?"

"It's a combination. Anxiety, depression, and panic attacks, and now a cold and flu."

Lisa assures her that making the effort is not a mistake and reminds her of all the challenges she overcame to get into school.

Marilyn thinks she has viral and urinary tract infections, so she is going to the hospital. The emergency room is her only option. She is worried about getting kicked out of school or failing. She feels she has missed so many classes. She is humiliated: One of her instructors told her that going to school was probably not a good thing. She is afraid that her mom and sister, too, will see her as a failure. Her sister believes that she creates her own problems.

Lisa helps Marilyn develop a plan to ask her social support network for help. She suggests that Marilyn call Ms. A from the PASSWAY office for her opinion and to call her instructor to inform him of her medical emergency. She then recommends that she ask the group home supervisor to find appropriate medical care. Marilyn listens, agrees, and then asks Lisa to hold while she answers another call. The call is lost. She does not call back.

* * *

The open road gives Lisa time to think. She wonders what the instructor said. Did he tell Marilyn that she should not be in school, or did he say this was not a good time for her to be in school because of her circumstances? Is Marilyn perceiving and interpreting the conversation accurately? Either way, the instructor's comment has shaken her confidence; what she feels is shame.

Reflect

There is a spectrum of feeling that begins with a dull shade of gray and gradually bleeds toward black. It begins with self-consciousness—the feeling of being watched and judged. It may be followed by embarrassment, shame, humiliation, and mortification. The root of the word *mortified* is *mors,* which means "death." At this end of the spectrum, one can easily feel there is no hope. And often when we feel mortified, we abandon hope, taking our own lives and sometimes the lives of others. We all regularly feel shame, and we sometimes feel mortified. It's a continuum. With Marilyn there is the sense that the world is pressing in like the force of gravity. Under this pressure, confidence cracks, and the self falls inward, from gray to more gray to black. Collapse. This is what happens when we collapse under the weight of sharp words, probing stares, the slap of a hand, the blow of a fist, disregard, disrespect, and disinterest. The root of the word *embarrass* means "to cut with a sharp tool."

* * *

Many of your clients experience the stigma of being labeled mentally ill. They have a diagnosis. They take medication. They have felt rejection by family, friends, co-workers, employers, or others in the community because of difficulties in communicating or interacting in socially acceptable ways. As a result, it is likely that your clients feel an anxious expectation of rejection; they will protect themselves from the potential of the shame that results from it. Can you recall a time in your own life when you felt the shame of rejection?

In this scene, Marilyn experiences anxious expectation of failure. She anticipates being seen as defective, as someone who, as her sister says, "creates her own problems." In moments like these, you may help your client with confidence by helping her recognize strengths. Marilyn is aware of difficult feelings. You might also consider standing by to admire. Here is what you might say: "I hear you loud and clear. You are struggling. You know what is happening inside. You took the initiative to call me. You are doing for yourself in feeling, thinking, and action. I am wondering whether you hear yourself the way I am hearing you." Ask how she might use her feelings to take steps to resolve her problem. Remember that the debilitating feelings are hers. She needs to find a way to transform them into feelings that will inspire positive action.

* * *

After a month's break, Marilyn calls Lisa.

Imagine times in your own life when you lose contact with important people. You are puzzled. So it is with Lisa. You might wonder whether the break in your relationship contributed to her missing seven classes. It is common in all case management, health and mental health, to feel helpless in situations like these. The job is often overwhelming. The mental health system demands from you productivity, billable time, client compliance, endless hours of documentation, and, of course, unreasonable caseloads. Feelings of helplessness are common; they are also quite painful and annoying. You may wonder, "Did I do or say something, what might it have been, and how can I fix it?" Talk to your supervisor about these feelings, and realize that your client may have needed a break from work with you. Case management is difficult for us all, managers and clients.

At other times a client who has cut herself off may be missing you. She may reconnect with you by making a crisis call. When this happens, it is important to stay calm. See this as an opportunity to reconnect. In short, don't let the immediacy of the crisis cloud your judgment. Let your client know that someone has been wondering about her. Let her know that you care. Here is an example of what you might say: "It is nice to hear from you. I have been thinking about you." This simple message welcomes your client back and invites her to pick up where you left off.

* * *

In reflecting on this scene, it is worth wondering how Marilyn's life experience may have contributed to her crisis at the community college. While she was growing up, how did she reconnect after separations to significant people such as her adoptive mother and adoptive father? Notice the process and the content of Marilyn's attempt to reconnect with Lisa. She says, "I am calling for some advice. Was it a mistake to go to college this semester?" She also reports that she is afraid of being expelled from school.

Talk to your supervisor about this and wonder together about the significance of the details. How do these current events relate to past ones? Consider this. Was Marilyn absent from classes in grade school and high school when she experienced separations from her adoptive parents? (Remember, she reported that her adoptive father became ill and died during her childhood, and later her adoptive mother became ill with a heart attack and stroke.) If Marilyn did miss school during these moments of crisis with significant caregivers, then old worries may be interfering with her goals with success and satisfaction in the present.

Lisa also thinks about the advice she's just given: a plan for her network, seeking medical attention. Is it too much, or too little? One needs to be cautious about giving advice. Why? What is advice? When you give advice, you are often telling someone what to do. Ask yourself: In giving advice, are you doing for? When we give advice, we should be aware of our motivations: Why? When? How? Do we give advice because we feel helpless to help others with their own solutions? Do we give advice because it is expedient, it seems easier? Do we give advice because we believe others incapable of finding their own solutions? Do we give advice during crises only or all the time? In short, are we advice-giving types? There may be times when our agencies and organizations require advice giving and when it is especially appropriate.

And many of us constantly seek advice, not only during crises but also in an everyday way. Explore the motivations of advice seekers. Wonder with them how, why, and when they seek advice. And surely there are times when we must give advice because we have expert knowledge or understanding. Consider this piece of advice: Explore first the reasons, your own and others', for seeking advice. Consider, too, the feelings behind advice seeking. It is not uncommon that when feelings are clarified, advice is unnecessary, and the advice seeker can then take full responsibility for his or her actions. Foremost, don't forget: Your advice may be wrong. You cannot know all possible courses and outcomes of a person's actions, and you are in a much better position if you help clients come to know for themselves what courses of action are best for them.

Observe

January 19

The early winter evening has painted a coat of darkness on the outside of the windows of the local McDonald's, turning them into mirrors for the few people who sit inside at tables under the fluorescent light. Lisa sips a cup of coffee while Marilyn enjoys a fried chicken sandwich, supersized fries, and a supersized Coke. She feels safe here. Anonymous. In the windows, their reflections are superimposed on the images of the storefronts that line the street. The dinner conversation is about Marilyn's holiday crisis. She spent Christmas Eve and Christmas Day at her mother's, with her mom, sister, and two nieces. She felt good about the visit. A few days later, she felt so down and so anxious that she did not go to work. Her head felt "hazy," she said. She was not thinking clearly. There was a new resident at the group home, a man she found very agitating. He made derogatory comments. It seemed there was nobody around to listen to her concerns: The group home supervisor was on vacation, and a substitute was on call for emergencies only. The new resident kept nagging. Finally he pushed her to the edge. She was in the kitchen, overwhelmed with anger, when she threw a coffee mug across the room. It shattered against the wall.

While some of her friends calmed her, another alerted the on-call supervisor. And after a brief visit and assessment, she was offered two options: a return to her mother's or a couple of days at a crisis shelter. Marilyn phoned her mother, who decided it would be best for her not to return home. The on-call supervisor took her to the shelter. There, the staff psychiatrist prescribed ten milligrams of buspirone twice daily for anxiety and instructed her to contact her psychiatrist at the community mental health agency after discharge, which she did, but the psychiatrist was on vacation. Instead, Marilyn met with the staff nurse, whom she sees weekly for counseling. She describes her as "pretty cool," because unlike the psychiatrist, she listens and understands. The nurse advised smiling in the mirror. She also suggested that Marilyn try to remember positive things. Marilyn doesn't like practicing in the mirror. It makes her feel self-conscious. The truth is that she was feeling terrible about herself when she went to the crisis shelter.

Marilyn is noticeably concerned about the intensity of her feelings, so Lisa inquires about them. "Are you feeling suicidal?"

"No. I just wasn't feeling good about myself."

"How are you feeling now?"

"I would like you to go with me to my next appointment with [the nurse]."

"When?"

"Friday at 3:30."

To Lisa it doesn't seem that the local McDonald's is the best place to have a conversation about something so private: terrible anxiety and the events that contributed to it. The tables are close. In other ways this is the perfect place. It is familiar to Marilyn. She is comfortable here. She enjoys the food. She does not seem self-conscious. She reveals some truths about her family, spontaneously, without the intrusion of Lisa's research questions. She explains that when she is not feeling well, she usually talks to her sister, who then talks to her mother. Although Marilyn does not mind talking to her sister, she does not want to burden her mother with troubles. She feels bad enough for the trouble caused when she lived at home. She cannot bear feeling that she took money from her mother, her sister, and her nieces—from piggy banks belonging to the children. She feels guilty about jealous and angry feelings, but she is happy that living away from home has given her the distance she needed to feel better about them, especially the children.

"The kids are a source of joy in my life," she says. "They accept me as I am. They don't hold the past against me. They make me feel good about myself, because I can play with them and make them laugh, and they give me love." She adds that when they get on her nerves, she responds differently. For instance, she removes herself by going for a walk.

Lisa commends Marilyn for responding constructively to the stresses of her relationship with her nieces. These stresses, she explains, are normal. She encourages Marilyn to use the same technique in relationships with adults, especially with her boyfriends.

Reflect

The earth rolls in its orbit around the sun like a ball on the rim of a bowl that is segmented and labeled with the names of months and the numbers of the days. Take a picture of that spinning ball on that spinning track on a date that is important to you, and you get a snapshot of significance—a holiday or an anniversary such as Halloween, Christmas, Hanukkah, the birth of a brother, the illness of a mother, the death of a father, the departure of a loved one to a new job in a faraway city. If you could peel that snapshot from the video screen in your mind, it might feel as if you are holding one flat piece of paper. Yet, in the mind, behind that one photograph are layers of snapshots stacked on top of each other like a deck of cards—Christmas 2002, 2001, 2000, and so on all the way back to the year you were born. It is true that with each new revolution of the earth around the sun, the snapshot of the significant holiday or anniversary evolves: Faces get older, fashions change, the circumstances of life become more complex. Memories change. Yet some elements of the anniversary or holiday remain the same, such as the angle of sunlight in this particular sector of the earth's orbit, the length of the shadows on the lawn and in the street, the character of the wind and the weather, the presence of people who gather.

Holidays are important. Think of the holidays and two things immediately come to mind: food and the feelings that come with being with others. Marilyn reported that Christmas began on a positive note in the presence of family. It ended badly three days later, with strangers: the new guy at the group home who was harassing her, the substitute group home supervisor, the substitute psychiatrist, and others who had sought refuge at the crisis shelter. As a reflective case manager, you need to wonder with your client about the significance of the shifting feelings and turn of events. It will help her recognize the difference between relationships that produce good feelings and ones that do not. It will help her recognize how she values certain kinds of relationships and to develop methods for staying connected.

Unfortunately, our public mental health system has not promoted relationships in recovery. Rather, ours is a manufacturing mentality: paying for throughput services, productivity, and the number of clients seen. And because the human psyche is not an object, it cannot be fixed like one. Automobiles can be lined up, steered into the repair bay, hooked up to a diagnostic computer, and disassembled and reassembled with a reliable set of wrenches and new parts. People cannot. Yet that is often how service professionals treat them. Clients show up for an appointment, get steered into the repair bay, are hooked up to a diagnostic computer-like mind that has been programmed with the *Diagnostic and Statistical Manual,* and are supposedly put back together with the latest regimens of medication or evidence-based technologies.

Fortunately, though, service systems have begun to change. As a reflective case manager, you must know that trusting relationships matter. We all rely on relationships for many things, including companionship, emotional support, and help. When psychiatrists, group home supervisors, nurses, counselors, case managers, and family members are not present or available, your clients will feel it. Moreover, feeling missed and feeling that somebody is missing can inspire a range of emotion and experience. Avoiding the pain does not make it go away; rather, it may be expressed in other ways, such as anxiety or depression.

When somebody important is missing from your client's life, feel the pain with her by paying attention to the process of your relationship as it unfolds. How is her loss being expressed in this moment with you? In this scene, you might try saying, "I can see and hear that you are aware of the importance of good relationships in your life, and you have learned how to manage some of those relationships. For instance, you appreciate your family most when you spend small amounts of time with them. So you had good feelings with your family during the holiday, and you had especially uncomfortable feelings with the new guy at the group home." Explore with your client what she notices about these relationships.

It is important to work with your client's guilt. Guilt, an especially powerful human emotion, may interrupt her recovery process. Be careful not to repeat or intensify this feeling by shaming. Stand back and admire her for connecting to relationships that matter: family and you. Try this: "You say that you were not kind to your mother, your sister, and your nieces. You are aware of this. Yet you are also aware that you have changed. You now relate to your nieces as the children they are. You know how to take a break from them and go for walks when you feel overwhelmed. You take care of yourself, and you are taking care of them at the same time. You no longer take things from them. In fact, you are giving them something. You are giving them space, and you are giving them respect. I hear in your voice that you might be missing somebody. Do you miss your nieces? Do you miss your family?"

* * *

During the holiday crisis, the mental health system fails Marilyn. First, at the group home a new resident appears, without preparation. For all of us, holidays are filled with big feelings, good and bad. What do you think about this sudden change at this time? Did the service professionals adequately prepare Marilyn and other residents? And the new resident? Would you make such a change over the holidays? Consider alternatives. Second, the new guy harasses Marilyn; instead of removing him, they remove her. Did they produce in Marilyn feelings of rejection, inadequacy, and shame? Could this have been handled differently? Remember that her mother rejects her by suggesting that she go to the crisis shelter. Third, at the shelter she finds herself in an unfamiliar place with unfamiliar people, talks to an unfamiliar psychiatrist, and takes unfamiliar medication. Marilyn does not report specifically how these changes make her feel. But is it safe to assume that she might feel anxious and ashamed, even overwhelmed? Take her place for a moment. How would these sudden changes and this new environment, social and psychological, affect you? How might you react? Imagine a time in your life when you faced a sudden change for which you were not prepared.

From Marilyn's report, it feels as if the service providers believe that significant people and places are easily exchangeable. They are not! Stand-ins do not produce feelings of comfort and safety. There is no history with them. There is no familiarity. There is no trust. In addition, taking medication, smiling in the mirror, and getting into a crisis shelter do not substitute for reliable relationships. And remember, advice giving is a potential problem. Separation, anxiety, shame, and aloneness can be meaningfully addressed in reflective relationships, where your client's hurt and effort to take care of herself are noticed and talked about. Try this: "I am sorry that you are being treated this way. You are being moved about, to a different home and a different psychiatrist, and you are feeling hurt and anxious. Most people would feel this way. You know, at the beginning of this conversation, you told me that you were so overwhelmed that you could not find words for your feeling. You threw a cup. But now, you are very clear about your feelings and about the relationships that matter to you. You made the effort to call me. You made this connection today."

* * *

Like important holidays and anniversaries, important places have moods. Consider the local McDonald's in this scene. Its decor is consistent and predictable, no matter where the restaurant is located. Its menu is consistent and predictable. And there are always customers; you can experience the presence of others without having to engage in conversation. For Marilyn, McDonald's provides continuity that she could not get from social services during the holidays. The familiarity of this place inspires her to open up.

We must return here to a discussion of place, privacy, and public spaces. Restaurants and coffee shops do not offer privacy and confidentiality. And although we can certainly feel with Marilyn the continuity and comfort of a public place such as McDonald's, this should not substitute for privacy. To respect and protect the relationship, a reflective case manager must talk about this with her client. You might consider saying something like, "You know, we're going to work together in the local McDonald's, and I cannot protect your privacy there. We have to have an agreement about working in spaces like this. It will remind us that your privacy is important, and you will remind me about how you are feeling about your privacy when we are there." This shows your client that you are careful and respectful. And you must address this each time you work in a public space. Your concern about privacy will also help her draw a mental line between her public and private selves. Often, especially in our public mental health system, we fail to recognize the importance of public exposure. Our bodies and selves are not public property, to be transported, revealed, announced, and exposed to scrutiny. Think for a moment. Would you want to talk with someone about your most private wishes and fears in a public place? Probably not. By reminding your client of how seriously you take privacy, you will remind her that her inner life, the life of her mind, does not have to be shared with everyone. This is essential for independence, which is a key ingredient for recovery. And it is the foundation of doing for oneself.

Observe

February 2

It's another tense day at a local mental health agency. A case management group meeting has just ended. Managers have learned that a local mental health levy has failed; they are likely to see an increase in their caseload. You can feel a tension in the air. There are five crisis calls for follow-up from last night. Two clients have been seen at a local emergency room. There's much to get done. Case managers are coming and going, hurriedly.

At a small reception window cut into the wall of the waiting room, visitors not only announce their arrival; they're also expected to speak the name of the doctor, nurse, or case manager. Lisa is sitting in a chair against a wall in a long, narrow room filling with people. She could kick the knee of the person sitting across from her. All eyes are directed toward the window, and with each new visitor, one looks and listens, almost like a voyeur. She wonders whether anyone else notices the absence of confidentiality. The entire room can hear your name when called and the name of the person you have come to see—the nurse, the psychiatrist, the case manager. This information reveals the nature of your visit. Visitors must pick up prescriptions from the window as well, so mentioning the name of your medication is like announcing your diagnosis—schizophrenia, depression, or bipolar disorder. Lisa quietly tries to preserve the privacy of others by purposely not looking at the faces and purposely forgetting their names. She is angry with the people at this agency for subjecting people to these conditions. She sits with her discomfort and tries to contain it while she waits for Marilyn to arrive.

People in crowded rooms are like molecules stuck inside a jar. The more that enter, the more nervous the energy becomes. The mood in the room is building toward repulsion and entropy. The bodies, the voices, the movements, and the noises multiply. The volume of the television on the wall and the persistent flash of images contribute to the chaos. Lisa tries to maintain her patience. She knows that people with severe and persistent symptoms of mental illness can come across as intrusive because their sense of personal boundaries—that invisible shield of energy that separates one from others—is not as clearly defined. Yet the increasing restlessness in the room makes her want to get out. As she struggles to contain her feeling, she thinks that most people in the community do not understand this about severe symptoms of mental illness and therefore do not form relationships with people who have mental illness. This is one of the reasons that clients are often so alone.

Shortly after Marilyn arrives, the nurse–counselor she has come to see calls them into her office. Lisa purposely sits a little behind and away from Marilyn to ensure that attention is focused on her. The nurse asks Marilyn how she is feeling, and when she answers, "Okay," the nurse asks what this means. She encourages Marilyn to describe her feelings more specifically.

Marilyn explains that she is feeling good about herself because she figured out how to fix her video game machine by herself and that she was so happy about this that she called her sister and offered to help her nieces set up their machine.

The nurse appears genuinely happy about Marilyn's ability to recognize her accomplishment. She admires her. "I like talking to you like this," she says. "When something good happens for you, I can tell that you feel good about yourself. You speak so positively." The nurse uses the opportunity to talk about a subject that is a little more difficult for Marilyn, namely her relationship with her former boyfriend. "How do you feel when he calls or doesn't call? Does it bother you as much?"

"Not as much. I keep myself busy with video games. Or I talk to somebody. Or I go out by myself."

"What else do you do in your spare time? Are you doing anything for others?" Marilyn says, "Not yet." She forgets to mention again that she will be helping her nieces set up their video game system. She tells the nurse that she has an appointment with an employment specialist next week. She's hoping they will help her figure out what kind of work is best for her, what she's suited for.

The nurse steers the conversation back to the boyfriend. "How did you feel about him showing up? Excited? Scared? Worried? Or everything all at the same time? Feelings are difficult. Strange."

There is a long pause, a long, uncomfortable silence.

"How about the mirror? Have you been practicing your smiles?"

"I haven't looked all week," Marilyn says. "I didn't want to."

"Was it just because you weren't feeling good? How have you been feeling?"

"I still have to force myself to go to work."

"But you went. That's great. You're getting to work, and you tell me you feel better."

"Yeah, but I fall asleep at work sometimes."

The nurse works with Marilyn to make a distinction between sleep as a symptom of being tired and sleep as a symptom of depression. "Are you getting a good night's rest, or are you falling asleep because you're depressed?"

"I just don't feel like getting up. I feel so comfortable in bed."

"You're feeling better about yourself but not necessarily feeling on top of the world?"

Marilyn nods in agreement, and the nurse looks to her calendar to set their next appointment.

On the way home, Lisa wonders whether the nurse is missing an important opportunity to help Marilyn with anxiety and depression by remaining on the surface of feelings. Also, she notices that the nurse did not give Marilyn an opportunity to talk about her desire for a meaningful job or her efforts to pursue a degree in culinary arts. She wonders whether anyone else understands the importance of cooking in Marilyn's life. She believes that if the service providers worked together around *her* interests and *her* service goals—and not their own—she might be able to recover and maintain her pride and self-confidence. She is going to need both to live on her own with success.

Reflect

You may find yourself waiting with your clients to see numerous service providers, such as nurses, psychiatrists and other doctors, probation officers, and employment and housing specialists. And each will have a different approach to the helping relationship. You will soon learn how the different helping professions (physicians, nurses, social workers, psychologists) approach their work, just as you are learning your own. It is important to develop close working relationships with your colleagues across the professions. You will need their cooperation. And they will need yours. Always remember: In all likelihood you know your client better than most. And if you carefully listen and observe (in a partnership with your client) the effects of their medication, the quality and nature of their relationships, and the realities of their everyday lives, you will also understand the effects these have on their symptoms.

And you will often find that many of your colleagues in the allied professions have as their principal goal the monitoring of symptoms. However, focusing on symptoms may reduce the individual—her feelings, thoughts, self-perceptions, personal goals, and relationships with others—to a list of problems, their appearance and disappearance. Remember that we are always more than our symptoms, our symptoms ebb and flow, and our symptoms always have a meaning. Imagine a time in your own life when you suffered a symptom, such as a headache. You went to the doctor. She found nothing wrong. You had a symptom: a headache. But you were also studying for final exams and getting little sleep. You were under a lot of pressure. You are more than your headache. You are a whole person: a student studying for exams and getting little sleep. Perhaps you have a boyfriend or girlfriend. In short, your are all these things, and they may each in their own way contribute to your well-being or to your symptoms. And in all likelihood you did not come to think of yourself as a person with a symptom. Your friends and colleagues did not say to you when you walked into the office, "There's the headache." No, you retained your identity as a person.

How can you become aware of a preoccupation with symptom monitoring? Listen for questions that encourage short answers. Here are a few examples: "Are you feeling okay?" "Are you doing better?" "Did you take your medication?" "How are your medications making you feel?" "Are you tired because you are not sleeping or because you are depressed?" You might find that symptom monitoring does for your client in the domains of feeling and thinking. In short, if you monitor the symptom, how does the client develop an interest in observing the ebb and flow of her mental life?

In this scene, the nurse asks one symptom-monitoring question after another. She also resorts to pep talks. How did the pep talk feel to you, as an observer? Does the nurse control and impose her own agenda? After an experience like this, it is important for you to use reflective case management skills to do with your client in the domains of feeling and thinking so she will reflect on her relationship with the nurse and her feelings and thoughts about it. You might try this approach: "I noticed that the nurse was asking you about your anxiety and depression and the time you are having with your boyfriend. I also noticed that she did not ask you about going to school or trying to find a job as a cook." Wonder with her about how this felt. By feeling with your client in this way, you help her observe that she is more than her symptoms. By helping her observe her strengths in the face of a humiliating experience of nonreflective symptom monitoring, you help her recover her confident self.

* * *

In this scene, Lisa is present with Marilyn, so she experiences the assault of the nurse's nonreflective questions. She is feeling with Marilyn and wondering whether anyone knows about her healthy side. The reflective case manager knows that there is always a healthy part of the self and helps her stay connected to it. The healthy side enables her to do for herself in the domains of feeling, thinking, and action.

If a nurse, psychiatrist, or other doctor feels that she must do for her client and initiate or change a prescription, she could talk openly about this decision. For example, she might say, "You have told me that you are feeling more and more tired and that you are missing classes and work because of it. You have also told me that you are feeling tired even though you are getting plenty of rest. I am not sure whether you are feeling tired because you are depressed or because the medication is making you feel this way. I think we should try changing this medication so you don't feel as tired."

A nurse or physician should also relate her decision to begin or change a prescription to the client's stated recovery goals. For example, "You have told your case manager and me that you would like to find a job as a cook because you feel pride and joy when you cook. I am going to do for you in the domain of thinking about your medication so that you can feel better about going to school and to work. However, we have to make an agreement. From this point on, we have to work together. You have to keep tabs on how you are feeling and report this to me. We have to work together to get this medication just right. The more you keep track of how you feel, the more you will learn to monitor the effects of your medication for yourself."

Epilogue

Lisa later learned that Marilyn dropped out of the culinary arts program at the community college. Marilyn felt terrible shame when her instructor told her that this was a bad time for her to be enrolled in classes. She never returned. Lisa discovered this after Marilyn received notices from the college about missing tuition payments. She did not withdraw from classes soon enough to avoid paying the fees.

On Being and Having a Case Manager Online

Please see our Web site (http://relationalcasemanager.com) for podcasts and additional resources on topics covered in this chapter.

SUGGESTED READINGS

Faust, J. R. 2008. Clinical social worker as patient advocate in a community mental health center. *Clinical Social Work Journal* 36(3):293–300.

Germer, C. K., R. D. Siegel, and P. R. Fulton. 2005. *Mindfulness in psychotherapy*. New York: Guilford.

Greenberg, L. and S. Paivio. 1997. *Working with emotions in psychotherapy*. New York: Guilford.

Topics for Discussion

1. In this exercise, imagine a home visit. Alternatively, reconstruct a visit you have made to a client's home. Write a paragraph describing your feelings when approaching the apartment or home for the first time. What actions would (did) you plan for the first visit? Next, reverse roles. Recall a time when you expected a new guest in your home.

Write a paragraph describing the feelings, thoughts, and actions you took to prepare for the guest. Finally, compare your two paragraphs and write a third paragraph from the point of view of a client anticipating your first case management visit.

2. We all exist in interdependent relationships: doing for, doing with, standing by to admire, and letting go. In a paragraph, think over the past month and describe interactions where someone did for you and with you. How did these types of interactions make you feel? In another paragraph, imagine an activity or ability where for the first time you acted independently. Did others compliment you? How did your independent action make you feel? Think about the multiple types of relationships you are engaged in and ask yourself the following question: Are some based entirely on you doing for someone, or someone doing for you? Can you characterize some relationships as doing-with-you relationships? Compare the feelings these types of relational activities evoke in you.

3. Recall a time when someone brought to your attention something about yourself or something you did when you felt embarrassed. What was the context? At first, how did it make you feel? In retrospect, how would you like to have had that person approach you with the suggestion? Did you feel shame or guilt? Write a paragraph describing how shame and guilt might be appropriately applied to how you felt.

4. Find a partner to discuss future goals: getting a job, moving away from home, buying a car, and finishing school. Have them first describe their goal-setting ideas and steps, and engage with your partner in all possible steps. However, do not make the content of the person's goals and dreams your focus. Instead, stay focused on how the person describes his or her goals, feelings, thought processes, and actions to achieve goals. Stay focused on how this person's goal-setting ideas and plans make you feel. Note what have you learned about their dreams. What did you learn about the person? What did you learn by focusing on the process of goal setting?

5. Social work researchers Stanhope and Solomon (2008:886) write, "The recent evidence-based practice (EBP) movement, with its emphasis on 'what works', has further encouraged researchers to put their energy into identifying interventions that can be manualized and applied consistently across settings, providers and clients. This type of evidence neglects a central part of social work practice and is limited in its ability to capture how social workers impact their clients' lives. Process may be an understudied aspect of services for the simple fact that it is hard to measure with current research

tools and the dominant methods. Sometimes referred to as the 'black box', social interaction is extremely complex and resistant to the 'inputs' and 'outputs' analysis that typifies so much of intervention research." What do they mean by "manualized" approaches? How do you understand what is meant by "process"?

Films

Frontline, PBS, "The medicated child." This PBS production has an excellent discussion guide and Web site; see http://www.pbs.org/wgbh/pages/frontline/medicatedchild/.

Skjoldjaerg, E., producer and director. 2001. Prozac nation [film]. Munich: Cinerenta Medienbeteiligungs.

Two

An
Apartment
of
Her
Own

Observe

March 18

There is a driveway between the brownstone apartment buildings that is more like an alley, barely wide enough to fit a full-sized four-wheel-drive pickup truck. It is always a challenge to get through. The parking lot behind the building is jammed with cars, so Lisa has to shift between drive and reverse, inch by inch, to avoid creasing sheet metal. Late for church, she's in a rush. Her phone rings. She hits the brake and answers.

"Hey, it's me." It's Marilyn. It is at first soft and slow and hesitant. She sounds a little depressed. "Can we get together? I need to talk with someone."

Lisa releases the brake and steers the truck into the alley between the buildings with one hand as she holds the desperate voice to her ear with the other. The timing of the request is bad. Lisa is going through a bit of a crisis of her own and wants to be alone today, but she agrees to pick Marilyn up after church. The call ends. She sets the phone on the seat next to her and drives into the city.

* * *

St. Malachi's is at the intersection of West 25th Street and the old Superior Viaduct across the river from downtown Cleveland. The 1947 gothic stone structure, built on the site of the original 1871 church, was dedicated as a parish in 1866 to serve the Irish community on Cleveland's near west side. Over the years its mission has changed and expanded along with the rapidly shifting industrial landscape. Today, in a fully deindustrialized world, the church runs a kitchen for the poor and homeless, a home for people with terminal illnesses, and a second-hand store to help those without money find clothes, appliances, and furnishings. The church is also host to Alcoholics Anonymous. And next door is a transitional housing complex that helps people addicted to alcohol and other drugs prepare for living sober in the community. A short walk to the north and to the south are public housing complexes. In a building one block away are the offices of Cuyahoga County's community mental health board. And about five blocks away is the Ohio City neighborhood, which is filled with historic houses and storefronts. Over the last twenty years, Ohio City has experienced a slow but steady migration of working professionals who are investing money in rehabbing old homes and storefronts and constructing new ones.

The Sunday congregation at St. Malachi's reflects the diversity of the neighborhood and the church's mission. Services are attended by people of European, Latino, African, and Middle Eastern heritage. There are biracial couples and members of Cleveland's gay, lesbian, and transgender communities. There are also recovering addicts, ex-offenders, homeless men and women, and those with severe symptoms of mental illness. Lisa likes this church. The building is old and simply decorated. The people are tolerant. They are friendly and sociable. They offer a glimpse of the good of which people are capable—when they make the effort.

* * *

After church, Lisa takes Marilyn to the local Blockbuster to return movies. Then it's to the coffee shop, where they sit at a table inside. Lisa drinks water and listens. Marilyn smokes, drinks coffee, and shares details about her life since they last met in February. The group home has threatened to evict her for not living up to the contract: She must keep her room neat and clean, she must help clean the common areas, and she must participate in shopping for groceries and preparing meals. The supervisor assigned a housing specialist to help Marilyn relearn tasks and a routine for getting jobs done. Marilyn has been tired and blasé. She feels like giving up. She hasn't, though, because the housing specialist helps her find the motivation.

Marilyn has other bad news. Her dream of learning to cook for a living has been interrupted. She was so behind in classes at the community college that she dropped out. There is hope, though, and she talks excitedly and rapidly about plans. She is working with a job coach at an employment agency who wants to get her into a twelve-week culinary arts course; the course would combine work with study and pay her $50 per week, and it would enable her to give up the job at the lumberyard. She can't wait to quit, she says, but she will be sad to leave friends. Marilyn jumps to the next topic. Her nurse–counselor left the social service agency. However, there is good news: The difficult man in the group home moved out.

Lisa wonders whether the changes occurring in Marilyn's life are adding up to a crisis, one leading to overwhelming anxiety and depression. This, Lisa wonders, may be the reason Marilyn called today, Sunday, but Lisa cannot understand why she didn't call somebody else in her social network. She asks, "Is there someone else you call when you're not feeling well?"

Marilyn names three: a friend at the group home, the group home supervisor, and her supervisor at the lumberyard. As she listens to the names, Lisa recalls that they are generally unavailable. The friend at the group home suffers from medication side effects for her schizophrenia. The group home supervisor, now in charge of two homes on opposite sides of town, is available after hours only for life-or-death emergencies. And the work supervisor is accessible only during hours that Marilyn works, which are few. Lisa has a hunch that Marilyn is in a crisis of loneliness. "How do you spend your free time?" she asks. "Do you fill your time, or do you feel bored?"

"Bored," she says, almost inaudibly.

"What would be helpful?"

"Trying new activities at the rec center. Having somebody go to the movies with me."

"You don't drive. Does this get in the way of doing something meaningful?"

"No. When the weather gets nicer, I'll be able to go to more dance clubs."

* * *

On the way home, Lisa reflects on the conversation and realizes that Marilyn is being passed from one institution to another and from one service provider to another and that there is no consistent person to help her with her internal (emotional) reactions to the external (social) situations. Marilyn is being passed around like a child in foster care. With the thought of those two words, *foster care,* Lisa believes she is finally beginning to understand Marilyn. For the first year of her life, Marilyn *was* a foster child. Could the experiences she described today be triggering emotions that link her to past experiences of being passed from one caregiver to another? Is she remembering that pain and trying to avoid it?

Reflect

A crisis call is a time of reconnection and an important moment for promoting recovery. Sometimes it is when we are in crisis that our social relations, thoughts and feelings, our reality, becomes remarkably clear: We reveal to ourselves and to those around us how we react or cope, how we adapt (or not), and how we change. This is true for you, the practitioner, and for your clients. Imagine times when you found yourself in crisis. To whom did you turn? What did your safety net look and feel like? Did you find yourself alone? What did you learn about yourself and those around you? How did you act, and how did others act toward you? Sometimes we produce a crisis to gather people around us. It's like an SOS signal. These are only some of the questions you might keep in mind. Add to them your own list of habitual ways of responding to crisis and how others around you respond, including your colleagues.

What is a crisis? A crisis is a turning point, a decisive moment or stage in the unfolding of events, internal and external. When taking the crisis call, resist the temptation to react and to do for your client unless it is clear that she is in danger of hurting herself or others. The phrase often used to describe this is *imminent danger.* What do we mean when we say something is imminent? Often it means that we've no time for thoughtful deliberation and reflection. If there is such a danger, follow your organization's protocol for crisis intervention; this will help you stay organized. If your client is not in immediate danger, allow time for evaluation. And if you feel urgent panic, take a step back to think about what is causing your feeling. Sometimes, in crisis, our tendency is to act. Slow down, deliberate, and get others to join you. It is quite possible that you've been drawn into the crisis and the panic. Where there is crisis, there is often panic. Panic, in Greek, comes from the word *panikos,* which means "of Pan." Pan, god of woods and fields, produced mysterious sounds and contagious, groundless fear in herds and crowds or in people in lonely spots. Watch out for Pan. Don't let a crisis turn to panic. Keep in mind that a crisis may occur in any one or all three domains of your client's life: feelings, thoughts, or actions. You can often evaluate (i.e., assign a value) the crisis based on the degree to which all three combine.

In this scene, Lisa does not understand why Marilyn needs so desperately to talk. So she first listens to the content of Marilyn's conversation. Then, she considers Marilyn's process of dealing with crises and discovers an emotional disconnection in her social relationships, especially with service providers who are meant to help her achieve personal recovery goals: going to school, learning to become a professional cook, and preparing to live in an apartment of her own. In addition, the nurse–counselor who was helping Marilyn manage her mental health symptoms is no longer with the agency. Marilyn feels abandoned. She is lonely. But she minimizes the feeling by using the word *bored.*

Many mental health service systems and organizations require case managers to carry large caseloads, which makes it almost impossible to stay in touch with clients in meaningful ways. In other words, caseloads contribute to the creation of anxious and hurried environments. Managers come and go. Clients come and go. In this way, *turnover* refers not only to frequency of staff change and interactions with clients.[1] It also refers to the nature and quality of relationships as they unfold in time and space. As long as organizations maintain this status quo, it is likely that crisis calls will occur regularly, especially if clients trust you and feel they have a good relationship with you. This is why the crisis call may be understood as a call for reconnection—a way clients manage loneliness and associated feelings.

* * *

No matter how prepared you are for the crisis call, when it actually occurs, you may experience a range of feelings that might conflict with your sense of duty and dedication to your clients. You might feel irritated, stressed, and overwhelmed with yet another demand for your time, attention, and energy. If these conflicting feelings occur, be careful not to unload onto your client. Here are a few clues to watch for. If you find yourself rushing to reassure your client that "everything will work out," you are doing for her in the domain of feeling. If you find yourself rushing to make a to-do list to help sort out the crisis, you are doing for her in the domain of thinking. If you find yourself rushing to make phone calls on her behalf or to drive her places, you are doing for her in the domain of action. Before you do or say anything, notice your own feelings, thoughts, and actions. Maybe you are feeling defensive, impatient, and angry because your client has a habit of calling you in a panic when there is not much of a crisis. Or maybe you are feeling defensive, impatient, and angry because you are experiencing demands for your time and attention from people outside work.

Once aware of your feelings and thoughts, use your mental energy to do with your client: Help her regain control over her feelings, thoughts, and actions. First, help her notice her awareness of the present situation and how she made the effort to get help. Here you are helping her recognize and develop observational strength. You help her observe how and when she seeks help. You might tell her, "I am sorry that you have had a run of rotten luck lately. I hear and understand your frustration. I notice that you've taken the first step to help yourself by calling me." Then, help your client turn attention to the emotion resonating beneath her troubles. Ask her, "I wonder if there is a feeling here that we are not noticing." If she has difficulty giving a name to her feeling, propose one in a way that invites her to do this work with you. Consider saying, "I wonder if you are feeling very lonely."

When your client makes the crisis call, she invites you to share in the process. There is a reason for this. In all likelihood it is a reach for a significant emotional connection, maybe a feeling of trust and safety with you and of hope for your understanding. This feeling of hope may exist simultaneously with the crisis feeling. Help her notice the simultaneity. It may seem odd to you that hope and crisis often come at the same time. You might say, "There must be a reason you called me. Maybe you feel something good will come from this call. What do you think?" If possible, explore the hopeful feeling.

* * *

Rarely does the crisis call end with the conversation or a resolution of the apparent conflict. Feelings and thoughts linger. For instance, in this scene Lisa reflects on the conversation as she drives away.

It is important to engage in some reflective work about your feelings and thoughts after a crisis call. Talk with members of your service team and clinical supervisor to process your feelings and thoughts; discussions will produce important insights to help you and the team provide more relevant services. Be sure to include your client's mental health counselor (if she has one) in your discussions. He or she may want to explore them further with the client.

After you have processed your feelings and thoughts about the crisis, consider a follow-up with your client along with a simple phone message or note in the mail. You might say or write something like, "I am pleased that you decided to call me, and I am happy we had a chance to talk. I am thinking about you." This simple message may give your client the feeling of continuing connection. It also demonstrates that you are keeping her in mind and helps her keep you in her mind. Do not underestimate the power of this simple act. Think about your own experience. How does it feel when you receive cards or calls from safe and supportive people in your life?

Observe

July 11

A family crisis has prevented Lisa from meeting with Marilyn for some time, but when she reconnects, the two converse as if they'd never been apart. They are sitting at a picnic table under a tree in Edgewater Park, which embraces the Lake Erie shoreline. They are near the parking lot. Lisa wonders why Marilyn has picked this table; others are much closer to the shore, where they would have a panoramic view of the water, the sky, and the industrial cityscape to the east.

Marilyn eats a sandwich and chips she brought in a brown paper bag. She drinks the usual—Pepsi—and talks openly and rapidly about a range of topics. First she tells Lisa that the employment specialist has not yet found a culinary training program. She is waiting for a letter from the Bureau of Vocational Rehabilitation (BVR), which is supposed to enroll her in a hospitality training program. She is on a waiting list for an apartment. There will be a unit open in mid-August, she says. (The building is owned by the same social service agency that owns the group home.) It seems Marilyn has proven that she can complete chores and keep her room clean. The housing specialist who had been helping her relearn the routine thinks she is ready. This surprises Lisa. She wonders whether the housing specialist and the group home supervisor are moving too quickly: Only four months ago they had threatened to evict her from the group home for not doing required chores. Lisa wonders, "Should they give her more time and test her ability to maintain the routine?" She also wonders how long it will take before Marilyn loses motivation.

Lisa also wonders how Marilyn might be dealing emotionally with pending separations from friends at the group home and co-workers. Although a new job and a new home will create new opportunities, they will also create losses and hence loneliness. Imagine times in your life when you felt the pain of loss from a change in residence, a move, or new job. Lisa asks for an update on relationships with people in her helping network and gets this summary:

- Her mom: Nothing to report.
- Her sister: "She listens to me. She decided that I did not want to fight with her any more. She helped me when my mother wasn't around. Took me to doctor's appointments and knew I needed help, even though I wasn't talking about it or acknowledging that I needed help."
- Her nieces (six and nine years old): "I can relate to them as a kid. I'm not a typical adult. I play and have fun with them. I don't want them to feel neglected. They are my world right now. I'd do anything for them. They can't get enough of me. They like me. They love me. They tell me they love me all the time."
- Group home supervisor: "She's like a mother to me. I can talk to her about stuff that I can't talk to my mother about."
- Work supervisor: Nothing to report.
- Housing specialist: Nothing more to report.
- Case manager: Nothing to report.
- Counselor (who replaced the nurse-counselor): Nothing to report.
- Psychiatrist: Nothing to report.
- Her friend Virginia: They met at social activities at the social service agency. They like to hang out together.
- Her friend Dolores at the group home (the backseat driver): "She's the first person who made me feel good about myself and comfortable when I moved into

the group home. She can relate to me. She's one of my best friends. We talk to each other. She listens to me. I don't have to sugarcoat what I say to her. She's kind of a role model for me. She's fifteen years older and grew up in the 1960s."

- Her ex-boyfriend, Frank: Marilyn has a lot to say about him. She says, "This is the best guy I ever met and the best relationship I've ever been in."

Marilyn met Frank at the lumberyard, where they both worked. He was polite. He was kind. They had conversations. They talked openly about family. They did not sit in her room and play video games and punch and wrestle like a brother and sister. This made her feel mature. They talked of marriage. She told him of her desire to be a stay-at-home mom and to cook fresh, hot meals for her children. They talked about the house they would own and how they would raise their children. The relationship was great. Then, one day, out of the blue, Frank told her they had to be "just friends." He explained that he was in his first six months of Alcoholics Anonymous, and the group discouraged romantic relationships in the initial period of recovery.

As Marilyn tells her story of heartbreak and loss, Lisa notices something significant. She does not seem overwhelmed. Frank had given her a good reason for the breakup—one for which she is not to blame—and maybe this has eased the hurt. Lisa wonders whether a battle is beginning to take place in the woman who sits across from her, a battle between accepting the separation for what it is and blaming herself. She wonders whether this is a calm before the emotional storm.

Lisa tries to assure Marilyn about the benefits of not being in a steady relationship. She says, "This will give you some time to get into the culinary arts training program and to get your life in order."

"Yeah, I know, but what if he meets somebody else?"

Marilyn changes the subject, suddenly, and tells Lisa that she has her temporary driver's license. Lisa, genuinely surprised and proud, admires Marilyn's courage and determination to achieve this milestone by herself. Lisa cannot contain her joy. Her smile is wide.

Marilyn smiles, too. She says, "I got it May fifth."

"That's awesome!" Lisa says. "How did you do that?"

Marilyn explains that a friend took the test for a temporary license and that she had gone with him for moral support. He convinced her that it was not hard. After the test, he gave her the study guide, and when he went back to take the driver's exam, she took the exam for her temporary license. Marilyn tells Lisa, "I want to get my license before the temp expires."

Reflect

In the Introduction, we wanted you to know something important about how we think about independence: It does not mean that our clients become rugged individualists. Independence is not the absence of relationships. Independence, for us, is a specific way of relating with others, one in which our clients identify what they want and need, set goals, and assert themselves to interact and negotiate with others to obtain, to achieve, and to live with success and satisfaction. Independence may occur when your client uses all three domains, feeling, thought, and action, to positively influence and be influenced by the people with whom they relate: family members, friends, co-workers, teachers, neighbors, landlords, and service providers. To achieve her goals of becoming a professional cook, living in an apartment of her own, and starting her own family, Marilyn must be supported by relationships.

You should notice in this scene how Marilyn reports nothing about her relationships with service providers, except the very significant one with the group home supervisor. She also talks with feeling about her friend Dolores. In these cases it is important to wonder with your supervisor and treatment team about the effect of such a move on your client's emotional well-being. There is no doubt that she will experience this as a significant separation from important people. In short, she will feel loss. The sadness and grief created by a separation like this may contribute to a crisis; it may cause her to miss work or important appointments or feel profound sadness.

Marilyn wants an apartment of her own, yet she also has important relationships at the group home. And although you can feel her ambivalence about the pending move, she does not put these feelings into words. Conflicting feelings are natural. We all have them. Sometimes we suffer with ambivalence, that is, we are in a constant battle with our own conflicting feelings. Imagine a time in life when you struggled with ambivalence: "I want this boyfriend, but right now I feel the need to finish school." You go back and forth, back and forth, unable to resolve the conflict. Soon, however, you work through the feelings. You decide to leave your boyfriend and go to school. You are sad at first, but soon you are studying hard and finishing your coursework. In short, you resolve or work through the conflict. Not everyone is so lucky. The conflict goes on and on. It is better to become aware of conflicts and to use them to your advantage than to let them hide and linger, like a ghost, sneaking around and finding expression in unpredictable ways.

* * *

There is more evidence of ambivalence in this scene. Marilyn has expressed a desire for independence, yet she is twenty-three and has not learned to drive until now. Most people, especially in this culture, begin driving in their teens. Some would argue that the car is crucial to our passage from adolescence to adulthood. It is significant that she has made this effort to learn. Notice, too, that she did this in relationship with a peer, who offers inspiration and encouragement. There is something important about the way Marilyn and her friend relate. Note it. When your client makes an unexpected step toward independence, help her become aware of it. Ask what was helpful about the relationship with her peer. This awareness will help her make constructive use of other supportive relationships.

Begin by helping your client understand the positive influence of this relationship in all three domains: her feelings, her thoughts, and her actions. Start with a general statement and question: "What a wonderful feeling you must have had getting the temporary driver's license. I wonder how you did that." Remember, this is your feeling, not hers, at this point. For example, in the domain of feeling, you might say, "From what you've told me, your friend was feeling proud about the exam. It seems to me that you were feeling pride with him and used that good feeling to study for and take the exam yourself." For thinking and action, you might say, "You studied for the test and remembered the rules. You also went to the Bureau of Motor Vehicles, took the test, and passed it. You did this for yourself, thinking and acting in ways that have given you good feeling. You understand that doing for yourself does not mean you have to be alone. Doing for yourself also means using the inspiration and support of people you trust."

Observe

July 14

An hour and a half of errands includes a trip to the bank, the video store, and the supermarket for Pepsi and snacks: potato chips, cupcakes, and cigarettes. The trip ends at Edgewater Park, where, this time, Lisa insists on sitting close to the water. The picnic table is on top of a hill, seventy feet above the Lake Erie shoreline. It is a stunning day: A dazzling blue sky and a few lonely, fluffy white clouds create an atmosphere. Some days, the lake is as still and quiet as a pond in the woods. Some days, it is like the ocean, with heavy, roiling waves. Today, there is only enough ripple to make windsailing fun.

Lisa is pleasantly surprised. Marilyn is quite calm, especially with the uncertainty in her life, which is bordering on a bureaucratic nightmare. She is on several waiting lists for a job training program and an apartment. No one among the myriad service professionals is preparing her for the move. In addition, her boyfriend has "downgraded" their relationship from romantic to "just friends." Despite this bad news, Marilyn seems content. She is making use of her social network. She is spending time with friends, Sophie and Dolores, from the group home. She is visiting with her nieces. She likes to watch them play softball.

Lisa is curious. She asks Marilyn which people in the community mental health system (i.e., which service providers) have been supportive, caring, and respectful. Marilyn does not relate the question to her current life. She explains that her new supervisor at the lumberyard has been lenient and understanding about her tardiness. And again, she speaks highly of the group home supervisor and the housing specialist who helped her understand difficulties with chores. Lisa asks about people who have shown her disrespect. Without hesitation Marilyn reports that her old supervisor at the lumberyard used profanity with the staff. "Fuck you," he would say. And he spent most of the workday talking to friends on the telephone.

Lisa steers the conversation back to the present. She recommends a to-do list for the pending move. She thinks with Marilyn about the move. There is a long pause, then a sudden breeze draws cool air over the lake. Soon Marilyn is actively identifying her priorities and concerns. She must work with her case manager to contact Consumer Protection Services (CPS) to help with money management. (Her mother is still legal payee. She wants CPS to take over this role.) She needs to save money for household items and to learn how to write checks. The group home supervisor has promised to help but has been too busy managing a second home. She also needs a toaster, cooking utensils, and a wastebasket. Lisa finds it peculiar that the service providers have not actively engaged Marilyn in planning the move to acquire necessities and help with the crucial task of money management. It is a perfect opportunity to do these with her. Accomplishing these would give her a sense of pride and help her recover her independent, confident self. Lisa is also concerned because Marilyn has access to credit cards, which her legal payee (her mother) cannot control. She has a Capital One Visa from Kmart, a Capital One Visa from JCPenney, and a Classic and Gold Capital One card. One has a $1,000 limit. Marilyn works a part-time job that pays $5.15 per hour. She regularly gets credit card applications in the mail, never reads the fine print, and is on the verge of being buried in credit card debt.

Despite the mounting debt, Marilyn is excited about the move. She is eager to shop for items on her list. Quickly she identifies the second-hand stores. Then Lisa reminds her that she will need help packing and moving boxes. She adds this to the list. Marilyn pauses, then says she will ask her friend Dolores to help pack, her case manager to carry boxes (although he might not because he has a bad back), and the group home supervisor to transport the boxes with the van. Again the wind brings in a cool breeze. Marilyn shifts restlessly as she contemplates the move.

"I don't know if I can ask you to help," she says. There is a long pause. Lisa and Marilyn look to the lake and the Cleveland skyline. "I didn't know if that would be rude."

Lisa knows that her truck will be useful and a much-needed backup, especially if the group home supervisor refuses help or is unavailable. "That's fine," she says. "You can ask. If you need help, I can see what I can do. I'll ask my supervisor."

Marilyn begins to talk, then hesitates; she seems uncertain about what to say next. Cautiously, she asks Lisa whether she would consider going this weekend to a church festival in the neighborhood where she grew up. It would be a good time for Lisa to meet her family; her mother, her sister, and her nieces will be there.

Lisa is not sure how this might affect their relationship. Will she cross a boundary? She does not want to cross that line and decides to stay in familiar territory. She tells Marilyn that she will check her schedule.

Marilyn responds with the stutter-start of another question that she is hesitant to ask. "What happens to me when the study is over?" she asks. "Do I ever get to see you again?"

Reflect

Marilyn has many responsibilities: chores at the group home, getting to work on time. And then there is preparation for the move and the ever-present threat of debt. Like Marilyn, your client might delay. She might not stay oriented to time and deadlines. She might not plan. You might feel the impulse to take charge and do for her in the domains of thinking and action. To-do lists are a common default. Resist the temptation. Instead, do with her; help her become aware of her ability to get things done. Recall, for example, that on July 11 Marilyn was motivated to learn to drive; she studied for the test and passed. Consider bringing this moment of success and good feeling back into memory.

Here is one way you might align yourself with the part of your client motivated to do for herself. Ask a simple question: "What have you done so far to prepare for the move?" Encourage her to elaborate on what she's done and how. Listen carefully, even for the most modest efforts. Remember, always: If you ask a question you'll get an answer. It's best to patiently and quietly wait for your client's words, thoughts, and feelings. What you might hear from her is something about the process of helping: who, how, when, why, where. You might learn about how one accepts help: willingly or with resistance, shame, or guilt. You might also learn something crucial about the helping network: when it functions, how it functions, where it functions. In learning about the helping networks you will also learn something about when the network kicks into motion. For example, you might see that the network is effective only during crises. And although crisis networks may be useful, they may leave our clients in a vacuum during the little and everyday moments of help seeking. And there are also times when the crisis network is especially dysfunctional. As soon as your client identifies accomplished tasks, you have strength to work with her. Name it. This will help her do more than just notice. Over time, along with your client, you will build a scaffold for understanding and using your powers to effectively and appropriately seek help.

Next, reflect with her about future activities. You could ask, "What else do you need to do to prepare for the move?" If she cannot begin a list, help her reflect on a typical day at her current residence. Does her day begin with the sound of an alarm? She will need to buy a clock or pack the one she has. Does she shower and groom and get dressed? She will need to buy or pack everything she uses. Review the activities of daily living. There is a list of products, utensils, and appliances that she will need to pack or buy. Encourage her to put these things on her list.

* * *

We live in an easy credit society. And easy access to credit is a problem for many millions of consumers. In this scene you see how easy access to credit presents numerous challenges, especially if your clients have difficulty orienting to external reality. For example, some of your clients will have difficulty thinking about money: how much they have, how much they need, how to organize or allocate it, and how to save or protect it. Others will spend with wild abandon. Remember, always, that this is not a problem unique to mental health consumers. Also, it is very important to know more about money management. You can use your own experience here. For example, some of us have difficulty managing money pervasively, that is, in every aspect of our lives. You will need to explore, with your client, how and when she has trouble with money management. For many millions, especially those who live on fixed income and in poverty, managing money is sort of like racing a horse without a jockey.

This might not be the best time in Marilyn's life to address the credit problem, especially if she is already overwhelmed with the imminent move. After all, you cannot address everything in one interaction. Remember times in your life when someone asked you to consider too many problems, too many questions, too many tasks, all at the same time. How did it make you feel? However, if your client is in economic danger and at risk of sabotaging her independence, you may need to call this to her attention. Be careful not to be critical. If you say, "Taking on this debt is irresponsible," for example, it may feel punitive, harsh, and judgmental. It may produce unnecessary guilt and shame. Too much shame will make your client ineffective. Recall that shame is an emotion that makes us ineffective. How might you say it differently? How might you observe without judging? What is the effect of being judgmental?

How might it affect your working relationship? Here's another way of thinking about this. Sharon Berlin (2005:485), a social work researcher and clinician, writes, "Honoring another's autonomy means acknowledging the things about the other person that are different, that one does not fully understand, and that perhaps one does not even like without trying to change those characteristics or otherwise control the person."

Work with the part of your client that has the desire and strength to notice and change spending habits. Remember to be reflective. Start by naming the discrepancy between goals and current behavior. You might say, "I wonder if you see what I am seeing. You have told me you want to live in an apartment of your own. However, you are spending money before you earn it. You will need that money to live on your own. What do you think about this? How do you feel about spending money with credit cards?"

It might be helpful to create an economic crisis intervention plan. Talk to your supervisor and treatment team members about your client's emotional and fiscal reality. Make sure everyone is consistent in his or her work with your client around money.

Observe

July 25

It is July in Cleveland. The hot, moist air from the Bayou is making its annual migration north on a high-pressure current that is so thick the air feels like water. There is no wind, only sweat. Lisa and Marilyn are at the same picnic table near the edge of the hill that stands seventy feet above the shore of Lake Erie in Edgewater Park. Marilyn reports that her belongings are packed in boxes. She is ready to move. Still, she waits for an apartment. She is told by social workers that there are no vacancies. For three years, Marilyn has wanted to move into an apartment of her own. When she first arrived at the group home, the staff asked her about goals. Moving was at the top.

"I am feeling more anxious and more stress about the uncertainty of the move. And work really stinks," she says, reminding Lisa that a lumberyard is not a good place for a woman who wants to cook. The place is dirty and dusty. The office is cramped. There is little ventilation. In hot, humid weather it is hell. If she were working in a kitchen, it wouldn't matter. She is so afraid she will be stuck at the lumberyard forever that she went out on her own yesterday to apply for a job at a local video store.

"I'm stressed because I don't think they'll hire me," she says. "I wore nice clothes yesterday so they would think I was clean. I'm just worried about what the staff at the lumberyard will say to the video storeowner about my tardiness. I'm worried. I don't have an appetite. I've got no taste for anything."

Lisa can tell that Marilyn's outlook and self-esteem are fragile. She is hopeful about positive changes—a new place to live, a new job, and a new training program in culinary arts—but she is anxious about potential failure. She shifts the conversation to a source of joy in her life. She talks about her boyfriend—the one in Alcoholics Anonymous, the one who needs to wait before he gets more serious about their relationship. She no longer feels awkward with him. He's been visiting at the group home, and they've been playing video games on her PlayStation. They spend a lot of time talking.

"I told my mom about him yesterday," she says. "She seemed happy for me. I just hate to burden her with my problems. I mean, I've gone to her with all my problems from all the assholes that I have dated. She told me that if I ever needed advice to ask my sister because she knows more."

Lisa asks where all these emotions come from.

"At the age of sixteen, I witnessed my brother choking my mother," she says. "I felt overpowered by my brother. I froze. I couldn't do anything except call for my sister. The police were involved, but they didn't do anything to help my mother."

Lisa waits in silence before asking, "How did that make you feel? What do you do with those feelings?"

"I bottled up my emotions until I would explode at my mother and sister."

Lisa recalls that these outbursts led the family to decide that Marilyn should move into the group home. "Where," Lisa asks, "do you learn now to handle your emotions?"

"From psychiatrists," she says.

Lisa asks whether there are others, and Marilyn explains that counselors have helped, especially the nurse-counselor who recently left the agency. She is having a hard time warming up to the new counselor, but there are other staff she can talk to. "I trust them," she says. "I know they won't hurt me."

"Are there others you can talk with when you experience overwhelming feelings?"

"The staff at the group home, but they are only available during business hours, between 8:30 A.M. and 4 P.M. The staff is on call after hours, but only for emergencies, like a medical problem or a fight. A breakup with a boyfriend is not an emergency."

Marilyn assures herself and Lisa that her relationship with Frank is good. She wants to stay in touch, even if they are just friends. She does not want to give up the dreams they share; she says,

It's better than before. I feel comfortable with him, and he seems to feel the same with me. We both still talk about feeling that we want to spend the rest of our lives together. I don't trust daycares too much, so Frank and I have decided that I'd probably stay home with the children, at least until they are a certain age. One thing for sure, all of my kids are going to learn how to cook. None of that frozen dinner crap. My mom always had a home-cooked meal for us as kids, no matter how tired she was from working all day, and I don't care how tired I am, I'm going to make sure my kids get good, home-cooked, nutritious meals.

* * *

On the way home, Lisa notes that Marilyn doesn't get excited about much, except cooking, even though the memories she associates with it are not always happy. For instance, Marilyn knows that her mother had been burdened by work and by cooking for her children. Yet Marilyn associates warm, safe feelings with the preparation of food.

Lisa thinks about how as people age, they find ways to channel negative emotion into positive action. It occurs to Lisa that although Marilyn feels like a burden to many people, she does not feel like a burden when she is cooking. There is pride and joy in the process. The outward (physical) act of cooking plays an important role in her inner (emotional) life. It might be a way that she manages problematic feelings. She wonders whether cooking might be therapeutic without anyone really knowing it. She wonders whether her social workers, counselors, nurses, and psychiatrist have ever thought about this.

Reflect

The person who has the most regular contact with your client is the one most likely to have access to her inner world: her most private thoughts, fears, inhibitions, and desires. In the public mental health system, that person is you, the case manager. As you work with your client, helping her with the activities of daily living, you will find yourself witnessing her expression of feelings, thoughts, and actions. This is why it is helpful to have clinical knowledge and skill. Keep in mind that your client's internal world will both support and inhibit her success with completing day-to-day routines and achieving recovery goals.

Generally it is not the job of the case manager to help the client explore in depth her inner world. This is most often the role of a clinical social worker, psychiatrist, psychologist, therapist, or licensed counselor. However, the case manager can and should help the client develop self-observation, which is necessary not only for successful living in the community. It is crucial for the therapist to have this support and for your client to have this support in building capacity for relationships. The case manager can and should also provide the treatment team with information about the client's day-to-day internal world. With your support the treatment team can develop treatment plans and improve their interventions.

In this scene Marilyn reveals her early exposure to violence in the home: an assault on her mother by her brother. It is not the case manager's task to explore feelings about these kinds of events. In fact, it may be especially inappropriate to encourage recall of intense and overwhelming experiences when there are few mechanisms in community-based mental health to help integrate, contain, or manage overwhelming feeling and intense affect. However, do not ignore these reports; they are important to our psychosocial histories, and they will help you understand and work with intense feelings and responses to aggression. Instead, let your client know that you feel the seriousness of the event. When you feel a client's intense emotion, you might simply say, "You must have been so frightened to see your brother attack your mother." In this way you become a witness to important events in a person's life, past and present.

Make a mental note of this interaction. Remember to share her story and your response with your clinical supervisor and service team members; work together to develop a plan to help her manage aggression. Over time you will get a sense of how your client responds to aggression, her own and that of others. You might find it helpful to get a sense of the size of a client's response. Sometimes, we feel even the slightest bit of assertiveness as too much, as attacking and destructive. At other times, when we should feel the too-muchness of aggressive acting out, we don't. When you feel another's natural and necessary assertiveness as an aggressive attack, it is in all likelihood the wrong size. Think of it this way. There are times when we need to have big feelings, when the situation warrants it. We may run to protect ourselves from attack, for example. On the other hand, if you tell me to clean my room (and my room is unclean), firmly, and I respond as if you are attacking me, it's the wrong size. As case managers we are every single day working with the sizes of feelings and their appropriateness. It's a very good idea for you to develop your own sensitivity to feeling sizes, a kind of mental map to help you navigate the everyday world of feeling.

* * *

Marilyn reports another instance of doing for herself. Last time, she passed the exam for her temporary driver's license. This time, she applies for a job at a local video store. Yet she conveys this story of positive action with a sense of shame. Read this episode again. How would you describe Marilyn's experience? Notice that the case manager does not try to relieve the shame; rather, she actively listens. This is an example of doing with and standing by to admire.

When you witness intense shame, avoid the impulse to reassure: "You're not bad, you're okay, don't be so hard on yourself." Some of us are "reassuring" types; we're constantly offering kind words. Remember, these are your feelings, not theirs. And in offering these words, you may be avoiding your own feelings of helplessness or fear. Resist the impulse to do for your client with reassurance; instead, help her notice her feelings *and* her assertive action. You are observing what is actually taking place. You might say something like,

> You made the effort to make a change in your life. You applied for the job yourself. You even put yourself in the shoes of the owners and imagined what they might want from a new employee. You felt uncomfortable feelings walking into the store by yourself. I

know you have experienced uncomfortable feelings in other new situations. Some call this feeling anxiety; it's a natural response to new situations. It is a feeling of anticipation. Sometimes you might anticipate a good outcome. Then you feel pride. Sometimes you anticipate a bad outcome. You might feel shame. Sometimes you might anticipate both at the same time because you have no idea how things will turn out. The important thing that I notice is that you took positive action. You have some feelings about this, and you are aware of it.

Standing by to admire plays an important role in recovery. You observe your client without judgment. She notices you observing her in this manner. Through time, she begins to observe herself without judgment. We have called this case management activity mentalizing (see the Introduction).

Observe

August 3

The first experience is always difficult. There is nothing to compare it to. There is no connection with anything. There is you, your environment, and the awareness of your separateness pushing against you. When you are shuffled from one unfamiliar person to another, time and time again, you become familiar with the feelings of rejection, abandonment, aloneness, and shame.

It is noon. Marilyn is to meet with her new counselor at the social service agency. She felt comfortable with the nurse–counselor, despite the affirmations-in-the-mirror technique. She's had three counselors over a short period. Lisa sits in the waiting room during the session and afterward takes Marilyn to the grocery store. Tonight is Marilyn's turn to cook. She is making her homemade chicken paprikash and has most of the ingredients, chicken and sour cream, but she needs a box of stuffing and brownie mix. In the checkout line, she tells Lisa she needs to talk.

* * *

The shadow on the patio in front of the coffee shop in Ohio City, the comeback neighborhood near St. Malachi's Church, offers a refreshing break from the sun and heat. As Marilyn starts her second cigarette, she tells Lisa that she and Frank have parted ways—for good.

Lisa is concerned. Just five days ago Marilyn talked of having a family and imagined preparing home-cooked meals for children they would raise together; today, she imagines, there is no one to share her dream.

"How are you coping?"

"I'm distracting myself with video games and movies. And keep busy preparing for the move. I still need to shop for household things." Excitedly, she asks Lisa, "Can you take me to buy household stuff and to the video store when I have enough money to buy new PlayStation games?"

Lisa agrees, then listens to a recounting of many current disappointments in her life. "Work still sucks," she says. She is still waiting for an apartment. And the only joy in her life, Frank, is gone. There is one comfort, though. Next weekend she'll be at her mom's for an aunt's retirement party. She needs an idea for a gift.

Reflect

In this scene, Marilyn is meeting her new counselor, one of many. Imagine a time when you were meeting new people. What comes to mind? No doubt you can picture many such moments along with the feelings. Perhaps it was the first day of class or on the playground or at a party. Perhaps kindergarten comes to mind. Suddenly it's the first day of school, and you are meeting lots of strangers. Or perhaps you can remember the feeling when you first ask someone for a date.

Do you find it difficult to meet new people? Do you avoid meeting new people? How do you respond when you meet someone for the first time? Do you tend to hang out with like-minded people, perhaps of the same ethnicity or culture, the same class, or the same part of town? Or with people who listen to the same music? Do you have a bodily reaction such as increased heart rate, sweating, or panic? In our public mental health system our clients are constantly meeting new people. Sometimes it is every day. Keep this in mind. Listen and observe. How do your clients feel and respond to new situations and people? In this scene, you learn that Marilyn feels the loss of an important relationship. Sometimes, after a loss, we're hesitant to meet new people.

Also, bear in mind that you can do something to help your clients when meeting new people and encountering strange situations. First, remember: Always prepare your clients for new situations and people. How can you do this? Begin talking about new encounters long before they happen, when possible. Consider saying something like, "Have you been thinking about what it will be like to meet your new counselor? What do you expect?"

Marilyn manages the hurt feelings resulting from the breakup. The feelings could be overwhelming, but they are not. She demonstrates resilience. What do we mean when we say that someone is resilient? Help her notice this strength. You might say something like, "Staying busy by preparing for your move and playing video games has enabled you to cope with this difficult time." By helping Marilyn notice her own coping, you are helping her remember this strength so that she can use it in the future.

Observe

August 10

Snow is falling on this hot August day in Ohio. It is falling on a decorated carousel horse—a unicorn. Marilyn is hypnotized. It seems she's been transported to another time, another place. Lisa notices that she shakes the glass globe several times—to make it snow again, and again, and again. Lisa and Marilyn are in the discount store, shopping for a retirement present for her aunt, who likes snow globes. Marilyn is reminded of her aunt and the special relationship they've had and of special times in the past.

The store is called Malachi Mart. It is behind St. Malachi's Church on West 25th, the one that serves the inner-city neighborhood. With proceeds from the store, the church funds social services for children, parents, families, and the homeless; Lisa explains this to Marilyn so she learns that there are different types of services in the community for people who need help. Marilyn is intrigued and plans to tell her friends at the group home. She'll shop here to furnish her new apartment. In this store she notices a difference. It's not a thrift store. There are no previously owned goods. Nor is it a dollar store. Most of the merchandise is new, just discontinued. It's like a T.J. Max or a Marshalls, but the store is not in the suburbs. It's in the neighborhood. Marilyn loves unicorns and wants to buy one. This is a moment when Lisa does some thinking for Marilyn. She reminds her that this might exceed her budget. The snow globe for her aunt costs $4. And Marilyn buys a card for $0.75.

* * *

Lisa shells out $1.25 for bottled water so she can sit with Marilyn in the local McDonald's and not feel guilty about not buying anything, even though Marilyn has purchased a Big Mac, supersized french fries, and a supersized Coke. Lunch conversation is dominated by Marilyn's displeasure with her job. Last week wasn't so bad, though. She was given the chance to work in the main office of the social service agency that owns the lumberyard. She loved it. Because the secretary was on vacation, they asked her to answer the phone.

"It was easy work," Marilyn says. "I actually got a Subway sandwich for lunch. Somebody was going out at lunch and asked me if I wanted anything. I felt like someone was including me as part of the group."

Marilyn is looking forward to the job interview at the video store. She would like this kind of work. She likes movies, and because the store is on a bus line, she could easily get there by herself. Marilyn feels good about the plan and her effort to get a new job. But Lisa notices that feeling quickly shift to shame. Marilyn begins to take inventory of everything that might go wrong with the interview and the job: She cannot work the night shift because it would not be safe to wait for the bus on the street at night. She has never worked a computerized cash register. She wonders, "Will it be too complicated?" These are valid concerns. But Lisa assures her that she can learn anything she sets her mind to. Lisa tries to flip Marilyn's shame on its head. She tells Marilyn that she has demonstrated a lot of courage and initiative to go to the video store by herself to express interest in a job and to ask for and complete an application. Lisa offers to help Marilyn rehearse for the interview.

* * *

The main street through the neighborhood where Marilyn grew up and where her mother, sister, and nieces still live is lined mostly with small post–World War II storefronts and bungalows. There are convenience stores, beauty shops, dry cleaners, and beverage stores. As Lisa drives, Marilyn points out familiar places. There is a school she attended and where her nieces now go, a stop where she used to get on and off the bus, a pizza shop where she used to hang out with friends, and there are buildings where she and her friends used to hide to smoke cigarettes. Marilyn is like a tour guide, or like someone much older who has returned to a place of youth long forgotten. There is pride in her voice. Excitement. And longing. Although Lisa is never quite sure what role she plays in Marilyn's recovery from symptoms of mental illness, today she seems a catalyst for making meaning—for connection. It is through telling her story that Marilyn connects her past with her present. She remembers. Today, she recalls a special relationship with her aunt. This happens in part because she is with someone who listens with genuine interest. Lisa knows that this is different from the work most case managers do with consumers of mental health services. Most focus on the tasks of recovery; they try to teach consumers like Marilyn how to manage daily routines such as cooking, cleaning, grooming, writing checks, taking medication to manage symptoms, and making and keeping appointments. They spend a lot of time teaching consumers the rules of living "independently" in the community and the consequences of failing to do so. There is a different kind of meaning in a teach-the-task relationship in which service providers do not have time to connect with the client's past and present lives, like the places in their old neighborhoods. Lisa knows that she could never have established this kind of relationship if she had the caseload of a typical manager. There would be no time to know sixty or maybe even a hundred people in this way.

As Lisa turns onto Marilyn's street, she notices that it is exactly as it was the last time she drove Marilyn home. Identical bungalows on small plots stand shoulder to shoulder as far as the eye can see. The lawns are neatly trimmed. The choice of flowers is the only evidence of their distinctiveness. Marilyn invites Lisa to meet her family.

* * *

There are three steps to the front stoop and door. To the right of the first step, there are three tiny handprints with the names of three children and the date they pressed them into fresh cement. Lisa points to them and says, "I remember you telling me about this."

Marilyn smiles with Lisa. And Lisa knows that paying attention to the details of their prior conversations has just paid off: The handprints have a very special meaning. There is an important memory and feeling embedded in the concrete. The handprints represent a time when the family was intact—when her father was alive and her brother was not ill. Lisa waits at the bottom step while Marilyn climbs and knocks. Lisa wonders, "does she have a key? If so, has she elected not to use it? Perhaps she doesn't have one." Lisa is puzzled. It feels to her as if Marilyn is not at home.

Finally, Marilyn's sister appears at the door balancing a portable telephone on her shoulder, talking loudly to someone. The two stand awkwardly on the steps for several minutes before Marilyn's sister ends the call and greets them. Marilyn timidly introduces Lisa; it feels as if she is expecting a negative response. She says, "This is that Lisa who I've been working with."

Lisa exchanges a "hello," but Marilyn's sister does not make eye contact. Without pausing or engaging Marilyn or Lisa, she unloads a list of tasks for the retirement party. The portable phone rings again. She answers. Lisa feels overwhelmed. She is being disregarded. She excuses herself. She tells Marilyn, "Maybe we can do this some other time when you're sister is not so busy."

Marilyn seems relieved that she, too, has a way out of feeling ignored. "Okay. Thanks for the ride and for helping me run errands."

Reflect

How does one stay connected amid distracting symptoms of mental illness? For Marilyn, the presence of important objects helps her reconnect. There is the snow globe in the discount shop, the buildings along the main street in the neighborhood of her youth, and the impressions of handprints in cement on the front steps.

Marilyn speaks of these objects with strong feeling; however, it is important to understand that the emotion may be less about the objects themselves and more about the relationships—the human connections—that the objects represent and enable. For instance, she has positive feeling about her aunt; she keeps her in mind and shops for a meaningful gift. So the content—the snow globe—initiates a process in which she experiences a mental representation of her aunt and, one might suspect, her family at large. And associated with this representation is a powerful feeling.

What is a mental representation? And how do feelings get attached to them? We all form pictures in our minds of things and people and relationships, past and present. Close your eyes for a moment and soon you will form pictures in your mind of people, places, objects. Some call these mental representations. And they are always partial, just as the camera captures only something that looks like us, and we always doubt the image. Is that really what I look like? Is that how you see me? In short, the photo image is an approximation of something or someone, just as our mental representations are always incomplete. And as we all form many mental pictures inside our minds, we also have as many feelings associated with them. For example, Marilyn has a mental picture, a representation, of the snow globe. For Marilyn, the snow globe stirs feelings associated with the past and present relationship with her aunt. The handprints in the cement evoke strong feelings about past and present. And you will recall that Lisa has her own feelings about the handprints that help her connect with Marilyn in a special way.

Notice that in this scene the case manager is not a guide or psychotherapist who leads the client. Marilyn does this work for herself. She is her own guide. Think of the case manager as a witness instead. And as a witness, the reflective manager observes and listens to the process her client uses to make connections with important people and helps her notice how connections are made, when connections are made, and with whom connections are made. And how she feels about making connections. In other words, you stand by to admire and do with by observing this process along with the associated feelings. If you find yourself in a situation similar to the one described in this scene, start your reflective work by helping your client notice the relationship between herself, the object (e.g., snow globe), and the people the object calls to mind. You might consider saying something like, "I see that you are keeping someone in mind. You know what your aunt likes. Maybe you feel a special connection." As a witness, the reflective manager acknowledges her client's internal strengths—to do for herself. You support her uniqueness as someone who can and does have positive relationships. This is the essence of what we call a working alliance (Angell and Mahoney, 2007). And as this alliance deepens, it is likely that your client will include you among those with whom she feels accepted, protected, understood, and respected. From this point, your client may recall her relationship with you and use the memory and feeling of connection with you to effectively engage with others (Bordin, 1979; Roth and Fonagy, 2005).[2]

Observe

August 22

Money is an object loaded with meaning. It is for all of us. And the way Marilyn deals with money is in many ways an expression of her internal world. But Lisa has not known her long enough to understand what money means to Marilyn.

The women are sitting at one end of the long dining room table in the group home, where Marilyn drags on a cigarette. Lisa listens as Marilyn reports on a recent visit to (CPS with her regular case manager. He helped complete paperwork to make CPS the guardian of her money; very soon her mother will no longer help with money management. CPS, she learned, will also pay monthly bills and give her an allowance. On this day, her monthly income, approximately $1,200.00, includes the following:

$900   Supplemental Security Income from her father, who is deceased, and Social Security Disability Income for her mental health disability

$250   from her job at the lumberyard ($5.50 per hour, fourteen hours per week)

* * *

Lisa takes the opportunity to explore some specific research questions. She wants to know who else in Marilyn's social network helps with money and medication. These are central concerns for all case managers. One might even say that this is the work of case management: money and medication. Marilyn reports that her mother, group home supervisor, housing specialist, and case manager help with money and medication.

Reflect

In our consumption culture, having the money and power to purchase has much to do with how we get along in life. For sure, it is about independence and self-control. But there is so much more. What we consume and how much we consume tells us much about who we are. And the failure to earn predictable income and manage money may result in great difficulty, social disapproval, and the shame of rejection: bankruptcy, poverty, homelessness, poor nutrition, and poor health.

We are everywhere encouraged to consume: in newspapers and magazines; on television, radio, the Internet, public transportation, and billboards. We are immersed in a world of advertising messages and images promising and coaxing us to meet our needs and desires by purchasing things, services, or experiences (e.g., fitness, spas, facelifts, teeth whitening, vacations). We live in an ad-saturated, fast-food world. Almost everything is available on demand and at the flick of a switch, including easy access to credit. Zygmaut Bauman (2007), a sociologist, argues that our very sense of self is defined by how and what we consume. We are what we consume. In short, ours is a consuming culture, and case management naturally unfolds within it. And because credit is available to everyone, managers inevitably face the management of client debt. They also face the challenge of working in a culture where that very same debt and all that is enabled by it defines who we are and what we might be. The message is loud and clear: Spending and consuming is good! Most of us do it quite naturally, and we often give ourselves permission to spend beyond our means. After all, our desires are always greater than our needs. So don't be surprised when clients come with conflicts between desires, needs, and income and decide to spend beyond their means. For example, you might anticipate there will be a time when they will spend money on a Big Mac and a supersized Pepsi instead of something necessary, such as a utility bill. After all, in the grand scheme of things, a hamburger and a cola is a small purchase and a small pleasure.

Most served by the public mental health system have little money; they must make important decisions about how to use limited resources. In addition, many, especially those with severe and persistent symptoms, have great difficulty with reconciling conflicts between income, needs, and desires. Who is to decide what is necessary? What is a luxury? Will it be your client? Or you? Imagine turning this dilemma into a partnership where you join to set the limits and possibilities of spending, saving, consuming, and desiring. You will often feel pressure to ensure that your client's money is in order, especially if you have a large caseload. And if money is not managed, there will be a crisis, such as an eviction, and your entire week (or next few weeks) will be consumed by crisis, leaving little time to attend to others. So what should you do? Take control or let it go?

Here are some questions to consider in the case management of money. Should I get involved in client decisions about what to purchase? Clearly there are times when this is necessary. Ask yourself, "Is this the right time? How should I do this?" Your involvement in the decision-making process may be viewed as paternalistic. If it is, will you trigger psychological defenses, which could destroy your working alliance? In this scene, did the presence of a third party, CPS, provide an important boundary between the case manager and the client? Also, was CPS working with the client to help her do for herself? How could this be done differently? Is it keeping her dependent by dispensing her money? How should the case manager work with the client and CPS to ensure that Marilyn benefits?

Most case management models do not equip managers with the clinical knowledge and skills to address entangled webs of desire and need. However, you can equip yourself with these skills and thus help clients with money management by respecting the inevitable and natural tension between desire and need and by recognizing the limitations of case management models.

Observe

September 26

Lisa steps through the front door of the group home into the collective shout of concern from residents, "Don't let Sparky out!" She hurries in, looking for the quick-footed ex–street cat longing for the freedom of his former life. The door shuts. The cat is nowhere to be seen.

Residents fill the living room, cigarette smoke hangs in the air, and the entire group excitedly trails Lisa into the dining room. Yearning for fresh air, she suggests that they open the door to the patio. A murder has been reported on the news; all at once they talk of feeling terribly unsafe. Marilyn appears not to share the worry. She talks instead about movies and television. Half an hour passes. Concerns have been vented, the residents disperse, and Marilyn and Lisa are left alone to talk about the job search and apartment hunting.

The apartment search continues. Marilyn met with a housing specialist to complete the paperwork. She received a letter from the BVR stating that there may soon be an employment opportunity. The letter makes no mention of cooking, however.

And because it was scheduled during the workday, Marilyn missed the meeting with the BVR. Because the BVR offices close at 4 P.M., Marilyn is trying to get permission to miss work. She never heard back from the video store about her job application. She is afraid of being stuck in her current job forever.

Lisa tries to encourage Marilyn by reminding her that there are always other opportunities. She says, "Why don't you go back to school?"

"I don't think I'll ever go back. I don't think college is a good idea for me."

"It may not be, but why do you think that?"

"It's hard, real hard, and I couldn't make myself go to classes."

"That's fine. As long as you know why it's not good for you to go to school. As long as you're not blaming yourself for not finishing last semester. There are a lot of people who start school and don't finish."

Marilyn does not seem comforted.

Reflect

While most residents express fear, Marilyn expresses disappointment. She is disappointed that her goals—getting a new job and finding an apartment of her own—are delayed.

Disappointment occurs when circumstances do not match one's desires and expectations. And sometimes disappointment can become a fixed or hardened attitude. For some of us, disappointment may organize our lives. We produce it. We expect it. We seek it. For Marilyn, school is too hard, getting the dream job is too hard, and getting the apartment is too hard. With everything and everyone she talks of disappointment.

If you find yourself in a situation like the one described here, there is little you can do. Resist the temptation to do for your client in the realm of feeling by reassuring her that everything will work out. Maintain your working alliance simply by being present with her. You might say something like this: "I hear that you are disappointed, and I can imagine how you have come to have this strong feeling."

Ask your supervisor about the evidence-based Supported Employment (SE) model. Unlike other vocational programs, SE works to help clients find competitive employment in the community as soon as they express the desire to work. A client like Marilyn would benefit from SE's emphasis on consumer preferences and rapid job-placement services. With SE, there are no pre-employment trainings or workshops, which delay the employment experience. Learning the job occurs in real time (Drake and Bond, 2008).

Observe

October 10

The City of Lakewood is one of the largest intact urban communities in northeast Ohio. Home to 56,000 people, it stretches along the shore of Lake Erie, a landscape dominated by a mix of residential, commercial, and industrial buildings. There are high-rise condos and apartments, brownstones, modest single-family working-class homes, row houses, duplexes, multifamily flats, and big old beautiful homes tucked beneath the shade of giant oaks and maples.

If you were to see Lakewood from the sky or drive through it without paying much attention, you might not notice that the land slopes northward in a gradual descent toward the water. You can feel the pull from the north when you're walking down Madison or Detroit Avenue, the two main commercial districts in town. You can hear it in the conversations in the bakeries, the butcher shops, the groceries, and coffee shops. You can see it in the stagger of the drunks as they trip out of the pubs. What is so magnetizing about the north is the serenity of the water. It is one of the reasons so many have not given up on the city of Lakewood the way they have on its neighboring town to the east, the city of Cleveland. Despite Lakewood's urban neurosis—its obsession with developing every square inch of land—the residential neighborhoods in this town, unlike those in Cleveland, are deeply connected to the lake. People here can walk or ride bikes to Lakewood Park on the shoreline, stare into the wide-open space, and breathe a deep sigh of relief.

Today, *errand* is a code word for cigarettes, soda, cash machine, and the music and video game store on Detroit Avenue in Lakewood. Although most of the time Marilyn runs errands by herself, today Lisa has agreed to drive her around. It will give them time to talk. Marilyn, preoccupied with her friend Sophie from the group home, recently hospitalized because of schizophrenia, recollects events leading up to the hospitalization like someone who has experienced a trauma. She puts the pieces together, trying to make sense of the situation. Sophie had been increasingly difficult to interact with at home and at work. One day at supper, she had taken a large bowl of food—the equivalent of several portions—before anyone else had been served. This surprised Marilyn. It was out of character. It also annoyed Marilyn because her friend was obviously being selfish. When Marilyn confronted her, Sophie didn't seem to care.

"She told me that it was too bad, that the others should have gotten to the food earlier. It was getting hard to help her around the house. She started snapping at me. One day, she was cooking chicken, and she took it out early. I told her that she needed to keep it in longer. She snapped. She yelled at me. So I backed off."

The small music and video game store on Detroit Avenue is housed in a storefront on the corner of a side street that slopes steeply north toward the lake. Inside, Marilyn is on a mission. She scans rows of compact discs locked inside tall glass cabinets. Without difficulty she approaches clerks and starts conversations. She gets what she wants. She does this for herself. She is effective. Lisa stands by to admire her assertiveness. Marilyn is obviously capable of using her emotions and thoughts, her social skills and money, to get what she wants. But Lisa is not convinced that this is what she needs. Marilyn buys three CDs and a video game for her PlayStation.

There is a coffee shop across the street, and because Marilyn likes to drink coffee and smoke cigarettes, this is where they head. Inside, there are open shelves with coffee kitsch: mugs, T-shirts, and coffee beans packaged in decorative bags. Marilyn is trying to decide. She's in the mood to spend. She holds a one-pound bag of whole coffee beans that costs $10 as she studies the brightly colored mugs. Lisa, concerned about Marilyn's urgent need to buy, especially as she prepares to move into an apartment of her own, discourages her. She will need the money. Marilyn picks a $12 coffee mug, along with a tall cup of coffee and a pastry. Lisa buys a bottle of water.

On the patio in front of the store there are plastic tables with umbrellas precariously stuck in the middle. It is surrounded by a metal fence. It is midday. The wind howls along with the cars on Detroit Avenue. The patio is crowded, but Lisa and Marilyn find a table. Lisa tries to start a conversation, but Marilyn picks up a video game and begins to read the cover.

Lisa pauses then persists with the conversation. She wants to know how Marilyn feels when she thinks about living on her own.

"It's the challenge of the unknown. The what-ifs," Marilyn says. She rattles off a list of concerns. She is afraid she'll have problems with her roommates. She wants to buy Dish T.V. but is afraid it might cost too much. She wonders whether the telephone could be connected right away. She's not sure what she'll do for transportation or how she'll get to work; she thinks she'll have to take a cab. Her case manager has suggested she buy a shopping cart for the grocery store, but she is not sure it will fit on the bus. She is applying for a food stamp card that works like a debit card so she can have money for groceries.

Lisa knows that, theoretically, Marilyn is doing for herself by exploring options, but she is surprised that none of the service providers in her support network have worked with her to develop a budget that will enable her to purchase a monthly bus pass. Lisa also knows that, theoretically, she is monitoring Marilyn's thoughts, which are scattered, and her feelings of anxiety. She feels overwhelmed by the conversation and noise and activity around her. She feels her head spinning. She wants to go next door for lunch. It's a Burger King. It's quiet there. By the end of the afternoon, Marilyn has spent a total of $62, none of it on what Lisa believes to be essential for the new apartment:

$40 = music CDs and video games

$12 = coffee mug

$5 = coffee and a pastry

$5 = chicken sandwich, large fries, and a Pepsi

_____

$62 = total

Reflect

Strong emotions drive our needs and wants. And at this point, we do not know Marilyn's. What we know is what *we* want for her or what our agency believes is most important among her needs. Maybe these apparently frivolous purchases have something to do with ambivalence about moving into an apartment of her own. Maybe she feels conflict: Some part of her wants to move on, and another feels the need to stay connected with familiar people and places, such as the group home. Maybe she feels change as profound loss. It is important to wonder about these possibilities. Talk to your supervisor and service team members to process your ideas.

Money is loaded with conflicting feelings for all of us. Try to keep your worry about money separate. In short, avoid feeling judgmental. You might think you know what is right and therefore apply an outside measure, such as a budget or a to-do list for the move.

It is possible that all the objects Marilyn wants to buy connect to important people and thus important feelings from her present or past. Maybe the video games remind her of hanging out in arcades along the main street in her neighborhood with friends from grade school and high school. Maybe the CDs remind her of hanging out in clubs with current friends. Maybe the fresh coffee beans remind her of hanging out at the kitchen table in her childhood home with her father and mother, or maybe they remind her of hanging out in the group home with the group home supervisor, a woman she has identified as a substitute mother. Maybe these objects are helping her reconnect to feelings. Maybe they are helping her avoid the pain of the pending change and associated feelings of loss.

Imagine that you are involved in this scene. When you finally sit down to take a break with your client, you might help her notice the objects purchased, the feelings, and the people associated with them. You might start by saying something like, "I notice you bought music and videos and coffee. What do you like about listening to music? What kind of music do you listen to?" After you reflect with her, you can help make the connections between these feelings and memories and her upcoming move. You might say something like, "I wonder how all of this might be connected to the move into the new apartment." Here, too, imagine times in your life when you faced a move to a new home, to school, or an apartment. How did you cope with these changes?

Sometimes clients will depend on your monitoring every purchase, especially if they are struggling. When this occurs, help them recognize you're doing for them. In this way you maintain their self-observation. You might say something like, "I am choosing to have you buy a cup of coffee instead of a bag of beans, because the cup of coffee fits into your budget. I am making this decision for you, because you have told me that your symptoms are a bit intense right now and that you have a hard time concentrating and making decisions. When you feel better, I will stand by and give you support as you make these decisions, once again, for yourself."

Observe

October 16

The cell phone rings. Lisa answers. She hears an excited Marilyn: "I'm calling to tell you the good news. I got the apartment. I'm scheduled to move on Tuesday, October 23, at 9 A.M. Does this time work for you? I'll see if Dolores can help too. I got a chance to spend some time with my mom and sister this weekend. We took my nieces to pick out a puppy from the animal shelter. I went to the Record Exchange on Saturday and bought a used PlayStation II and a few games and memory cards. The whole thing cost four-hundred-and-something."

Lisa listens in disbelief. Marilyn has just spent more money. Now she's even deeper in debt. Yet she has no hint of concern. Her case manager must not be keeping tabs on her spending. She wonders whether anyone knows that Marilyn's experience with the move is being expressed as a financial self-bleed. Lisa lets her breath out easily, along with a very softly spoken question. "Is there anything you need to do to prepare for the move?"

"No, but I'm relieved that I can get cable hooked up. I've got a DVD player, but I need a small TV with a built-in VCR because I've got so many tapes. The only thing I have to figure out now is how to get to and from the grocery store."

October 20

Lisa calls Marilyn to ask how the packing is going.

Marilyn says, "Slow."

"Do you need any more boxes?"

"No."

"How many do you have?"

"Three."

October 22

Marilyn calls. She is procrastinating. She wants to know whether Lisa can still help with the move and whether she plans to bring her truck. Lisa asks her how she is feeling. She says, with hesitation, "Fine." The call ends, and Lisa has a gut feeling that Marilyn doesn't know how to express her worry, especially when it is intense.

October 23

Interstate 77 between Akron and Cleveland is a thirty-mile stretch of northbound highway that gradually slopes downhill along the Cuyahoga River Watershed toward Lake Erie. This stretch of highway through wooded suburban districts gives you lots of time to think. Lisa is making a mental list of what is needed for Marilyn's move. She is supplying the truck. She has bungee cords in a bag behind her seat, but she doesn't have a cap for the bed, just a tonneau, and it is supposed to rain. She reminds herself how much she despises moving and wonders, momentarily, why she agreed to help. Deep down, though, she knows the answer. She hopes this will go fast. Marilyn lives in only one room in the group home, and she doesn't own much except video-tapes.

At 8:45 A.M., her cell phone rings. It's Marilyn. She is happy to report that she called the telephone company all by herself yesterday and got the service turned on. Lisa assures her that this is a good thing and tells her that she will arrive shortly. At 8:50 A.M., she backs her truck to the door that leads into the kitchen. She is eager to get the job done. Marilyn's room is on the second floor. Lisa climbs the back staircase, the one they'll use to carry the boxes down.

Imagine that everything in your house or apartment has been picked up and thrown into the air and landed in one big mess. This is what Marilyn's room looks like. There are mounds of clothes chest-high with videotapes and papers sticking out: scraps of paper, full sheets of paper, mail order catalogs, old bills, old receipts. There are a couple of moving boxes. However, nothing is packed, labeled, or stacked, ready to be moved. Marilyn is sitting on the floor, staring at one of the boxes. She appears lifeless.

Stunned by the scene, she stops in the doorway, uncertain about what to say or where to begin. It is clear to Lisa that the burden of the move is hers. She remembers that Marilyn must be at the new place by 9 A.M., so she reminds her of the deadline and asks whether they have time. Marilyn remains silent and makes no effort to find out. She stares at the floor. In the meantime Lisa puts her anger to use by sorting through the mess, separating the essentials—like clothes and video games—from the apparent junk. She wants to lighten the load by throwing out the junk. At first, she asks for permission to toss things, like tangled balls of wire hangers and mail-order catalogs, but after getting the answer, "I think we should keep that," one too many times, Lisa decides to make her own decisions. They will have to hurry to beat the rain. She hopes they can move everything in one trip by packing all the boxes and miscellaneous stuff into the open bed of the truck.

Lisa sorts through plastic tote boxes filled with videotapes and finds videos from Blockbuster. She inquires about the due date.

"I've seen two but not the third. I have yet to see that."

Lisa finds the receipt and notices that two are a week past due. "We should stop on our way to return the videos."

Marilyn disagrees. "We should drop them in the night box and pay later."

"Won't they freeze your account until you pay them off?"

"I suppose." Marilyn shows no sign of concern.

Dolores, Marilyn's friend at the group home (the backseat driver on the trip to the community college), arrives to help Lisa sort and pack. Marilyn stands silently in the door, watching impassively. When she speaks, her words have nothing to do with the task of moving. She says, "Since I don't have cable yet or an antenna for my TV, I'm wondering if my new roommates will let me watch *Roswell* [a television show] tonight." With this comment Lisa is ready to explode. She uses the energy to sort faster and to begin packing.

At 9:30 A.M., Marilyn decides to call; she reports that they have time, until 10:30 A.M., to get the apartment keys; the manager is attending a funeral, she says. Once they get the keys, they are free to come and go. Still, she sits on the edge of the bed and watches as Lisa arranges and rearranges the contents of boxes to maximize carrying space. She says, "Wow. You're good at this."

Lisa conveys her displeasure with silence. Fifteen minutes pass before Marilyn asks, "Am I being helpful?"

Lisa makes eye contact and says, "No, not especially, but I'm guessing that maybe you are feeling really overwhelmed or something else like that, and it is making it very hard for you to help with the move."

She says, "I guess."

Eventually, Lisa and Dolores get the truck loaded, drive to the new place, get the keys, take the boxes to Marilyn's new room, dump the contents, and take the boxes back to the group home to pack yet another load. There, it begins to rain. Lisa throws the boxes into the kitchen and hurries to snap the canvas tonneau onto the bed of the truck, but the sky lets loose, and she is caught in a downpour. Dolores watches with concern from the kitchen door and yells to Lisa, insisting she come into the house.

Lisa finishes the job and runs into the kitchen, soaking wet, where Dolores is waiting with a hair dryer. Another resident boils water and offers tea. Marilyn shows no sign of concern. She sits, smoking, in the living room.

When the rain lets up, they drive the second load to the new apartment. Lisa was hoping to have time to take Marilyn to the grocery store, but it is now 2 P.M. and she must go. As soon as the last box is dropped, Marilyn says, "Maybe I should go to the group home to watch *Roswell.*"

Lisa bites her lip. But Dolores speaks up: "You need to go to the deli, buy some food for lunch and dinner, and start working on this room."

Reflect

Marilyn does not want to move. She wants to stay at the group home and watch a favorite television show in the company of friends. The mess in her room is evidence of her resistance to the move and the loss of the camaraderie she's felt with those in the group home.

It is important to ask whether Marilyn really wants an apartment of her own. Or is this an expectation of and compliance with the service system? Here, it is the responsibility of the case manager and the service team to sort out the recovery goals of the service system from those of the client. There are plenty of clues throughout this story that signal Marilyn's reluctance (or ambivalence) about the move. She drags her feet: She does not plan, she does not save money and direct her spending toward the apartment, she does not pack.

In retrospect, it is clear that Marilyn struggles with separations. She takes steps toward independence yet acts in ways to undermine this goal; in other words, she has internal conflict. She needs support from her case manager during painful and potentially debilitating moments of separation and loss. Marilyn needs help preparing for transition events, not just economically but emotionally. Separations may produce overwhelming feelings of abandonment, aloneness, loss, and shame. She will also need the support of her social network of family and friends. In other words, she will need others to do with and stand by to support.

* * *

The crisis of moving is an everyday affair. That's what life in the community is all about. It is true for everyone. There are deadlines. The job must be done.

It is helpful to be aware that when your client feels paralyzed in stressful situations, she may transfer feelings to you, and thus you might feel paralyzed. Help connect her inaction to her feelings. You might ask, "What is happening here? There appears to be a feeling that is overwhelming you."

Allow yourself and your client time to process the stuck feeling, then be reflective about the need to do for your client to get the work done. You might say something like, "We've got to get this done by 10:30. You have to get keys to the new place. Today, you must lean on me for help, and that's okay. I will do this for you, because it must get done. I know that you are capable of doing this, but right now you are overwhelmed."

Be prepared to spend a lot of time after this crisis doing reflective work to help her process feelings and thoughts about this important life event.

Observe

October 24

Marilyn pushes her cart up and down the grocery aisles, erratically plucking boxes and cans and jars and cartons. Periodically Lisa stops to review the cart and encourages returning what Marilyn does not need—most of it. Marilyn is accustomed to shopping and preparing meals at the group home for eleven; the home had ample space in its commercial-sized refrigerator. She will now cook for herself. She will share the apartment with two women, and she will have only one shelf in the fridge and one-third of the freezer. Lisa looks at the grocery cart. It's overflowing. She says to herself, "It will fill the shelves and most of the freezer." Marilyn returns items. Most she stubbornly keeps. She ignores Lisa.

In the checkout line, Lisa packs groceries and puts them into the cart. Marilyn pays, then pilots the cart around Lisa, who asks her to pull it aside. "Stop," she says. She insists, "Please stop." She does, dead in her tracks. Now that the shopping is done, Lisa feels, it is time to confront Marilyn. Lisa steps into her space, so close that Marilyn backs against the cart.

"Please don't take this the wrong way," Lisa says, "but I've never seen you this disorganized. I'm really concerned. The past two days, I've been trying to point out the reality of your new living environment, like how you're going to get your groceries home from the store and how you're going to put them away and how you are going to get to and from work. What is going on?"

To this, Marilyn replies, bluntly and looking away, "Oh, I kind of try to avoid reality."

Lisa is speechless. The two return to the truck, in silence, load the groceries, and drive to the apartment. There's a long, uncomfortable silence.

After a few minutes Marilyn begins to talk. She explains that over the past days and weeks she has sensed a change. She feels different. She's not sure what it is. She pauses, then begins to stammer, as if preparing to make a confession. She's not been taking her medication. And because she missed the last appointment with her psychiatrist, she did not get a refill. She ran out of pills weeks ago. She's told no one—not her mother, her case manager, or the supervisor at the group home—because she is afraid they will yell. Lisa feels that Marilyn is truly scared about getting in trouble. For Marilyn, yelling was expected. Yelling was all around her. Yelling was an everyday thing. Yelling in her family was a way of life. Lisa assures her that she will not get in trouble. She then seeks to determine whether Marilyn's symptoms have worsened.

"Did you notice changes when you stopped taking medication?"

"No. Not really."

"Did your mood change? Did you lose your appetite? Sleep too much or not be able to go to sleep? Were you more irritable? Did you find it hard to focus on what you were doing, or did you find it hard to make sense of things?"

"Yes. You know, I took a pill during the move. I found one when we were going through all of that stuff."

October 25 to 31

Lisa helps Marilyn develop a plan for getting in touch with her psychiatrist. She telephones daily to encourage follow-through. She stops calling after the appointment has been scheduled. She takes time to reflect on what has occurred. In the public mental health system, missing an appointment with a psychiatrist can produce a cascade of problems. If you miss one, it may be weeks before somebody tracks you down. Once they do, it may take weeks to get another appointment. The supply of community-based psychiatrists is low. The demand is high.

Reflect

In these scenes, there is more evidence of Marilyn's reluctance to leave the group home. She fills the cart with enough to feed everyone, even though she will no longer cook for them. On the surface, it may appear that Marilyn is simply being unrealistic about her new downsized living arrangement. However, without words to describe her fear of being alone and of losing the connection to and safety in the group home, she acts out the feelings.

Here, we learn how Marilyn defends against powerful feelings. The consequences are costly. Symptoms increase, especially anxiety and depression; she spends recklessly; she avoids taking action to achieve desired goals; she abandons her observing self and thus becomes ineffective in making decisions and taking care of herself.

It is no coincidence that Lisa witnesses Marilyn's conflict and ambivalence about the move. Marilyn feels safe with her: Lisa offers a level of attention that others do not. As a reflective manager, you will find yourself in similar situations. When this occurs, take time to help your client reflect on and become aware of conflicting feelings and thoughts and her defenses against them. Stay in touch with her behavior, her feelings about life transitions, and the process of her relationship with you as it occurs in the here and now. You might try saying, "I notice you are filling your shopping cart with more than you have room for. You are doing this with me. You appear to feel frantic right now. What is this frantic feeling about?" Remember, what you are doing here is a kind of mentalization: By observing with her, you are using your mind to help her observe her own mind.

* * *

After you reflect with your client, you might try to problem solve with her. You might say something like, "You are valued by your friends at the group home, and you know it. You enjoy cooking for them, and they like it when you cook. Have you thought about how you might stay connected with friends in this way?"

It might be obvious to you that your client could maintain relationships with the people at the group home by cooking on occasion, and it is a wonderful idea. However, refrain from telling her to do this. Give her some time to realize this for herself. If you suggest that she cook for friends, she might feel you are imposing your thoughts and feelings—that you are doing for and doing to her. That's the last thing you want to happen. Help her find her own solutions.

* * *

There is more evidence of Marilyn's ambivalent feelings in this scene, in her use of psychiatric medication. She stops taking meds and misses an appointment for refills. For people with persistent symptoms of mental illness, failure to take medication or get refills may exacerbate symptoms. Therefore, many mental health providers will view this behavior as noncompliant and see it as an unhealthy choice. However, in the context of the events leading to and included in this scene, it is apparent that Marilyn is ambivalent not just about her thoughts and feelings about living by herself but also about her recovery in general. Right now, she needs help naming these feelings. She needs help becoming familiar with having many feelings at the same time, some in conflict with one another. Like Marilyn, your clients might not easily tolerate good feelings about becoming more independent at the same time they are experiencing uncomfortable feelings about it. They seem to contradict one another.

In your work, try approaching medication noncompliance as an expression of ambivalence about recovery and wonder with your client about the timing of missed appointments and forgotten pills. You might try saying something like, "I wonder why during this stressful time, you forgot your medication and your appointment?"

If your client expresses a fear of being scolded by her psychiatrist or by others, as Marilyn does, this may be a legitimate concern. We do not know how others will treat her. However, right now there is no yelling. So help her notice this. In this scene, it is safe to suspect that Marilyn's conscience is doing the yelling and that she is defending against this internal assault by projecting it into the future and on others. Help her notice. Say something like, "I am wondering who is doing the yelling here. Are you yelling at yourself about missing your medication and the appointment? What is this yelling about?"

* * *

As a reflective case manager who strives to be in tune with your own feelings, thoughts, and actions while you are in touch with your client's, remember that life transitions are hard for all of us. Think back to the last time you moved to a new apartment or house or to a time when you first moved out of your childhood home, away from your most familiar environment. Keep these feelings in mind when you help clients work through important life transitions and know that their ambivalence about change is not just a symptom of mental illness.

On Being and Having a Case Manager Online

Please see our Web site (http://relationalcasemanager.com) for additional resources, podcasts, and readings.

SUGGESTED READINGS AND OTHER RESOURCES

National Association of Social Workers Web site links to information and resources on safety:
http://www.socialworkers.org/pressroom/events/safety1006/default.asp.

Newhill, C. E. 2003. *Client violence in social work practice: Prevention, intervention, and research.* New York: Guilford.

Singer, J. B., host. 2008, March 3. Client violence: Interview with Dr. Christina Newhill [Episode 35]. *Social Work Podcast.* Podcast retrieved from http://socialworkpodcast. com/2008/03/client-violence-interview-with-dr.html.

Topics for Discussion

1. Try this brief exercise. Pair up with another person in class, workshop, seminar, or your agency. Interview one another about a recent event in your lives. As you do so, pay attention not only to the content of what you learn and say but to the process. After completing this exercise, share with your partner what you learned. How was the information conveyed, for example? Was there eye contact? Anxiety? Change in tone of voice? Body movement?

2. On one page list all the people who are making a difference, good or bad, in your life today. Write several sentences describing how they are making a difference and how they make you feel.

3. Take a minute to write a short paragraph about a time in your life when someone pointed out to you something embarrassing. We can all remember these events, even from early times in our lives. If possible, discuss this with a peer or supervisor.

4. Anna, a case manager for Hope Mental Health, Inc., has been asked to visit Donald, a young man with a long history of difficulties, mental illness, and problems with the law. Her supervisor is out of town and the case record offers no detail. Should Anna take precautions to remain safe? What should she do?

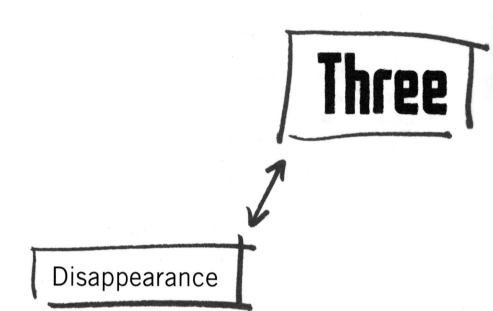

Disappearance

Observe

November 1

The office of psychiatrist Susan Brown, M.D., is located in an old house on the second floor of the social service agency that employs Marilyn's full-time case manager. Dr. Brown's office is a small room whose only protection from the cold Ohio winter air is a thin layer of plaster and a large window, which lets in plenty of natural light. Marilyn sits at a table in front of the window. They face one another. Lisa sits nearby. She is uncomfortable with the doctor. She seems so starched. Her facial expressions are stiff. So is her posture. She thumbs through Marilyn's chart, trying to find notes about her former boyfriend, Frank. Marilyn has informed Dr. Brown that she and Frank broke up a while ago but are friends again. Now they are just enjoying each other's company.

"Refresh my memory," Dr. Brown says, with her head and eyes melded to Marilyn's file. "How long ago were you boyfriend and girlfriend?"

"Oh, a long time ago."

"How long?"

"Last August or so."

Again the doctor shuffles through the file looking for the right page. The record seems to replace the relationship: The doctor is interacting with the file. The doctor is searching for clues in the file, for a place to start talking with Marilyn, for some hidden meaning. Lisa is wondering why the file has become so important. Finally, she finds a page to read, aloud, "I see you got angry a lot with Frank and threw fits."

"No. We're not like that any more." Marilyn protests in her usual quiet voice. She insists, losing hope in her reach to be understood, that the note does not accurately describe their current relationship. "We're like brother and sister now. We're best friends."

"What do you mean, 'brother and sister'? Is he pressuring you to be a girlfriend?"

"No," she says with greater emphasis. Marilyn is noticeably uncomfortable and changes the subject: "I moved out of the group home."

The doctor is surprised by this news, even though she has easy access to information about Marilyn from other service providers located in the same building. Marilyn feels the failure in communication. The doctor says, "Oh. When did you move?" Marilyn falls silent, so Dr. Brown asks another question. "How is it going so far? Are you living by yourself?"

"Pretty good so far," Marilyn answers. She quickly changes this subject. She reveals that she is having some difficulty concentrating.

"How?"

"I'm staring off into space and not knowing about it."

"How long does it last?"

"About five seconds."

"How long has this been going on and how often?"

"About four years ago. It started when I was living with my mother."

Lisa remains silent but wants to interject to inform Dr. Brown that she is missing the point: Marilyn's current lack of concentration started about four weeks ago after she ran out of fluoxetine, after she missed her last appointment and therefore did not get her prescription.

Dr. Brown asks whether she has been experiencing a loss of consciousness.

Lisa is afraid the conversation is drifting way off course, so she asks a question. She asks Marilyn whether the lack of concentration is similar to the episodes she experienced during the move. Marilyn says, "Kind of," so Lisa suggests that maybe too much or too little medication would make this happen.

"I don't think this has anything to do with too little or too much medication," Marilyn interjects. Her tone is defensive.

Dr. Brown asks, "Have you ever had a seizure?"

"No, but they think I had one when I was living with my mom."

"Do you have a primary care physician who can refer you to a neurologist for tests?"

Lisa knows for sure that the conversation is adrift. Again, she asks Marilyn whether her difficulty with concentration relates in any way to the conversation they had in the grocery store after the move.

"I've been having difficulty concentrating," Marilyn repeats. She addresses her psychiatrist directly.

"Do you forget to take your medication?" Dr. Brown asks.

"Sometimes. I took one last week. I found it in my room when we were packing to move."

"Did you lose them?"

"Yeah. Kind of."

"Where do you keep them? Someplace where you can see them?"

"In my bedroom."

"Someplace where you can get them?"

"On my dresser."

"Do you think the move caused you to lose your meds?"

"I think so. I was feeling pretty overwhelmed and anxious about moving."

As Lisa listens to the exchange between doctor and patient, she cannot imagine the doctor does not know about the missed appointment in September. Is it possible that the chart does not contain a note about something this important? Marilyn is so afraid of getting in trouble that she is not talking about it. Lisa looks across the room, out the window, at the doctor. She thinks to herself that this conversation should not be about Marilyn's inability to remember medication. "Marilyn let the prescription expire," Lisa mumbles.

"I'll give you samples and write a prescription you can fill later," the doctor says.

Marilyn nods her head in agreement, and Dr. Brown leaves to get samples. She returns to ask whether there are other medications she needs. Marilyn is silent. The doctor hesitates before saying, "Birth control shots?"

"No," she says bluntly. Marilyn, now defensive, has one more question: "I was wondering if you could set me up with another therapist? I think it would be good to talk to somebody regularly again."

Dr. Brown asks Marilyn to refresh her memory about past counselors, so Marilyn reminds her that both have left the agency. The doctor mentions that a new female case manager has recently started, and she would be good.

Lisa immediately feels the increasing disconnect. Marilyn has asked for a *therapist*. The doctor recommends a new *case manager*. She then gives Marilyn samples of fluoxetine and a prescription for more; she calls the new case manager, leaves a message, and schedules the next appointment. The meeting ends.

Reflect

Some psychiatrists are physicians of the brain. For them, symptoms of mental illness are rooted primarily in biology, as diseases of neurons and neurotransmitters or chemicals that transmit feeling and thought signals throughout the body. Others are physicians of the mind and brain. For them symptoms of mental illness express feelings and thoughts that develop over time and that we experience in relationship with others.

Psychiatrists and other mental health and human service providers who use the relationship method approach mental health holistically to understand the emergence and persistence of symptoms; for them, symptoms may have biological roots, but they may simultaneously have psychological and social ones. And even if they have biological origins, they always have social and psychological implications. And because of this complex dynamic between our minds and brains and our symptoms, we must always help clients understand and negotiate the complex relationships between internal (biological and psychological) and external worlds—between themselves and others. In short, reflective practice is holistic because it accounts for the whole person: mind, brain, body, and interpersonal relationships, in neighborhoods and communities.

Let's look at how Marilyn has reconnected with Dr. Brown. She wants help with her mind. She talks about her relationship with Frank. She asks for a referral to a new therapist. Dr. Brown, instead, focuses on the body and brain: She offers pills and recommends a neurological exam. She also sets in motion a forced separation from the current case manager, with whom Marilyn has worked for three years.

Stay alert. Notice when other mental health and human service providers fail to help clients understand and clarify the complex relationships between their thoughts, feelings, actions, needs, and desires. And although you may not be able to change colleague approaches or attitudes, you may help your client advocate. For example, after the meeting described here, you might consider directing attention to the exchange between the doctor and patient: "I noticed that you asked for a new therapist. But the doctor insisted that you try a new case manager. I wonder how this made you feel?" Remember, if the doctor proposes a change in case management, Marilyn will probably feel another loss: you. So you might want to explore this with her: "Being asked to change your case manager means that you will have to end your relationship with me. I am wondering what feelings you have about leaving me."

* * *

Here is something else to consider in thinking about this scene. Marilyn may have stopped taking fluoxetine because she is struggling with and seeking relationships. Similarly, if your client stops taking medication, explore with her the feelings about the change of course. Always wonder, "Why now?" For example, what might be happening in the world of relationships? You might begin your reflective work by saying, "I notice that you're seeking a therapist. I am wondering what this means? Why now?" Note that you first observe with your client by asking whether she notices what you notice. In short, "Do you see what I see?" Then you may wonder with them. You might also reflect on difficulty with medication management by observing with her:

"I also notice that you stopped taking medication at the same time you're asking for a new therapist. Do you see any connections?"

* * *

Psychiatric medication has played a crucial role in the recent history of public mental health services in the United States. It emerged as a treatment option in the late 1940s and early 1950s and set the stage for deinstitutionalization, which began in the 1960s. Soon, with the help of medication, many thousands of people, once confined to mental hospitals, were able to live productively in communities. Medication is a complex topic, yet here is one way to understand its importance in community mental health: Medication may help people live in the community by reducing the severity of symptoms. Medication often provides a way of managing otherwise unmanageable feelings, thoughts, and actions.

In reflective management, however, we do not treat clients as passive agents in the management of medication. We see medication management as an unfolding process that involves many people in complex and overlapping networks: doctors, nurses, family, friends, psychotherapists, peers, and case managers. And your client may not always be at the center of the network or the most effective, active, or powerful member of the medication network. In reflective case management, we like to think about the degree to which we are active or passive in the medication management process (Longhofer et al., 2003). For example, some in the network may have a greater desire for medication interventions than others. Sometimes your client may desire and seek medication, while others do things to undermine her efforts. We look at who in the network is active or passive. And why? Ultimately, it is the goal to move our clients toward the active side of the continuum. If some in the network are too active, they may be disempowering your client. Often, however, we must become active, especially when symptoms worsen. When we do so, we must remain vigilantly self-observant about the reasons for and degree to which we become active. At other times symptoms may have so dramatically improved that your client (and others in the medication network) become less observant. When this happens, we may help others in the network to become active. In short, there are times in the management of medication when we must do for and other times when we must avoid the temptation to take over. Prescribing pills without the opportunity to reflect on feelings and thoughts about the pills turns clients into objects. Moreover, if your clients passively consume drugs, they may lose the incentive to explore and use their own internal resources, their own feelings and thoughts, to get better.

In this chapter we describe in detail the medication management process. Before we start, however, it's important to note that this is not a linear process. First, there is the assessment or evaluation. Unfortunately, case managers are not consulted often enough during this phase of the process. This is most often the work of psychiatry. It includes the diagnostic interview. Second, there is the prescription and delivery phase. Here, managers are directly involved. Among other things, you may offer transport to and from pharmacies. In this phase you are often involved in what is sometimes called the med drop, and for many in our public mental health systems, med drops dominate the daily work. They may also be among the least rewarding activities. In the third phase, you stand by to monitor for compliance and often observe with your clients how the medication is working. Here, you may find yourself observing for the effects of medication and, when necessary, doing for your clients. This can also be felt as the most intrusive intervention. How would you address this feeling? Imagine a time in your life when you were forced to take medication or when you took medication while a parent stood by to monitor, coax, or even coerce. Finally, there is the reporting phase. Here, you report to your clients, supervisors, physicians, or team members concerns about medication effectiveness, compliance, and symptom reduction. And often it is the manager who is best positioned to see problems in this unfolding phase of the medication management process.

Here is where the real work of medication case management begins: observing for effects. When case managers, psychiatrists, and other providers empower clients to verbalize thoughts and feelings about medication, they give them power over that medication. And it is in this way that they may become active participants in caring for their bodies, brains, minds, and relationships. They use feelings and thoughts about the drugs to work with providers to find the right combinations in the right dosages. In your working with clients on medication concerns, start with obvious questions: "I was wondering what you think and feel when you take this medication?" If your client does not know, consider a simple and direct question: "Do you have any fears or hopes about it?" Often you will find it necessary to patiently observe with your client the effects of medication over time. Remember, try not to become a detached, impersonal observer but a partner. No one likes to be observed. Think of times in your life when you felt the intrusive gaze of the observer. How did it make you feel? Together, consider keeping a journal to describe the unfolding medication experience. Answers to these questions might offer information crucial to deepening the reflective case management relationship. First, if your client cannot describe her experience with medication, it may well be that it's having no effect or perhaps a detrimental effect. Or it may be that she's not observing or letting herself know something important about the effects. Second, if she offers detailed information such as "It makes me sleepy or causes me to eat continuously," you may need to work with doctors and the service team to address side effects. And remember, side effects are often as severe as the symptoms they are meant to address. They are not just side effects; they are *undesired* effects.

If she says, "I think my symptoms are much improved, but I feel so fat that I don't like myself," you may need to work with physicians and therapists to deal with concerns about self-image or other emotional states produced by changes in self-perception. If you don't address these concerns, compliance may become a problem. And sometimes, lack of compliance or questions about self-image will work against medication effectiveness. Remember, too, if you feel as if you're monitoring and enforcing med compliance, you have altogether abandoned reflective management; you no longer have a partnership.

Consider asking your client what she hopes the medication will do for her. Often, what we hope for does not match what is realistic or possible. If our hopes and the reality are too far apart, there will be disappointment. And disappointment breeds its own problems: anger, frustration, noncompliance. You should also know what the physician and other providers hope for the medication; they, too, may be very unrealistic about what is possible, or they may participate with clients and others in producing unrealistic expectations. And certain disappointment. Medication can do only so much work. The rest is left to us.

Observe

November 7

Roger has been Marilyn's case manager for three years. They connect; there is a casual, friendly rhythm to their conversation. Nothing seems to divide them—not gender or social class. They sit in his office on the floor just below the psychiatrist's. Roger shares his with three other managers. The desks, all within earshot, often leave managers and clients feeling too close. Today, however, nobody is in, so Marilyn and Roger will enjoy the quiet, uninterrupted by the bustle of case management. Her confidentiality will not be compromised. Roger sits facing Marilyn. She is talking about her finances. She says with great concern, "I guess my credit card situation is out of control. I can't pay them off."

Roger reviews options. She could file for bankruptcy. Or she could cut up her credit cards. Another option is to enroll in Consumer Protection Services (CPS), and CPS will manage her money. All her income will go to CPS. In short, they will take control. They will pay her monthly bills and debts and provide a cash allowance for spending. This, Roger imagines, might help her control spending. As Marilyn considers the options, Roger shifts the conversation. Medication is on his mind. He reminds her that she needs a new Medicaid prescription card. She might have to reapply. In the meantime, Marilyn will get samples from her psychiatrist. After a few minutes, Marilyn, with shame, admits that she stopped taking medication. She wants to know how she will feel without it. She informs Roger that Dr. Brown has recommended that she see a neurologist about her concentration. However, she needs a referral from her primary care physician, who is available only on Thursday, a day she must work. Missing another day might cause her to lose her job. Roger calls Marilyn's supervisor at work, and her primary care physician, to arrange the appointment.

About her medication, Roger assures Marilyn that it is normal for people to want to know how it feels not to take pills, but he recommends that she take them as prescribed.

Reflect

Marilyn is comfortable with Roger. She trusts him. She reveals a difficult, hidden, potentially shameful feeling: She stopped taking medication. She wants to know how she'll feel without it. She expresses the desire for a new understanding of herself and her mental illness, yet this escapes the attention of those around her. They are focused, instead, on the external world: insurance cards, credit cards, prescriptions, neurological exams. What is missed here? Her feelings, her internal world, the backdrop against which her external world is measured and understood. If you find yourself in a similar situation, try something different. Become a careful observer and listener for what is missed. We learn from our mistakes when we stay open to what we've not seen or heard. For example, what is missed when Roger simply reassures Marilyn that "it is normal for people to want to know how it feels without meds"? Was this an opportunity to listen to Marilyn's worry about the effects of medication? Or might this be a moment to listen to what Marilyn expects from medication and how she feels differently on medication? Here, too, is an opportunity to listen to her concern about the difference between what the medicine (and its proponents) promises to do and what it actually does. It is often in this gap—between what is promised and what actually happens—that we find ourselves (clients, case managers, family, physicians) especially discouraged and disappointed. And sometimes we may act out our disappointment in destructive ways. Noncompliance is only one of the many ways we may act out our feelings. We may also get depressed or anxious. Also, we might want to consider the possibility that, with careful medical supervision, this is a moment that Marilyn might want to try living without medication. All of these questions, and many more, might be considered in listening to Marilyn's story.

Notice that Roger has been respectful of Marilyn's privacy. More often than not case managers and clients have little access to private space, and we should do everything possible to create social and psychic spaces where we respect the individual's need, indeed right, to privacy.

Finally, we should avoid at all costs engaging in what are sometimes called split treatments. Split treatments occur when the psychiatrist, the social worker, the psychologist, and the supported employment worker find themselves working on the same issues, with the same person. When this occurs, the client will at the very least be confused about goals and advice. Often, clients find in the split treatment a way of avoiding or effectively using the treatment. Sometimes, when contradictory information or understandings are conveyed, clients will abandon the treatment altogether. Just as often the split treatment results in a lack of engagement with all the providers. And beware: This may be the way they've had to lead their lives. In short, no one is there, really there. You saw evidence of a split treatment when Marilyn so easily capitulated to Dr. Brown's recommendation that she get a new case manager. It is not uncommon for some clients to have dozens of case managers over short periods of time.

Take a few moments and imagine yourself in Marilyn's position. She was asking for a counselor, someone who could attend to her mind, not her brain or body. What did she get? How would you respond? Indeed, instead of seeing this as a real opportunity for Marilyn, the physician dismissed her. Indeed, one might ask, was this a very special moment when Marilyn was showing a genuine interest in her internal world, in her mind. An opportunity missed?[1]

Observe

November 8 to 13

Lisa has a series of telephone conversations with Marilyn, encouraging her to find copies of her income statements and monthly bills, so that Roger will have all the information to evaluate her financial situation and help her develop a plan. Marilyn cannot find some bills or her apartment lease. They were misplaced during the move.

November 14

Marilyn hands Roger a stack of paper. She says nervously, "I was afraid you weren't going to be here. I called yesterday and you weren't in."

"I don't have too many sick days left," he says.

"How's the baby?"

"He's doing great. Thanks for asking."

Marilyn points to the stack of receipts and bills that Roger holds. "That's most of them," she says. "I couldn't find some because of the move."

Marilyn's new case manager, Janet, walks in. Her presence reminds everyone that this is the last day Marilyn will work with Roger. He reviews the case transfer form with Janet, then reads to Marilyn the reason for the transfer, which has been written by the psychiatrist, Dr. Brown. Roger is uncomfortable. He reads softly. Sadly. "The client would be better served by the new position of case manager working with clients at high risk of HIV." When he finishes, he tells Marilyn that she can write a response to this reason for transfer. She appears nervous, does not question what the doctor has written, and without objection signs the form. Roger updates Janet about Marilyn's recent move and informs her that CPS is now her legal payee. He updates her about Marilyn's Medicaid spend-down (Medicaid pays the social service agency to help Marilyn, so she must keep her appointments to remain eligible for the insurance).

Janet directs her attention to Marilyn. She says, "I am sorry, I have to leave for another appointment. Is there anything you would like to tell me?"

"No."

"Would you like to see me on the same day that you see Dr. Brown?"

"Yes."

"When is that?"

"December fifth."

Janet opens her calendar. "That's two weeks. Do you think that's soon enough? Would you like to see me sooner?"

"No. December fifth is okay."

"If you have any questions or need to get hold of me, don't hesitate to call."

"Okay."

Janet leaves, and Roger asks, "Is there anything else we need to cover?"

Marilyn responds in a hurry. "What about the Medicaid stuff? I'm out of meds and need to get my prescription filled. What about food stamps?"

Roger reads a letter that has been sent by the Department of Human Services (DHS) that states she still has medical coverage through Medicaid, but her prescription card will not be activated for another day. He places a call to DHS to ask about food stamps and is informed that Marilyn has been assigned to another representative who is currently not available to take the call.

Roger hangs up. He says, "You're just getting shuffled all over the place, aren't you?"

Marilyn shrugs her shoulders and says, "That's okay."

Roger calls the psychiatrist's office and asks for more samples, then asks Marilyn, "Is there anything else we need to talk about?"

"No." Marilyn abruptly grabs her purse and walks toward the door.

"Wait. I don't want to end like this. Please sit." He gestures toward her chair. "Let me get the samples, and I'll be right back."

When Roger returns with the fluoxetine, he reminds Marilyn to go to the pharmacy and ask the pharmacist to verify that her card has been reactivated. He then begins to review her financial statements, the ones she brought with her. He tells her that the credit card bills are a significant amount of debt but assures her that CPS can help her develop a plan.

"I'm thinking about giving the cards to my mom to hold, but she lives so far away if I need them."

"For what?"

"For an emergency."

"Put a rubber band around them and keep them in a drawer out of sight. Don't use them."

Marilyn nods in agreement.

"Do you have enough money for groceries?"

"As long as I don't do what I did last weekend."

"What happened?"

"I went drinking with friends."

"Does the drinking affect your medication and your mood?"

"I haven't noticed."

"Did you tell Dr. Brown about the drinking?"

"No."

"You should tell her. She needs to know because it might affect your medication."

"She'll get mad at me."

"It's your right to drink if you want. Dr. Brown just needs to know because it might affect your medication. She'll keep an eye on that. She'll be pleased if you tell her. She can help you minimize the bad effects on the medication."

Marilyn seems to understand, but she does not say whether she will comply with Roger's suggestions. He begins to close the conversation. "I've enjoyed working with you. I'm sure it will work out fine with Janet, but if you find you're not getting what you need, let me know and we can work on it."

"Okay." Marilyn picks up her purse and walks out. Lisa follows. She is stunned. She cannot believe Dr. Brown has transferred Marilyn to a case manager who specializes in AIDS prevention without evidence that Marilyn is at risk for AIDS. Marilyn is not a drug user. She's had no history of intravenous drug use. She's never talked about being sexually active. The fact is that Marilyn was trying to take care of herself by asking her psychiatrist to refer to another counselor, so she would have someone to talk with about personal matters. What she got instead was a forced separation from her case manager.

Reflect

To some it might appear that Marilyn does not have strong feelings about the termination of this very important relationship with Roger. She is congenial. She signs the form. She is ready to leave. To some this might even suggest that Marilyn is "resilient." Yet she is feeling deeply at this moment. At the beginning of this exchange, we learn how afraid she is. She worries that he may not be at the office when she arrives. Already she is missing him and anticipating the ending. When the conversation ends she is visibly upset, grabs her purse, and begins to walk out. She is hurt. Is she embarrassed and ashamed, sad, or all of the above? Does she feel the shame of rejection? Does Roger feel shame along with her? After all, he too is being replaced. How do these emotions, Roger's and Marilyn's, facilitate or inhibit independent living in the community?

Your clients need to know the meaning and impact of separations and goodbyes in their lives. And it is the role of the reflective manager to develop the skills (in working with clients) to construct these understandings. This is especially important when our clients experience rapid turnover of managers and even more significant when they've formed close working relationships. You might start by thinking about your language. Imagine being referred to as a "case to be transferred." Your client is not an object to be passed from one person to another. Nor is she a Medicaid card to be activated, deactivated, and reactivated. She is a human being in a meaningful relationship, and this means that she experiences difficult beginnings and endings, along with an assortment of associated feelings and thoughts.

When your client has little choice but to abruptly end the management relationship, try not to let her acquiesce to a recommendation for termination without reflecting with her on the feelings and thoughts. However, if she wants to end, help her develop a plan for transition. Set a date for termination. Consider with her the time (days, weeks, months) needed to say goodbye; some will need more than others. Consider, too, your own thoughts and feelings about termination. Recall a time in life when an ending came too quickly, without preparation or without a proper way of saying goodbye. What happened? How did you feel? Also, do not be surprised if a client wants to end immediately. However, do not agree to an unplanned or sudden ending without reflection with her. Consider saying, "We have been working together for three months. We need to reflect on what we have accomplished and how to say goodbye. When you say that you want to end this relationship right now, it feels so sudden. What do you think?"

At some point during the termination process, shift your attention to a review of your client's successes. Try saying, "Let's talk about our work together. What have been your most significant accomplishments?" A reminder might be helpful. You might say something like, "I am remembering the work we did on your personal finances; what do you think was most significant to you?" Consider, too, her expectations for the new relationship: "I am wondering what you might want to accomplish with your new case manager? Would you like me to introduce you, or do you prefer to do this?"

Finally, do not give your client the impression that she might be able to continue a management relationship with you. In this scene, Roger informs Marilyn that she may call him "if things don't work out" with the new manager. A gesture like this might interfere with the engagement phase of the new relationship and with the formation of a working alliance, which are essential for supporting recovery. It might be appropriate to say, "I have enjoyed working with you. I will miss you."

* * *

Your client is not the only one with strong feelings about termination. You will also have them. We will have good and bad feelings about those we work with. And with some clients we will be eager to terminate. It is our job to manage feelings and to manage them in such a way that our clients can benefit and we can grow in our skills. For instance, in this scene, when Marilyn grabs her purse in haste and begins to leave, Roger feels bad. The ending, for him, seems unplanned and abrupt. He asks her to stay. In a sense, he asks for a chance to say goodbye with understanding. Maybe he feels sad or guilty or both. We do not know. We do know, however, that he is uncomfortable. He is anxious, and he slips into doing for Marilyn by offering advice about her medication, Medicaid card, credit cards, and drinking habits. Imagine yourself in this situation. You've just been told that you will get a new case manager. You will say goodbye, today, just hours after you've been told. Picture a time when you were faced with saying goodbye to someone you cared deeply about. We all face losses, large and small (jobs, friends, pets, family members), and we all find ways of dealing with them. Sometimes we're left alone to manage our most profound losses in life. Take a moment to explore your own reactions to endings. How do you end significant relationships and start new ones? Think back to a time when you said goodbye to a boyfriend or girlfriend. How did it make you feel? What do you remember of the good endings and the bad? What made them "good" and what made them "bad"? Were they sudden or abrupt, or did they happen over time with explanation and discussion? Your way of managing feelings during these transitions will influence the way you interact with others. Also, ask your clinical supervisor to reflect with you on the progress you have made in the relationship with your client who is leaving. Remember: You also have strengths that have emerged in this relationship, and you need to notice them, own them, and add them to your growing sense of a professional identity. Don't underestimate for your client the meaning and value of your relationship. And make sure, if at all possible, to allow time to prepare with your client to say goodbye.

Observe

December 4

To get to the desk of the intake worker at CPS, Marilyn must sit in a makeshift waiting room in a narrow, dark, and crowded hallway in the basement of an old building at the intersection of East 30th Street and Euclid Avenue and fill out paperwork. If social services in Cleveland were a video game, waiting rooms would be chambers of limbo; paperwork would be the magic key that opens secret doors to adventures in bureaucracy, where dens of seemingly well-intentioned people insist that Marilyn tell her story over and over again.

CPS acts as legal payee for anyone with financial difficulties. And people with mental illness are not alone among their customers. Here's how it works. CPS accepts income and allocates it to pay creditors, utilities, and landlords; it puts money into savings; it distributes an allowance to pay for living expenses such as food and transportation; it negotiates with creditors, such as credit card companies, for lower payments and forgiveness of debts. CPS is a busy, bustling place. One gets the feeling that the business here is urgent. One also feels the heavy burden of shame: "I'm so damaged and flawed that I can't manage to pay bills and now, like a child, I'll receive an allowance, if I'm lucky."

The intake worker is not in an office. There are no walls. She's in a large room filled with heavy, old steel desks. One feels here the complete absence of privacy. Faces are heavy with desperation. Some cannot face this, so they stare at the floor, waiting for their number. The worker, a middle-aged, petite African American woman, tries to assess Marilyn's financial situation so she can refer her to the appropriate credit counselor. Marilyn fumbles anxiously through papers and then offers up the documentation of income and expenses. She is embarrassed. She is fidgety. Here face is flushed. She has charged so much on credit cards, and she could not find some of the statements.

"I couldn't find my cell phone bill either," she admits, as if she's expecting to be punished. "They shut off my phone. I owe them a lot, about three hundred to five hundred dollars."

She does not scold. She is sympathetic. She's been in Marilyn's shoes. "Girlfriend," she says, "I'm with you. I've been there, done that."

"I want to buy Christmas presents, but I can't on this budget. The last time I talked to my mom, she said I did not have money for Christmas presents."

The intake worker feels with Marilyn the shame, and with feeling she says, "It doesn't matter how much money somebody makes, girl, everybody gets into debt." She recommends that Marilyn order credit reports. She gives her the phone numbers to the credit agencies, then calls the secretary of a budget counselor to set the next appointment.

Marilyn has listed the following income and expenses but cannot account for most:

INCOME

$862 = Supplemental Security Income (SSI)

$242 = work

She is in the process of applying for food stamps.

EXPENSES

$253 = rent and utilities (water and electricity)

$62.50 = security deposit (× 4 months = $250)

$??? = cable

$??? = telephone

$300 to 500 = cell phone

$??? = Heritage House (mail order catalog)

$??? = Franklin Mint (mail order catalog)

$??? = Stephen King Library (videos)

$??? = Lane Bryant credit card

$??? = Capital One (#1)

$??? = Capital One (#2)

$??? = Capital One (#3)

$??? = Capital One (#4)

$??? = Capital One (#5)

Reflect

Money is the object with which we manage our day-to-day lives. It is the ultimate source of our living independently in the community. No other object seems to carry as much emotional weight, yet that weight is not its own. It is ours. In short, we make money meaningful. And money is more often than not the object that stands between us and the realization of our most basic needs and our most profound desires and longings. And because our needs and wants are so often different and at odds with one another, how we make money meaningful will vary widely. This will be especially true as you navigate with your clients the complex world of managing money. And because you often hold deeply held beliefs and values and have very different understandings of money, you must be careful not to impose your own views. Imagine for a moment a time in your life when someone controlled your access to money. Or a time when you wanted something badly but you could not afford it. Or a time when your needs competed with your desires. Or a time when you spent money you should have saved for school or retirement. Or a time when you used your credit card recklessly. Or a time when you went shopping just after some intensely disturbing interaction or emotional upheaval. Listen carefully to your clients' needs and desires and learn, with them, to make distinctions between them.

Most service organizations and providers do not work with clients to explore the meaning of money: spending, saving, bingeing, debt, credit. It's never as simple as a two-column ledger of debts and credits. In short, money is meaningful. And because it means something different for each of us, we must be in a constant dialogue with ourselves and our clients. When we aren't, we will resort to the management of behavior. We develop spending plans; in short, we do for. And when behavior management fails to address the *meaning* of money, economic crises deepen and one finds recurring cycles of economic dependency and budget crises.[2] Indeed, recovery will always be limited by our failure to address the meaning of money. Recovery involves knowing how feelings and thoughts relate to and influence behavior, including behavior with personal finances.

Although there is a role organizations such as CPS can do for clients during a crisis, providers should be reflective about doing for. We should all be aware, with our clients, that there will be a time beyond the urgency of the crisis, and with the end of the crisis we will return to doing with. And eventually we will let go so the clients can do for themselves. We might even call this hope. Stanhope and Solomon, social work researchers, have recently written about the relationship between hope and recovery:

> The transformative process is created by a sense of hope—a choice about one's path to recovery, empowerment and a sense of place within one's chosen community. As symptom reduction becomes replaced by these more holistic personal goals, diagnosis has less influence over how clients perceive themselves and how care is organized in the community. (Stanhope and Solomon, 2008:887)

In this scene, the CPS employee tries to ease Marilyn's shame by making debt seem normal. She says, "Girl, I've been there, done that." Everyone gets into debt from time to time, she says. Even she has experienced it. In short, she reassures Marilyn. Informing your client that debt is common may ease her shame, which is helpful, but it will not eliminate the feeling. Here are some ideas and questions that might help you help your client reflect on her relationship with money and thereby begin the process of self-determined money management:

- "What do you know about your expenses?"
- "There must be something that gets in the way of your wanting to know more about these expenses and your ability to manage your own money. This might be worth exploring together over time."
- "Tell me about your past relationships with money. Have you ever managed your money by yourself?"
- "When your mother was in charge of your money, what did you feel about that arrangement?"
- "You tell me that you do not remember all your expenses. Is there something you would like to remember?"

Observe

December 5

The first meeting with the new case manager, Janet, is held at the social service agency. Unlike the previous manager, Janet has her own private office, probably because she is assigned clients who are at risk for HIV.

Janet is young, a twenty-three-year-old kind of young. She has an innocent face— no stress lines. Her dark brown hair is cut short and trendy, and she wears hip clothes: high platform shoes and bell-bottom black pants. She is just out of college, where she majored in psychology. Although she has no experience in the public mental health system, she exudes a refreshing kind of undergraduate confidence. She is polite, friendly, and respectful. Like others before her, Roger and the worker at CPS, she is trying to assess Marilyn's financial situation. Marilyn tells her that her SSI check is about $800, but Lisa knows it is $862 and that the $62 per month will make a big difference in her budget. Marilyn tells Janet that she's been playing telephone tag with the DHS about qualifying for food stamps. Janet encourages her persistence; it will improve her chances of a response, she says. Marilyn would like to take care of this now, so Janet places a call. She leaves a voicemail. Then she asks Marilyn about how she's doing at the new apartment.

"I was up to 1 A.M. doing laundry."

"You must have had a lot."

"Yes. I got distracted with phone calls and taking breaks to play video games. It's difficult to sort, fold, and put away laundry in such a small room with so little storage space."

"Is it a quiet neighborhood?"

"No. There are a lot of doors slamming, and one night I heard gunshots."

"Do you feel safe living there?"

"I feel cramped in the apartment. It's so small."

"Have you talked to anybody about the gunshots?"

"I have somebody come by to check to see if my chores get done."

"Is she someone you can talk to about the noise?"

"I can talk to my friends. I can't stand and wait for a bus without guys pulling up in their cars and trying to pick me up. I tell them they have the wrong person. That I'm not interested in being picked up."

"That's a good response."

"I have guys hitting on me all the time when I go out with my friends to bars. I tell them I'm not interested."

"Good for you. It sounds like you know what you want from a relationship. It sounds like you handle unwanted advances pretty well. How do you deal with rejection?"

"I don't like it too much. It's been a big issue that I've been working on. It's getting better, but it's still painful."

"Are you feeling okay?"

"I was up late last night."

"You're eyes look watery."

Matter-of-factly, Marilyn says, "I had problems at work with my eyes. I saw an eye doctor. My supervisor asked for a written explanation about my excuse from work. My eye doctor sent him the results of my exam."

"What did the results say?"

"I didn't get them. I figure I'll wait 'til my supervisor gets the letter, and he'll tell me."

Janet informs Marilyn that the time will end soon.

She says, "Is there anything you can tell me that would help me get to know you better?"

Hurriedly, Marilyn responds, "I have a birthday coming up. I'll be twenty-six. I have a twin brother. Right now he's doing stuff I'm not really happy with, and pretty much the whole family is disowning him, and I don't want to talk about it."

Marilyn has a meeting with Dr. Brown today as well. She says goodbye to Janet and goes upstairs.

* * *

In the psychiatrist's office, Marilyn says, "I'm tired. I stayed out late with friends."

The doctor, with the same lack of interest and long list of formulaic and tedious questions, says, "Do you still have headaches? Can you concentrate?"

"I'm concentrating okay."

"Did you see your primary care physician? Did you get the referral for the neurological exam?"

"She said I'm having tension headaches, that it's not neurological."

"Do you go to your doctor's appointment by yourself, or did your case manager take you?"

"I go by myself."

Dr. Brown turns to Lisa. "Do you go with her?"

"Only if she wants me to. Do you want me to go?"

"Okay," Marilyn says.

Dr. Brown writes a note for Lisa to give to the physician: "Neurologist? Rule out seizures."

"Does being tired make it hard to go to work?"

"No, because I have less work. I only have to clean the kitchen now."

"Have your responsibilities changed?"

"Yes. Since I moved out of the group home."

"Oh. What about your work at the lumberyard?"

"I'm still working."

"How are you with cleaning the dishes?"

"I get complaints."

Marilyn has been in the new apartment for only six weeks, and already her room-mates are complaining that she is not keeping up with chores.

"How many times has the staff talked to you about it?"

"Just twice." Lisa knows that they have talked to her twice in six weeks, which is more frequent than Marilyn leads Dr. Brown to believe.

"When was the most recent time they talked to you?"

"Last week."

"How are your moods?"

"My friends, Jessica and Frank, fight all the time. They drive me crazy."

"That would be difficult if you're romantically involved."

"We're just going out to clubs to drink."

"Some studies show that just one beer per month can affect Prozac. It's better that you don't drink at all."

Marilyn changes the subject. "I'm getting counseling once a month."

"Only once per month?"

There is an obvious misunderstanding. Marilyn believes that her new case man-ager, Janet, is also her counselor, because she had asked Dr. Brown for a new coun-selor, but Dr. Brown transferred her to Janet. Lisa tries to clarify. "Janet is her new case manager."

Dr. Brown, still confused, says, "I think you should see somebody weekly. What is giving you the most trouble? This will help me refer you to the right person. Are there any stresses?"

"I got some bad news. My mom says I have no money for Christmas presents."

"I can see how this troubles you."

Marilyn lists all the presents she would like to buy and for whom.

"I'm going to try to get you to focus."

"I'm sorry."

Dr. Brown places a call and leaves a voicemail for a therapist. Then she writes another prescription for fluoxetine. She sets an appointment for Wednesday, January 30—eight weeks away.

Reflect

In this scene, the new case manager, Janet, is trying to determine how she will relate to Marilyn. What do you notice about their emerging relationship? Take a few minutes to write about what you hear. Try not to be judgmental. Notice when you start to feel you're making a judgment.

Marilyn, too, is figuring out how to relate to Janet. Again, write about what you see. How would you describe their developing relationship? Observe and listen. Often there is discomfort, awkwardness, and uncertainty at the beginning. Starting something new may be scary and destabilizing. You see the confusion in Marilyn's interactions with the manager and psychiatrist. What are the possible reasons for the confusion?

Imagine for a moment how you have managed beginning new relationships. Have there been times when you found yourself surprised and confused by an unexpected change in relationship with a friend, family member, or co-worker. We face beginnings and transitions with different degrees of preparedness. And we may often find ourselves confused when we are unprepared. This is a good time to talk about the four phases or moments in the case management relationship: preparing, connecting, working, and ending. Think of them, always, as nonlinear; for example, we may find ourselves at one moment working and in the next, with the same person, preparing, or at one moment ending when all of a sudden we are preparing. So it is that our lives are lived—never in a straight line.

During the first phase, preparation, we prepare ourselves and others. What does it mean to be prepared? First, to be prepared means that we have considered what might happen. In short, we anticipate. And we all have feelings about what might happen. Some of us worry a lot about what the next moment—minutes, hours, days, months, years—will bring and others not at all. We also anticipate what we'll need as we face a future task. Imagine a plumber who forgets to bring important tools, or a student who brings too much, filling his backpack with pounds of books and papers. Too much or too little! How prepared should we be? For what? With what? For example, what should you know about a person's history? Or current relationships? Or family? Or history of hospitalizations? Or what should you know about personal safety?

And we must especially prepare for the possibility of surprise. Things do not always go as planned. We can begin by observing with our clients how difficult change can be, especially when they've been abrupt. Imagine saying something like, "Starting a new relationship is difficult for everyone, for me too, and it must be very hard to say goodbye to Roger and start yet another relationship." Marilyn needs to know the reason for the transfer. And we need to know what she feels and thinks about it. With truth comes trust. So in this example, the case manager must be clear. She might say, for example, "Dr. Brown has referred you to me because I am an HIV counselor. I work with people who are believed to be at risk of HIV. What are your feelings about this? What do you think?"

Notice that Marilyn begins her new relationship by describing unsafe scenes from her daily life: gunshots in the neighborhood, strange men trying to pick her up, a potential neurological problem, insufficient funds. Although Marilyn is talking about her experiences outside the office, the feelings themselves are also inside the office: inside her and in her relationship with Janet. Indirectly, Marilyn reports feeling unsafe with this new person. When you find yourself in a similar situation, do for your client in the domain of feeling by observing with her what she reports. Stay with the unfolding process of the communication in the moment with you. Consider saying, "I hear that you feel very unsafe. I am wondering if you are feeling unsafe with me." Give your client some time to respond. In the right moment, it might be appropriate to follow up with, "I am wondering if there is anything I can do to make you feel safe."

Also, take some time to reflect with your client on her previous relationship. Consider asking, "In your relationship with your last case manager, what worked for you?"

Clinical supervisors should take time to help their staff prepare for new relationships with clients. Use the reflective method to help them get in tune with what you and they are feeling. Here are a few ideas and questions to ask of yourself and others:

- "When you're in a new situation, what makes you feel unsafe? And what makes you feel safe?"
- "Is there something about your clients that makes you feel unsafe when you first meet them or have been away from them for a while?"
- "What are your thoughts about your own need for comfort and safety?"

In the second phase, connecting, follow the client's lead. Here, you should respect the tentativeness of the relationship. During these moments, your goal is to be present in a quiet way. Visits might be brief and should be without agendas. Here, you should be a caring observer willing to patiently listen and learn. Imagine this: You are being paid to be a student, and your client is your teacher. During this phase you may do nothing more than offer a helping hand, a ride, or a cup of coffee. There will be disappointments, missed appointments, and setbacks. During this phase of your relationship you should become increasingly aware of your client's current circumstances: How she sees herself, how she perceives the world, her ability to accept help and to keep herself safe. You do this not by asking endless questions but by carefully observing and listening. You will no doubt learn about your client's strengths and deficits. Your notes may read, "Saw Marilyn today, one hour, for coffee, first time in two weeks." You may during this phase be doing for. Very gradually, as your relationship deepens, you begin a third phase.

In the third phase, working, you should find yourself sharing the client's recovery journey: You are recognized, greeted, welcomed, and trusted. You will not only listen to Marilyn's story. You will observe with her. You will wonder with her. Remember, it's not easy to wonder about something unless you have first observed it together. First, observe and notice, then wonder. During this phase, you are working with one another. You are an advocate, yes, but in a special sort of way, always striving to do with. Here, as well, you are helping your client connect with others in her helping network: psychiatrists, nurses, psychotherapists, social workers, supportive employment, housing specialists, CPS. Here you are working together to reach recovery goals. And the movement from connecting to working can also be seen as a transition from a dyadic relationship to a triadic relationship. It is also during this phase of the work that we find ourselves standing by to admire.

Finally, there is ending, or letting go. Endings, like beginnings, are fraught with difficulties, intense emotion, and a tendency to avoid. No one likes to say goodbye, even when it's important to do so. Here, perhaps recovery goals have been reached—living in an apartment of one's own, developing daily routines, work and recreation, effective use of helping networks and relationships—and it's time to prepare to say goodbye.

* * *

Observe

December 13

The office of the primary care physician is located some 150 blocks from the agency. Lisa is driving. The drive, through endless, monotonous stretches of suburban shopping strips, ends just where one imagines a doctor's office at the edge of the city to be: at a dying strip mall. Nothing fancy. Clean.

The physician is a young woman, a recent immigrant, probably from the Middle East. She stands about five feet tall. Her hair is long, black, and beautiful. She wears a white coat and moves quickly but not abruptly. She is purposeful but not in a rush. When she sits, her attention stops with her and is focused directly on Marilyn. Without doubt, she is completely present. There are no distractions here. She asks Marilyn whether Lisa is her case manager.

"Would you like Lisa to stay or wait for you outside?"

"She can stay." Marilyn reports that she has a stomach pain and pain in the ear that shoots to the jaw.

The doctor looks into Marilyn's ears. "The jaw pain may actually be caused by wax buildup in your ears. Tell me about this abdominal pain."

Marilyn points to her stomach and answers the doctor's questions with a simple "Yes" and "No."

"It seems like your bowels. You've had problems with that in the past. Have you been eating your fruits and vegetables?"

"I love fruits and vegetables. I'm trying to drink more water. I'm better about not eating as much at fast-food restaurants."

"Good, then you're almost there with your diet."

As Lisa listens to this exchange, she has vivid images of Marilyn eating Big Macs, Whoppers, french fries, and potato chips and drinking liters of Pepsi and mugs of coffee.

"What about those headaches?"

"Stress."

"What kind? You're so young. What are you so stressed about?"

"My brother. He's acting like an ass. The family is disowning him. I'm getting a lot of grief from my supervisor at work for missing work."

"Why do you miss work?"

"Because of appointments like this one. I have to come in to see you."

"Tell me about your headaches. Are they different?"

"I stare off into space. It's like I'm not aware of people and activity around me when this happens."

The doctor explains a diagnostic procedure done with magnetic resonance imaging (MRI). "It is highly unlikely it will show anything," she says, "but to be on the safe side, we should do it."

"Okay, as long as I don't miss work for it. Then I'd really be in trouble."

The doctor leaves the room, returns with the order for the MRI, and advises Marilyn to "call right away" to make the appointment. She gives Marilyn an eardrop solution and shows her how to use it. She wants to see Marilyn again in one week.

Reflect

Sometimes there is a physical explanation for physical pain. Sometimes there is not. Sometimes physical pain is an expression of emotional experience. Sometimes this is called somatization. This is important for you to know because it will help you in your reflective work with clients as you navigate with them the medical and mental health systems in search of relief from pain and suffering.

It is *not* the role of reflective managers to determine (for clients) which pains have physical causes. Rather, you must help your client understand and navigate the complex medical system. Often our clients need help to see how different people function as partners in the search for causes and remedies. If a test comes back positive for a physical illness, help your client integrate this new information about the self. How do we integrate? First, we integrate when we have accurately perceived and remembered (not always possible, even for the healthiest among us) what's been communicated. If you've been told that you have a benign (harmless) skin rash but instead you hear "cancer of the skin," you will probably need time or help or both to integrate. Case managers often need to listen for our clients so that the information conveyed is accurately perceived; here, for example, you may find it necessary to be with clients during medical appointments. We may also need to function as an auxiliary (supportive) memory; in short, you may need to remember for your client, especially when new information about the self is overwhelming. Here it is important to remember that what may be overwhelming to your client might not be for you. Second, we have integrated when new information about the self is not so disturbing that its causes overwhelming anxiety (not always possible). For example, if a benign skin rash causes us great anxiety or severe depression, we've probably not integrated. And sometimes doctors do not offer us explanations (e.g., they may be too complex or the appointments too brief or the information too scary) that can be integrated; then it is the job of the case manager to offer help. How? You might need to seek clarifying information from the doctor or nurse. Or you might need to consult with a supervisor. Third, we have integrated when we have incorporated the new sense of the self into our daily living (not easy).

If tests come back negative and physical illness is ruled out, you should explore with your supervisor how to bring this to the attention of a qualified professional: a psychiatrist, social worker, or psychologist. Exploring emotional issues behind physical suffering is not the job of the case manager. It is the job of the therapist or counselor. However, the reflective case manager should help clients prepare for this work. When somatization appears, it is important to talk about it and to find a language for it. Otherwise, your client—and all those involved in the medical and mental health systems—will aimlessly circle around it.

In this scene, Marilyn reports to her doctor that she is stressed about her brother's behavior. The physician does not explore this, mainly because it is not her role. However, it is the client who links her physical pain to this stressor. This is an opportunity for reflection. If you find yourself in a situation like this, talk with your client after the appointment and encourage her to explore this with her therapist. Try saying, "I notice that you have a clear sense that there is some kind of connection between what goes on in your body and your mind. You seem to know that there's a connection between your headache, your stomachache, and your stress about your brother. I think it's a good idea for you to explore this with your therapist."

Observe

January 11

Lisa answers her cell phone. There's no "hello." The voice she hears is filled with nervous energy.

"Things have gotten a little worse for me. I got fired." It is Marilyn.

"Have you gotten written notices about your attendance?"

"Yes. I signed a contract saying I would attend. The staff thinks I'm bored and not challenged. I've been there three years. They said they would make a referral to an employment agency and not say anything bad. Maybe if I tell Social Security next week, they'll give me more money."

"It doesn't work that way."

"Yeah. Nice dream, huh?" Marilyn replies. She is aware of her wishful thinking. "I need a meeting with Social Security about food stamps. I need to get those checks taken care of. I can't afford to have those checks stop. I got another collection letter from a credit card company."

Lisa makes arrangements to meet in a few days.

January 15

It's 9:45 A.M. Marilyn bounces off a series of cellular relay towers and lands in Lisa's truck. The ringing of the phone seems like an alarm. Marilyn is not feeling well. She wants to reschedule her appointment at Social Security. Lisa convinces her to keep it. She is only fifteen minutes away.

Marilyn's apartment is in an old brownstone on the west side of Cleveland, where she shares a four-bedroom suite with two women. As soon as Lisa enters, she can tell that Marilyn is struggling. Her clothes are a tangled mess. Her hair is disheveled. Dishes from the night before are in the sink. Because personal things are not to be left in common areas, the mess is a breach of her contract. A few unpacked boxes are in the dining room—another violation. There is a trail of clothes in the hallway leading to her bedroom, where it looks as if a bomb has exploded. Piles of clothes and papers are everywhere, leaving only a foot-wide path for walking. Dresser drawers are open. There are no clothes in them, only papers. Her bed, stacked with blankets and clothes, leaves no impression where a sleeping body may have lain.

"Where do you sleep?" Lisa asks. Silence.

Marilyn needs her termination letter from the lumberyard for her appointment with Social Security. Lisa helps find it; she separates papers into bills and letters, magazines, and junk mail. Lisa knows she has to do this work for Marilyn. She is in crisis. She is not thinking clearly.

Marilyn says, directly, "Now that I lost my job, Social Security's gotta give me more money per month. That's why I need the letter from work. They need to know how badly I need my money." There's a long, painful silence.

"You have enough for necessities," Lisa says. "That's what they cover. Social Security won't cover credit card debt and dance clubs. Your lumberyard money was used for those things."

Lisa is holding a stack of unopened envelopes. They appear to be bills. She asks Marilyn for permission to open them. There's a mail order catalog statement with a balance of $42 and an order confirmation for a $245 ceramic figurine. Lisa cannot believe what she sees. Annoyed, she shows Marilyn the bill.

"What were you doing? You owed money."

"But they didn't send it to me."

"Of course not, they sent you a notice. I thought you gave your credit cards to your mother."

"I did. My mom's holding my credit cards."

"How did you order this?"

"They didn't send it to me."

"There's no room for it in here."

"I thought the manager would let me put it in the hutch in the common area, where we keep our bread and stuff."

Lisa opens more envelopes. Many are unpaid bills.

Marilyn offers an explanation. Lisa wonders whether she is feeling guilty. "I know it's all bad news, and there's nothing I can do about it, so I just stuff it, hide it in my dresser. I'm supposed to have an inspection from the agency. They'll write me up if I don't have all my stuff in my room and if I can't close the door. They might evict me."

After an hour of looking, they can't find the termination letter. Lisa recommends that she keep her appointment and drives, as planned. On the way, Marilyn confides that she's in trouble. She needs help. Now that she's not working, it would be a good time to get into a partial hospitalization program (PHP). It's a psychosocial program to help consumers learn to manage their internal (emotional and psychological) worlds and their external (social) worlds. She attended one a few years ago. It helped. She believes it will again.

* * *

At the Social Security office, a few blocks away in an old storefront, Marilyn and Lisa sit on old plastic chairs. The room is packed, shoulder-to-shoulder. One after another is called. An hour passes. Lisa is counting and feeling the stress of the situation. She feels like a needle at the bottom of a giant stack of unkempt clothes and unopened bills. She goes out for a breath of fresh air and calls Janet, the case manager. She tells her about the mess and the impending inspection. She tells her that Marilyn has asked to enroll in a PHP. Janet says she will visit Marilyn later in the day to help clean for the inspection. She asks Lisa to relay the message.

Reflect

We all go through periods of disorganization and reorganization. Think about your life at home or work. You may spend so much time responding to day-to-day demands that chores pile up: laundry, dishes, dusting, vacuuming, sweeping out the car, paying bills, filing receipts, and completing paperwork. Sometimes, things get so backed up that you have to take a few days to get everything sorted, put away, and completed. You recover. Yet if you stay disorganized long enough, you will become overwhelmed and lose track of yourself—and others. In other words, disorganization can cause disappearance.

This is what happens to Marilyn. She is becoming increasingly disorganized. She is disappearing. She disappears from her job. The termination letter disappears from her room. She loses track of personal hygiene (self-care). Her personal belongings disappear. Yet, amid the crisis, there is reappearance. Somehow, for Marilyn, people reappear. They clean for her. They rush to do for her in crisis. Where does this feeling come from? Why do others feel compelled to rescue? Why does she expect it?

In your work with clients, you might feel the pressure to rush in and do for them, especially during a crisis. Maybe you are afraid the crisis will lead to hospitalization. Perhaps this will make you and your organization look bad in the eyes of your county board or state department of mental health. Maybe the county and state are keeping a close eye on client outcomes; staying out of the hospital and in independent living situations are quantifiable measures of success. Maybe you are afraid it will seem that you and your organization have failed.

Resist the temptation to act out of fear of failure and shame. Talk to your supervisor. Use the reflective method to explore your own feelings and thoughts about rescuing clients. In short, stay in touch with your organized self. Always keep an eye on your strengths as a reflective case manager. This will enable you to help your client keep an eye on her strengths, her recovered sense of self, and her abilities to manage her crises.

Work with your client to develop a strategy for noticing periods of disorganization and a plan for managing crises. For instance, you might say, "I have noticed, and I wonder if you notice, that before you know you are feeling overwhelmed certain things start to happen. You do not open mail. You lose track of mail. You spend money you don't have. You do not clean and fold clothes and take care of chores around the house. Is it possible that these are signs that you can use as your own internal warning system? I think we should develop a plan for you to notice when this stuff starts to happen so you can talk about it." In sum, help her anticipate crises, and by observing the warning signs with her, you may help her use your observing self to observe her own crises and habitual reactions to them.

Keep in mind that physical symptoms may also be a warning sign of oncoming disorganization or relapse. By working reflectively with your client in all aspects of her life, you do with her in developing a relapse-prevention strategy so that she can do for herself to call for help. When this happens, the power is in her hands, not yours or the system's.

Observe

January 30

The psychiatrist is her same stiff self; the tree is losing its battle with gravity. Her questions are matter of fact. Marilyn's posture and the tone of her answers mirror her psychiatrist's. The exchange drones on:

"How's it been?"

"I've had good days and bad days."

"What's going on?"

"I got fired from my job."

"Why?"

"Attendance and absences."

"Did you not want to work there anymore?"

"No."

"So you didn't mind?"

"I had a panic attack when they told me. I think I should go back on something for my anxiety."

"We stopped that because of the side effects."

"I thought maybe we could start at a lower dosage, five instead of ten milligrams. Maybe I won't have side effects."

"How about the Prozac? Have you been taking it?"

"No."

"Tell me why you stopped taking it."

"I don't know. Lately I feel people stereotype when they find out you take medication and see a psychiatrist."

"Do you have an example?"

"When I worked at Wendy's."

"Can you think of a recent example?"

"It just makes me feel not normal."

"Is there an event that prompted you to stop taking it?"

"Not really. Sometimes I do things without thinking, or I want to see how I would do without medication."

"The problems with work, with not attending, when did that start?"

"I missed eight days in December." Marilyn does not tell her doctor that she had to work only ten days in December and was supposed to work five days in January but missed them because she was sick.

"Have you been feeling irritable since you've been off the Prozac?"

"A little."

"Sleep?"

"About twelve hours a day."

"Drinking a lot?"

"Just at clubs. I go twice a week on weekends, but I haven't gone in two weeks."

Janet, the case manager, knocks and enters the office.

"So you're looking into the PHP. Have you been talking to Janet about this?"

Janet says, "They've got room for her if she needs it now."

The doctor responds, "It's a good idea."

Marilyn agrees, and the doctor sets their next appointment.

Before they get up to leave, Lisa asks Marilyn whether she's had the MRI. Dr. Brown looks for a response. Marilyn shakes her head.

Dr. Brown says, "It'd be a good idea to get it done. The hospital is just down the street."

Reflect

What does Dr. Brown focus on? Medication, the MRI, and the PHP. Moreover, she prepares to pass Marilyn off to the pharmacy, the hospital, and the PHP. Marilyn, on the other hand, filled with feeling, says she does not like her status as a "client." She talks about the stigma associated with meds; she wants control over her symptoms. She hates her job. But she is frightened about not having enough money.

In moments like these, remember your client's strengths. Reflect with her about them. Help her remember her healthy self, which has experienced periods of disorganization and uncertainty before. You might say, "Does this experience remind you of another time of change in your life? Do you remember how you felt then? You made it through that experience. How did you do it?" Remember, always, when you ask questions, you will get an answer, even if it is silence. Your purpose here is not to fire question after question but to create an environment where it's safe for your client to wonder with you about her stronger self and times when things really did work out. This, also, produces a mental space for hope.

Notice that in this scene Marilyn reports to the psychiatrist good days and bad. This might be an opportunity missed. It is especially helpful to know about what contributes to a good day. Be straightforward. Say something like, "Tell me about the good days. How do those days go?" Learn as much as you can about the good days. When we don't learn about how, what, when, where, and why things go well, it is easy for us to sink into despair, along with our clients, focusing almost exclusively on the worst times and the most urgent crises.

Remember, the current crisis was triggered by Marilyn's dismissal from work. So talk about it. Start with the obvious: "Tell me about the job; what happened?" She is panicked about not having a job, yet she might also be relieved. Maybe she feels good to be free to pursue a meaningful career, such as being a professional cook. Remember that recovery goal? That, too, seems to have disappeared. Here's a perfect opportunity to make it reappear in her mind and to work with her to make it a reality.

Observe

February 1

Marilyn's voice waits behind the ringing of the cell phone like a quarter horse at the starting gate of Ruidoso Downs. Lisa answers. Words stampede.

"They cut my SSI check to only $72 for the whole month. They sent me a letter, and my sister said she'd call Social Security to find out what's going on, and I'm waiting to hear from her. I'm so anxious; I'm panicked." Her pace picks up. "I just can't get this amount of money for the rest of the month. I'll be stuck inside my apartment. I want to go out. I already made plans to go to the clubs this weekend. I need the money."

Marilyn drifts. Lisa can hear the television in the background. "I gotta go," Marilyn says. She hangs up.

February 9

Lisa's cell rings. Again, Marilyn's speech is rapid and her tone full of panic. She reports, "I'll start the PHP on February 11. Janet is taking me to the Social Security office to straighten out the SSI mess." She answers call waiting. It's her mother. "Gotta go."

March 11

It has been a month since Lisa heard Marilyn's voice, so when the phone rings, she is surprised. As if no time had passed, Marilyn says, "I'm in the bigger room now."

Lisa is confused. She can't quite place the voice. "Yeah?" she asks.

"Yeah. The bigger room."

"Marilyn," Lisa says, "I forgot you only have two roommates. How did you swing that?"

"It was empty, so I asked."

It is 8 A.M., unusually early for Marilyn, who sleeps most days until 11 A.M. Lisa mentions this, and Marilyn explains that she's up early for PHP. Group therapy starts at 9 A.M., but she gets together with friends from the group at 8:30 A.M. to smoke cigarettes and drink coffee. It seems that new friendships are providing emotional support.

"How is PHP going?" Lisa asks.

"Good. It's been a month since I started. I've been sharing lots of personal stuff in group."

"Great. It sounds like you're getting something out of it."

"Yeah."

"How's everything else going? Are you still working with Janet, Dr. Brown, and your new counselor?"

"Yes."

"Is there anything else you want to talk about?"

The question opens a door to Marilyn's inner world. She explains that she is talking more in group therapy about feelings. She is learning how to be more responsible for her actions. However, when she shares feelings with her mom and sister, she feels like they baby her. She feels invalidated and controlled. She is twenty-six and has lived out of the house for a few years, and she would like to make her own decisions. The disapproval bothers her. She feels judged and notices contradictions. Her mom tells her not to go to clubs without money, yet her mom will stay home with her sister's children so she can go out with friends to bars. Her mom also keeps bothering her about the cost of cigarettes; but she, herself, has smoked for a lifetime and continues even though she suffered a stroke and the doctors blamed it, in part, on smoking. She feels her mom and sister encouraged her to leave home but keep reeling her back. She feels guilty when she doesn't submit to them. Her brother shames the family, and she wishes they were not related. Recently, after he badly beat a resident, he was expelled from the group.

Marilyn shifts the conversation and asks Lisa whether she's heard news about Sophie, her friend from the group home—the one who was hospitalized. She also wants to know about her friend Dolores, who recently moved out of the home into a less expensive place. Sophie, Lisa says, is now in a nursing home.

"I don't need Buspar any more," Marilyn proudly reports. "The group at PHP is great and it seems to be helping, especially with my anxiety."

April 1

As part of the study in which Marilyn participates and for which Lisa works, each mental health consumer, like Marilyn, is participating in social network training. The purpose of the training is to help consumers explain their support networks to family members, friends, and service providers and their goals for recovery. They can then develop recovery plans together. Marilyn has identified a list of helpful people. And with Lisa's help, she is slowly making plans for the training at the end of the month. Lisa receives a call and expects Marilyn to talk about this, but she does not. Lisa asks, "How are things at PHP?"

"Good," Marilyn says. "Veronica is going to join."

"I guess you'll be learning a lot about yourselves."

"Yep. Did I tell you I got my hair done? It's black with red streaks."

"Isn't that what you had last year? Or was it red with black streaks."

"No. This is the first time I have black in my hair."

"Are you managing okay now that your SSI check is lower? Are you okay?"

"Kind of."

"Are you getting enough to live on without working right now?"

"Well, yes and no. I could definitely use the extra money from working."

"But you're doing okay, right? I know you'd like the extra money and that your mom is kind of pressuring you to start working again, but like we talked before, you thought it might be better to stick with PHP and get yourself on solid footing again before starting another job."

"Yeah. I still think this is a good way to do this. I wanted to ask you when we're going to do my network training so that we have time to get everyone together."

"Mid- to late May or June."

"I'd say that'd be just about perfect. By the way, I'd like you to come when I graduate from PHP."

"Keep me posted about the day, and I can see what I can do."

"Okay. Maybe when you get some time we can get together and I can catch you up on things."

Reflect

Marilyn is in a panic about money. But today it seems that she is unusually calm and confident about PHP. Like Marilyn, some of your clients may benefit from structured group environments to help contain anxiety and to explore feelings and their relationships. In this scene Marilyn talks of insights about relationships with family. She is making friends (she hangs out with them to drink coffee and smoke cigarettes). It seems buspirone has been replaced by group work at PHP. In a situation like this, help your client notice the connections between the group work, the new insights, and her expanding social network. Help her notice, too, her ability to do for herself. Noticing this now will help her do this work for herself in the future.

We also learn that Marilyn keeps others in mind: her mother, her sister, her friends from the group home (Dolores and Sophie), and Lisa. She reconnects with those she has in mind. After all, it is Marilyn who places the calls to Lisa. This is one of her great strengths: She keeps others in mind and reconnects. What does it mean to keep someone in mind? This means that you can form a mental picture of the person even when he or she is not present. And generally, the mental pictures we form have feelings attached to them. When your client makes efforts like these, help her notice the feelings that motivate her to pick up the phone. You might say, "I am so glad to hear from you. It's good to hear your voice. You know, this call feels significant. I wonder why you chose to call me now. What's going on?"

If your client is feeling good about something—as Marilyn feels about her group at PHP—name the feeling for her (if she does not). You might say, "I hear that you are proud of taking care of yourself and of learning new things. What do you think?" In addition, help your client notice strengths as they occur in the moment with you on the phone. State the obvious: "It is a great to call people you know and trust when you have strong feelings. They can listen and share your joy and pride when you feel good, and they can help you sort things out when you feel overwhelmed and confused." With consistent reminders like these, over time, your client might be in touch with you to say, "I called because I just need to stay in touch. I have mixed feelings about my life right now. I feel pretty bad about my financial situation, but I feel pretty good about taking care of myself. I'm a little lonely, and I was thinking about you, and I just wanted to say 'Hi.'"

Observe

April 24

Marilyn calls to update Lisa about the network training on May 21. She wants to invite a lot of people from the social service agency, where the PHP is held, but the director of the program is giving her a hard time. She demanded to see information about the research study and the network training. Marilyn had given her the information, but she never responded. Marilyn and Lisa set a date to meet to prepare the invitations.

April 29

Lisa picks up Marilyn at the social service agency. It's just after PHP lets out, around 12:30 P.M. At Marilyn's apartment, they look for a place to work. The dining room table, it seems, is too cluttered. There's a microwave. There is an ashtray spilling over. And there are dried sticky rings from soda cans. Marilyn removes the ashtray and wipes the table. She sets out a stack of envelopes, a stack of invitations, and a stack of directions printed from MapQuest. Lisa stuffs envelopes. Marilyn addresses. It is important that people see her handwriting: It conveys the seriousness of her desire that they attend. While they work, one of Marilyn's roommates comes home. She is excited about participating. A neighbor from upstairs, Pam, a sixty-year old woman, heavy and in poor health, comes down and talks about the event, which she will also attend. Pam tells Lisa that she suffered a stroke a while ago and her legs are swollen, which gives her a limp. When they are done stuffing the envelopes, Pam leaves and Marilyn and Lisa walk to the corner deli. Lisa is longing for fresh air. And Marilyn is seeking a pack of cigarettes.

May 6

Lisa calls. She is happy that Marilyn sent her an invitation to her network training.

"I didn't know you were going to send me one."

"I wanted you to have specifics about the meeting time and place."

"I'm planning to be there. Should I return this card or what?"

"You can do what you want, but I'm counting on you being there."

"I'll be there."

"Dolores called. She received her invitation and plans to be there. Veronica will be there, too. I talked to my sister and she's still deciding. I talked to my mom and she's still trying to decide."

"I hope they can make it," Lisa says. "You might want to remind them that, although it's scheduled from 5 to 8 P.M., they can come whenever they want. Remind the people at PHP who you want to participate that they can come and go when they want."

"Okay."

"Hey. I heard that Sophie found a group home. She's not in the nursing home anymore."

"Good. They found her something. That's good. I'm glad for her. She should be happy."

May 11

Lisa is driving on a stretch of Interstate 271 built on the highlands between the Cuyahoga River and Tuscarawas River watersheds. This stretch of road is lined with woods and old farms. It's a peaceful drive. Lisa is headed toward Mansfield to meet family. Her phone rings.

"Hey, it's me. My best friend in the whole world came and visited me today."

"Veronica?"

"Well, she is my best friend, but it was another kind of friend, that special female kind of friend that I was talking about."

"I see," Lisa says, remembering that this is Marilyn's code name for her menstrual cycle. "Sorry to hear you're not feeling so well. So, is there anything else going on?"

"Veronica is definitely coming to network training, and Dolores wants to come."

"So that makes six 'Yes' and four 'No.'"

"What should I do about inviting my friends from PHP?"

"I have extra invitations and RSVP cards. I'll get them to you. You can hand them out."

Marilyn is happy with this. "Yeah. Yeah. I can tell the people that I want from PHP."

"I'll mail the stuff if I'm not going to be on your side of town anytime soon."

"You know, I've been thinking about upgrading my cable."

Lisa gets impatient. "Is there anything else you needed to talk about?"

"No. Not really."

"I'm sorry you're not feeling well. It sounds like a kind of day to lie around and watch TV."

"Yeah. That's what I was pretty much thinking of doing."

"Take care of yourself. I hope you feel better soon. I'll talk to you on Monday."

"Okay, you have a good weekend."

Reflect

You will probably not invite your client's entire network of social support at one time. However, it is useful to familiarize yourself with the people in the network and the strengths they bring to your client's recovery process. Collaborate with your client to evaluate the strengths of each person and decide who might provide support. Use the reflective relationship matrix (see table I.2 in the Introduction on page 14, and Appendix 2, page 217) to understand who might be suited to do-for, do-with, stand-by, and letting-go activities. Sometimes your client will need someone to do for her, for example, during periods of psychiatric crisis (e.g., to pay rent and other bills, to manage money, to manage medication). Sometimes your client will need someone to stand by for support, for example, during periods of stability (e.g., to encourage her during doubts about work or school).

Collaborating with your client to evaluate her support network, using the reflective relationship matrix, should be an ongoing case management activity. In times of economic crisis, for example, your client may have a sister able and willing to do for her in managing her money. This same person, you might find out, may not be particularly adept at doing with, standing by, and letting go. If you find someone like a sibling, willing to be an effective member of the support network, work with your client and sibling to prepare a plan for activating the network when needed and for stepping aside once your client has recovered capacity to manage finances again. The same strategy should be used with other activities of daily living, such as medication management, medical care, and employment.

Work with your client to develop an action plan for crisis, such as relapse. This will be an important opportunity to do with your client in the domains of thinking and action; it is an opportunity to help her engage in conversation with family members, friends, and service providers about her recovery and to teach them about the reflective relationship language. In this context, the action planning process becomes an opportunity for you, your clients, and the people in her network to do with each other—to collaborate for future action. Without action planning, crisis interventions are aggressive doing-for activities. However, with proper planning, future doing-for activity will eventually give way to doing with. Why? Because clients have made decisions about their care in collaboration with others.

* * *

Remember that each person in your client's network of support has a different story to tell about your client's life—her personality, her symptoms, her recovery. These stories are based on many factors, some of which relate specifically to your client's present circumstances and personal history and some of which contain evidence of the storyteller's biases. The reflective case manager listens carefully to the story that each tells about her client and carefully evaluates how each might use the reflective relationship method to navigate his or her relationship with the client.

All human relationships function with a constant exchange of expectation, assumption, and interpretation in which there are many and varied dispositions, including assertiveness, passiveness, and disinterest. Ideally, there will be constant communication about the shifting dispositions to ensure that each person knows who expects what, when, where, and how much intervention will be needed. When possible, educate all members of your client's network about the reflective relationship method so that everyone is equipped with a commonsense, everyday language that enables them to navigate their relationships with each other clearly and compassionately.

Observe

July 2

Marilyn is happy. Relatives of her friend Veronica are going to have their own fireworks on the Fourth of July. Veronica has asked Marilyn to go, so she is buying fireworks to contribute. Lisa is glad that she has someplace to go. Ordinarily Marilyn spends holidays with her mom and sister or with residents at the group home.

July 4

Marilyn is disappointed. She is not going to the July 4 party. Her friend Veronica has canceled the plans. Lisa recommends that she call her mother to visit with her family, especially her nieces. Marilyn says she will call friends from PHP to celebrate the holiday. She is going to set off the fireworks that she bought for the party.

July 10

It is 12:35, Marilyn is done with PHP for the day, and she's joined Lisa at the coffee shop in Ohio City. It's muggy, so they decide to sit inside at the bar, where it's cool and less crowded.

Marilyn's eyes are heavy. She seems depressed and confirms it with the news that Dr. Brown has increased the fluoxetine to thirty milligrams. She's had no appetite; she has little energy. She saw Janet, her case manager, yesterday and felt comfortable enough to talk about her twin brother. At first she felt awkward about disclosing, but by the end of the conversation she felt better. Janet called CPS to request $200 so Marilyn could buy new summer clothes. She is looking forward to shopping and wants to buy clothes in time for the July 25 PHP talent show. She is going to read a poem, "Dream of You."

Marilyn says, "It's about being alone and the fear of being alone. It struck a chord with me."

Marilyn asks Lisa to go on the Internet and get PlayStation codes for her from http://www.cheatcodecentral.com. The codes will enable her to advance to higher levels of difficulty in some of her favorite games and beat the machine. Lisa encourages her to go to a local library and ask a librarian to show her how to use the Internet.

Reflect

At first Marilyn is happy. There will be fireworks. Then you notice a quick change in her mood. Your clients will experience disappointments for different reasons. For Marilyn, this occurs often when she is cut off from those with whom she is trying to be active. There is separation. There is loss. A reflective case manager must be prepared for a client's disappointment and be prepared not to become too active in doing for to make the feelings go away.

Disappointment occurs when experience is out of line with a strong wish or a confident expectation. Disappointment may be a reactive feeling, or it may be a defense or a secretly sought-after pleasure. For some of us, it might be easier to feel disappointed than to evaluate our circumstances, devise a new plan, or initiate the relationships with others necessary to execute positive action.

Disappointment may be one of the more prominent feelings in recovery. Clients may wish for many things, including symptom relief and success and satisfaction with living independently in the community. Yet because recovery is cyclical and nonlinear, clients often become discouraged.

When you find yourself in moments like those described here, help your client reflect on her feelings and how they might be used to change her circumstances. You might say, "Do I hear disappointment in your voice?" If your client feels that she does not want to be alone during the holiday, help her notice how this feeling may inspire a solution. "I hear what you're saying. It is disappointing to be alone, especially when you already had plans and were expecting to be with others. When this happened in the past, how did you respond? What did you do so you would not have to be alone?"

* * *

Know that your clients will not just be disappointed about the circumstances of their lives. They will also feel disappointed in you from time to time, mainly because it is not possible for you to meet their expectations and needs. Be prepared for the feelings you will experience as they express disappointment in you. Be prepared not to react. Use the reflective method to help clients understand the limitations of case management relationships. Also, work with your clinical supervisor to reflect on your feelings and to develop strategies for constructive responses. The nature and quality of your response to their disappointments will make a difference for everyone.

Observe

July 25

Lisa calls Marilyn in the morning to tell her she won't be able to attend the talent show and asks her to share the videotape so she can watch. Marilyn calls after the show, elated about her performance and her supporting performances in the other skits.

"You don't have to worry about missing it," she says, "because they videotaped it. I did a real good job."

July 31

Marilyn calls Lisa to tell her about the meeting with Janet and Dr. Brown on the 29th. She told Janet that she is struggling with depression and wanted an explanation of bipolar disorder. Janet gave her a brochure, and Dr. Brown changed her medication. She told her to stop taking fluoxetine and in four days to start each night five milligrams of olanzapine. She gave her samples and a referral for a psychiatric evaluation at MetroHealth Medical Center. Marilyn is scared about the change in medication. She is afraid that if she doesn't take the fluoxetine, she will hit rock bottom. She is also afraid of the psychiatric evaluation. She has heard stories about people going in for an evaluation and never coming out. She is afraid she will be committed. Lisa knows that as young children Marilyn and her brother had been hospitalized for a psychiatric evaluation. Marilyn has told her about her brother's "weird behavior." And because they were twins, they included her in the evaluation. Lisa assures her that the medication will stay in her system for four days, so she will be okay, and that she will not be held involuntarily. Lisa assures her that many care about her and will make sure she gets home.

August 5

Marilyn calls. She has resolved recent differences with her friend Veronica. She attributes this new ability to her work in the PHP. It has helped, especially, with interpersonal skills. She could have finished the program this month but plans to stay longer, especially with the pending psychiatric evaluation and possible new diagnosis of bipolar disorder. She is proud that she has taken the initiative to enter the program.

"Two years ago, I don't think I would have asked for help. I would have waited until somebody did it for me."

August 16

Marilyn calls. She wants to learn how to use a personal computer. She wants to buy one so she can use the Internet to get access to the codes for her PlayStation video games. Lisa suggests that by using the public library she'll save money. Marilyn refuses. She does not want to ask for help because she is afraid she'll look stupid. Lisa assures her that the librarians will not make her feel bad. They are there to help. She encourages her to ask someone in her helping network to go to the library with her, maybe her friends Dolores, Sophie, or Veronica.

August 18

Marilyn calls again. She took the initiative to go to the library. The librarians showed her how to use the Internet and how to access a few sites where game codes are located. She tells Lisa, "I'm proud of myself."

August 20

Marilyn is upset. She calls Lisa and tells her about a new roommate she does not like. She is inconsiderate. She has guests stay overnight. One of the guests stole her PlayStation and broke her television.

August 22

There is a voicemail from Marilyn: "Um, Lisa. I was wondering. I did not know if . . . maybe I could pay you if I have to. . . . . I'm going to need some help and was wondering if you might be able to help me."

The message ends abruptly. Lisa suspects that Marilyn is planning to move out of the apartment. She returns the call, and Marilyn confirms her suspicion. She is moving back to her mother's. Lisa does not commit to helping. She encourages Marilyn to ask her case manager for help.

The call ends. Lisa thinks the disappearance of the PlayStation has led to a crisis and a strong desire to return home, to a safer place. It must have felt like such an assault on her private space. She needs help from people who will accept her need for safety.

August 27

Lisa calls Marilyn to tell her that she can help with the move. She can hear Marilyn's smile through the phone.

August 30

Marilyn calls. Janet has two hours on September 5. She has a small car that won't hold much, so Marilyn asks Lisa to bring her truck. The moving day is less than a week away.

"Have you started to sort what you will move from what you will throw out?"

"Yes. I've already started packing."

The phone call ends, and Lisa feels satisfied that Marilyn seems to have taken the initiative to plan for and execute the move. She has identified people to help, has arranged for transportation, and has coordinated with her help to identify a moving day.

September 2

Three days before the move, Marilyn calls. Lisa is surprised to learn that most of Marilyn's belongings have been moved. Her mother asked a neighbor and a deal was struck: an old-fashioned barter of time. The neighbor, the mother of a girl Marilyn grew up with, agreed to help, as long as Marilyn would help her daughter with a move home from college. Lisa notes that this is the first time Marilyn has received this kind of help from outside her professional care network. It seems a good example of how a case manager could encourage consumers and family caregivers to build new social relationships. But for this to happen, the case manager would need to spend enough time with the client and the family to know the networks exist.

Reflect

In these vignettes, Marilyn reports that she is taking independent, positive action: She resolves a conflict with her friend Veronica, she goes to the library, she learns how to use the Internet, she decides to move to where she will feel safe, and she manages the details of the move. In addition, she is curious about her diagnosis and wants to know more about bipolar disorder.

Unfortunately, despite abundant evidence of these strengths; and despite her curiosity about her internal world, the mental health system insists on doing for. Dr. Brown, using the same tired way of looking at and responding to her mental life, prescribes a different medication and a psychiatric exam. Today, she adds to the list an illness identity: bipolar. Marilyn had never thought of herself as bipolar. Notice, too, that the exam frightens Marilyn terribly. One might suspect that this fear worked against recently reported positive action and good feeling. One might wonder, was she losing touch with important aspects of herself—her own strengths? She drifts.

When you find yourself in situations like this, resist the temptation to do for in the domains of feeling and thinking about a new illness identity. Instead, align yourself with the strength of her curiosity; do with her. Resist the temptation to focus on the content of her inquisitiveness—that is, the facts about bipolar disorder. Rather, focus on the process: She is inquisitive, she wants to change, she asks you to help her understand. You might try saying, "You are asking me about bipolar disorder. You are wondering about your diagnosis. You have a curiosity about yourself, which is very positive. Why now? Tell me about your curiosity and your desire for me to help you figure this out."

* * *

As a case manager, you will find yourself immersed in the changing moods of others: states and swings. It is helpful to know how the moods of others affect you. Otherwise, you will react for them or to them instead of reflecting with them.

Observe

September 5

Moving day. Lisa arrives at the apartment at 1:30 P.M. She stands in the kitchen, talking with Marilyn, who is washing dishes.

"So, how's it going?"

"I'm so overwhelmed. I'm so exhausted." Marilyn has been doing physical labor all weekend, making room in her mom's house for her belongings and moving boxes.

"That is a lot of work," Lisa says. "But isn't it great that you can recognize that you're overwhelmed and exhausted? You know you're aware of what's going on and what you need to do about it."

"Yeah, I guess."

"You recognize things. You know when to take a break instead of getting burned out."

"Yeah, I think that's because I'm taking my medicine."

"Exactly. Do you see how it helps you manage your symptoms under all the stress of moving?"

"Well, the medication makes me so tired. It just wipes me out. So I come home and sleep. The other day I slept from 7:30 at night 'til 9:30 the next morning."

Lisa notes that this is a common reaction to olanzapine. Marilyn's sleeping through the night is not typical. She is usually a night owl.

"I was fussing with my mom about getting a job, about needing money to pay for things, but my mom was like, 'Oh no, I think you should just focus on finishing that PHP for now. Worry about a job later.' I think this is the first time my mom has ever told me not to worry about getting a job and to finish something else first."

When Janet arrives, Lisa volunteers to finish cleaning the bedroom to give her time to work with Marilyn—to build their relationship. The bedroom is empty. The hardwood floor is coated with dust, scraps of paper, and loose change. Lisa sweeps the floor with a broom, then mops.

"You didn't find any damage, did you?" Marilyn asks.

"No. You're set."

Lisa dumps the dirty water and carries the remaining boxes to her truck while Marilyn and Janet take out the garbage, return the keys to the manager, and sign an exit form. Marilyn was on a month-to-month lease, so there are no financial penalties for moving out.

* * *

The small porch on the front of Marilyn's mother's house is stacked with boxes and plastic bags and old furniture. This is all of the stuff that Marilyn and her sister removed from the basement, which is being converted to Marilyn's bedroom. The stuff is all trash. The porch is a holding bin for garbage day.

There are two very large dogs blocking the path to the garage, where boxes of Marilyn's belongings are being stored until she has the time to arrange her room. The dogs are pacing nervously and barking. Marilyn, Lisa, and Janet stand on the driveway at the tailgate of Lisa's truck. Marilyn looks at the pile on the front porch. She says, "I never sweated that much before, probably because I've never worked that hard in my life." She turns to face Janet. "I think this is going to work out. I worked for three hours with my sister, and we never argued. I like my nieces, but when they start to bother me, I know I can go to my room."

September 23

Lisa calls Janet to check on Marilyn. Janet has no update. She hasn't talked to her since the move.

Reflect

Marilyn is doing a lot of work, but it is not just the physical work of preparing for and executing the move into her mother's house. She is also doing the emotional and cognitive work of noticing her feelings, naming them, owning them, and using them as motivation for positive action. Notice how Marilyn thinks about her current strength. It is the medication, she says. Medication can modulate the extremes of our emotional states, of course. But medication cannot do the work of feeling, noticing feeling, thinking about and making plans for change, and picking up dish towels and boxes and carrying them where they need to go. You might say something like,

> You have mentioned how medication helps reduce the impact of big feelings. But I also notice that you, not your medication, have done the work of taking care of yourself. You experienced a violation of your privacy when someone stole your PlayStation. You took action to protect yourself, to find a safe place. You explored ideas for making yourself feel safe. You initiated a plan. You are now moving boxes and cleaning. That sounds exhausting to me. That is a lot of work. That kind of work makes me tired, too.

Notice in this scene that there is substantial evidence of positive change in Marilyn's relationships. She has an improved sense of reality. She does not argue with her sister and knows to avoid conflict; she values the relationship with her nieces and knows that when she reaches an emotional limit with them she can retreat to a quiet space to avoid conflict. In short, she has an overwhelming feeling but does not become disorganized.

Observe

October 23

Four quarters in the belly of the parking meter limit the conversation in the coffee shop in Ohio City to one hour. It is 1 P.M. Marilyn just graduated from the PHP. Today was her last day. She doesn't talk about the feelings she has about ending. Nor does she talk about the feelings she has about the research study coming to an end. Instead, she talks about her disappointment with CPS. She is thinking about firing them as her payee. They are disorganized. Every time she visits the office, she has to talk to somebody different and explain her situation all over—from the beginning. The counselors believe they have done all they can to reduce her debt; some of the credit card companies will not forgive debt. They recommend filing for Chapter 7 bankruptcy. She doesn't know what to do. Her mother refuses to be her legal payee. Lisa recommends she take personal financial management classes so she can become her own payee.

Marilyn disagrees. "I just can't handle it. I can't do it. I'm not good with money. My sister said she might do it for me. She warns me that she will be very strict."

Lisa steers the conversation to Marilyn's new living environment and learns that the room in the basement is a bit cramped. She recently put her name on a list for an apartment through an organization that provides affordable housing. They can find something close to her mother's. She likes the idea of being close to family. She also likes the idea of shopping at the dollar stores with her mom.

"My mom doesn't want me to talk about leaving yet, at least for another year."

"What will you be doing now that you will not be in PHP five days a week?"

"I've got an appointment with an employment agency. They'll help me find work in a hotel or a restaurant."

"What about your medication?"

"Dr. Brown asked if I wanted to stop the Zyprexa; it's making me so tired, so I stopped. I'm taking Prozac. Twenty milligrams."

Lisa looks at her watch, which has been synched with the parking meter. Marilyn borrows Lisa's cell phone and calls her mom to tell her that they are on the way.

* * *

There is a car in the driveway at Marilyn's house. Lisa turns in and stops near the sidewalk. "My mom's home. Do you want to meet my mom?" Lisa puts the truck in park and shuts down the engine.

Marilyn's mother is sitting on the couch in the living room. She shakes Lisa's hand and says, "It's nice to finally meet you."

The living room is narrow. The furniture is old and almost threadbare. Lisa sinks into a love seat decorated with faded floral patterns. There is a day bed against the wall. The mattress is folded in half. Lisa wonders whether the living room doubles as someone's bedroom. There are three adults and two children living here. She wonders whether everyone gets the privacy they need.

Mrs. R asks Marilyn to turn on lights. The room does not seem brighter. The light is absorbed by the thick tar of cigarette smoke that clings to the walls and furniture. Piles of paper litter the room. Marilyn sits on the couch next to her mother. She is holding a bag of materials from the PHP. She tries to show her mother something in it, but her mother pats her on the knee as if to say, "Not now, Honey. We have company."

Mrs. R tells Lisa that the social service agency that manages the apartment where Marilyn was living is not willing to take action on the missing PlayStation and damaged television. She is relieved that her daughter is home; the neighborhood where she lived was unsafe. And she is enjoying her daughter's company.

"On my days off, Tuesdays and Wednesdays, I try to make sure I do something with her," Mrs. R says. "We don't have a lot of money so we can't go out to eat, so we go shopping."

Mrs. R has noticed a difference in Marilyn since she joined the study and the PHP. Her attitude is different. In the past, when confronted about leaving her clothes lying around the house, Marilyn would throw a fit. Now she doesn't. Hopefully, she will not get bored and backslide now that PHP is over.

Lisa uses this opportunity to explain how the episodes of messiness are related to her emotions. "The piles of clothes are a sign that she is stressed and overwhelmed. It's like her emotions pile up. They get to be too much."

She is not sure that Mrs. R understands. She explains that the network training in May was designed to help her understand when and how to give her daughter help. Mrs. R is intrigued and would like Lisa and the case manager to do the training in the house on her days off, on Tuesdays at 11 A.M., when the children are at school.

Lisa is impressed with her eagerness to learn and addresses her immediate fear that Marilyn will get bored. She advises Mrs. R to encourage her to go to the local library to learn more about using the Internet, to volunteer at a soup kitchen as a way to build her résumé for a job in the hotel or restaurant business, to make an effort to visit her good friends Dolores, Sophie, and Veronica, and to use public transportation as a way to exercise her independence. Mrs. R listens, nodding her head with approval and understanding. After a moment of silence, she says, "What do we call you?"

Lisa refers the question to Marilyn. "What do you want to call me?"

Marilyn does not answer. She gazes at the floor.

"I'm a research assistant."

Mrs. R admits that she and her older daughter want to make their relationship with Marilyn a good one. She seems genuine about this. Lisa can tell. There is tenderness in her eyes and a tremor in her voice, as if she were bracing herself against the thought of losing something. She begins to explain. She says in a soft yet matter-of-fact tone that the family has gone through some difficult times and that her son, Marilyn's twin brother, is not doing well. He has schizophrenia.

Reflect

Take a moment to write a page or two about what you think is happening in these interactions. Just keep writing. Don't worry about the order or organization of your thoughts or writing. You'll do that work once you've finished. After you have finished writing, draw a circle in the middle of a blank page. Inside the circle, using single words or simple phrases, jot down what you consider to be the main themes, thoughts, and feelings expressed in this observation section. Describe. Try to focus on what you actually see, feel, and observe. Consider asking the reporter's questions: who, what, when, where, and how. Do the answers to these questions generate new ideas? Or do the answers to these questions suggest a new way of understanding these interactions? Consider them. Jot them down. Avoid the tendency to ask why. Try at this point not to explain what you see. Consider, too, your senses: What do you see, hear, feel, smell, taste? Then, from each idea inside the circle, draw a line to a point outside the circle. At the end of the lines, try to imagine how the ideas inside the circle connect to what you know about Marilyn. For example, you might consider her experience with work, or housing, or her relationships with family and her social network. Your task here is to try to connect what you know of Marilyn's daily life and history to the interactions you've observed. Write whatever comes to mind. For example, you have learned more about Marilyn's mother and her relationship with Marilyn. Perhaps you've placed something like this in the center of your circle: "Mother seems worried." Is there a way that this observation connects to themes or ideas you've learned as you've read Marilyn's story.

Now, step back from your circles. Look at them from a distance. Do you see patterns? What patterns emerge? How would you now describe the patterns? For example, do you see a pattern of doing for, doing with, admiring, letting go? Now, you might begin to think about how and why certain patterns in relating exist. It is helpful to discuss the patterns you see with a colleague or supervisor. Over time, you will form pictures of how your client interacts and forms relationships with you and others.

On Being and Having a Case Manager Online

Please see our Web site (http://relationalcasemanager.com) for podcasts and additional resources on topics covered in this chapter.

SUGGESTED READINGS

Bentley, K. J. and J. Walsh. 2006. *The social worker and psychotropic medication: Toward effective collaboration with mental health clients, families and providers.* 3rd ed. Pacific Grove, Calif.: Brooks/Cole.

Bradley, S. 2003. The psychology of the psychopharmacology triangle: The client, the clinicians, and the medication. *Social Work in Mental Health* 1(4):29–50.

Cohen, D. 2002. Research on the drug treatment of schizophrenia: A critical appraisal and implications for social work education. *Journal of Social Work Education* 18:217–239.

Cohen, D. 2003. The psychiatric medication history: Context, purpose, and method. *Social Work in Mental Health* 1(4):5–28.

Dziegielewski, S. F. and A. M. Leon. 2001. *Social work practice and psychopharmacology.* New York: Springer.

Floersch, J. 2003. The subjective experience of youth psychotropic treatment. *Social Work in Mental Health* 1(4):51–69.

Longhofer, J., J. Floersch, and J. J. Jenkins. 2003. The social grid of community medication management. *American Journal of Orthopsychiatry* 73(1):24–34.

Walsh, J., R. Farmer, M. F. Taylor, and K. J. Bentley. 2003. Ethical dilemmas of practicing social workers around psychiatric medication: Results of a national study. *Social Work in Mental Health* 1(4):91–105.

Topics for Discussion

1. Consider, in small groups, how you have arranged to say goodbye to a close friend or family member as they prepare to leave home or for a long absence (e.g., school, vacation, work). Appoint a group member to record your discussion. Then consider how Lisa and Marilyn arranged to say goodbye. Describe. How could this have been handled differently?

2. In medication treatment, compliance or adherence to the regimen is an outcome of a relational process between numerous people: psychiatrists, nurses, case managers, group home supervisors, employment specialists, family members, and friends. Imagine how each person in a client's medication grid may have different expectations and make different promises about the work medications do for the body and mind. What

does it feel like when others have expectations for you and those expectations are not met? Discuss how the client and others may feel disappointed when medications don't always work to meet the promises or have undesirable side effects, yet others want your client to continue anyway?

3. Most of us have had experience taking some kind of medication, so use that experience and imagine taking a psychiatric medication for depression, anxiety, or manic symptoms. Ask yourself the following questions: What do you want the medications to do for you? What do you want a medication not to do? How do you know the medication is working? How do you know when you have had too much or too little medication? What is gained by taking the medication? What is given up by taking medication? Will I become dependent on medication? How can I attribute to medication its proper role in producing effects, and how do I attribute other changes to me? These are just a few of the many questions to ask your clients. Often, no one takes the time to feel and think with them about what it is like to live with psychiatric medications. Try always to imagine with your clients the myriad ways medications become meaningful to them.

4. All case management relationships eventually end. Think about the kinds of feelings, experiences, or events that have occurred when a relationship you have had with a mentor, teacher, instructor, or coach has ended. How were you prepared for the goodbye? Were you tempted to avoid talking about a final goodbye? What feelings do you have when you think of never again seeing someone who has taught you an important lesson about life?

Four

Realizing the Promise of Case Management

A RELATIONAL APPROACH TO RECOVERY

In this final chapter, we will look first at how deinstitutionalization, the rise of the case manager, and community support services have evolved. We will show how they follow from and require one another. We will then consider how the relational method proposed in this book relates to this history. For fifty years, the prevailing policy for care of the mentally ill in the United States has been deinstitutionalization. Today, for most, the large state mental hospitals are a distant memory and mostly the subject of historical study. However, in 1975, when *One Flew Over the Cuckoo's Nest* (an Oscar-winning film, starring Jack Nicholson, depicting the lives of the mentally ill in the "total institution") appeared, it was for many, struggling to adapt and survive in communities, an all-too-present reality.[1] Today, former hospital "patients" (our clients or consumers) must live, eat, travel, work, play, and seek help in a radically decentralized and often imagined institution called the community.

And in the transition from hospital to community, a new mental health practitioner was invented: the case manager. Along with the case manager and case management, entirely new practices and vocabularies emerged. These practices, often invented in the moment of working with consumers, have over time been organized into models such as strengths and assertive community treatment (Angell et al., 2006; Floersch, 2002). What is consistent across the many mental health practice models is the presence of the new practitioner called the case manager. Indeed, the idea and history of deinstitutionalization and the history and idea of management go together; they need one another (Mowbray and Holter, 2002:139–142). Inside the "total institution," management was not the concern.[2] Inside the large, bureaucratic state hospitals, the mentally ill were subject to highly rationalized forms of control and surveillance. In hospitals, the object was to control and to treat, not to manage need and desire. In short, there were patients, not cases. There was treatment, not management. Daily needs (e.g., food, housing, healthcare) were not only provided, they were required (Grob, 1995).

Moreover, hospitals were restricted environments. What do we mean by "restricted environments"? First, one could not freely circulate inside the hospital. You were not just confined to the hospital, a specific ward, a locked room, or the surrounding grounds. You were also under the constant, watchful eye of the nurse or orderly. Michel Foucault (2006), a French philosopher and social theorist, called this the medical or psychiatric gaze, or panopticon. In the panopticon, you were watched and monitored from a central observing point, such as the nurse's station or prison watchtower. Your movements and location were monitored in the interest of your treatment. Second, you were not free to work or earn an income. Third, moment to moment, your life was routinized: bedtime, mealtime, therapy, exercise, leisure. One could and often did live a lifetime in the hospital, abandoned by family and buried on hospital grounds. Eventually, critics and social reformers saw these environments as warehouses, as places of horrific human experimentation, where human dignity and freedom were entirely compromised.[3]

In sum, in the absence of the total control offered by the total institution (e.g., hospitals, prisons, schools), one needed management. And management was to take place in communities, where shelter, housing, and other basic needs had to be met through existing social safety nets (Medicaid, Medicare, Social Security, other entitlement programs, county and city government, charities, and family) and the market. With the decline of the large public hospital, case managers replaced doctors and nurses in the daily lives of those with severe and persistent mental illness.

Looking back over the half-century since the beginning of deinstitutionalization, we can see a tendency to rigidly oppose institutional care with care in the community. However, care in the community did not eliminate institutions, nor did it occur seamlessly, nor without its own, perhaps more subtle forms of control, surveillance, and inhumanity: homelessness, overmedication, poverty, and warehousing in jails (Abramsky and Fellner, 2003; Angell et al., 2006). It seems that less visible walls, called catchment areas, replaced hospitals and locked wards. Indeed, many have argued that the movement has been a dismal failure (Fuller-Torrey and Miller, 2002), nor were the barriers produced by social stigma removed (Hinshaw, 2007).

Emptying mental hospitals presented numerous and tough challenges to former patients like Marilyn. Her needs were many: housing, education, employment, medication, meaningful relationships, and mental health and social services. For Marilyn life in the community required constant movement in and out of community institutions: mental health centers, partial hospitalization programs, supportive employment, community college, family. And her case managers were at the center of this unending psychological and physical circulation (Floersch, 2002). Although many like Marilyn lived in their own apartments and homes in neighborhoods, they also, like Marilyn, rotated in and out of intermediate care and residential care facilities: nursing homes, jails, shelters, and transitional living apartments. Indeed, a whole new set of institutions and problems developed around the so-called deinstitutionalized patient (Torrey, 2002). And in this way one might argue that deinstitutionalization is a myth. Why? We are always in institutions, necessarily so, in a creative and continual tension between strivings for dependency and independence.

By 1979, the National Institute of Mental Health had convened a series of meetings that culminated in new policies and practices, known collectively as community support services (CSS). CSS was aimed at mobilizing resources to coordinate the movement of discharged patients through variously organized community spaces (e.g., group homes, supervised temporary apartments, crisis facilities) to "higher levels of independent living" in "least restrictive environments," that is, to independent apartments or homes. Indeed, community support service administrators and policymakers correlated the success of deinstitutionalization with reduction in hospital admissions, resource acquisition, skill development, and service coordination. For several reasons this view limited deinstitutionalization practice. First, it privileged the socioeconomic world (especially successful employment and training). Second, it often placed new consumers or clients in communities with insufficient safety nets—social and psychological. Third, it assumed that these imagined communities would somehow embrace the newly discharged and welcome them into the worlds of work, leisure, and neighborhoods (Leff, 2001). Fourth, it was assumed that stigma (Hinshaw, 2007) could be neutralized by propinquity: The idea was, "We'll live as neighbors and easily adjust to our differences." Finally, it produced a backlash against models of the mind and self and related clinical practices that have always offered useful understandings of human relationships. Soon, under the influence and ideology of evidence-based practice these clinical approaches were discredited or subsumed under the antipsychiatry movement. For some, clinical practice was opposed to community practice, as if one could occur without the other, and even in some schools of social work, clinical social work was set in opposition to community mental health practice. One popular and Whiggish writing of history, written by Harry Specht and Mark Courtney, *Unfaithful Angels* (1993), argues that social work abandoned its historical mission by turning to individual solutions.

There was yet another crucial turn in the history of mental health case management. By the late 1970s, the National Institute of Mental Health, together with a host of activists, researchers, policymakers, and practitioners, charged that fragmented community services and the lack of service coordination were the central barriers to successful deinstitutionalization. They concluded that case management was essential to the task. Case managers would provide the essential coordination of client services, a function necessary to avert hospital care. How, then, were models of case management to do the work of coordination?

In the early years of community support services (1970–1985), managers created their own practice models. They invented knowledge by relying on a "learning by doing" philosophy (Floersch, 2002:43). In the second phase (1985–2000), administrators, policymakers, and researchers sought to standardize community work to meet the growing demand for accountability and evidence-based practice. Moreover, standardization was achieved through fidelity implementation of single models of practice: rehabilitation (Boston Center for Psychiatric Rehabilitation), assertive community treatment (Wisconsin ACT or PACT), broker, and consumer models (Angell and Mahoney, 2007; Simpson et al., 2003). And in general there was a movement away from clinical or psychological conceptions of the mind, self, and human relationships (considered to be hopelessly problem focused or oriented to a person's deficits) toward pragmatism: the management of behaviors and the teaching of social skills.[4] The management of behavior, in turn, could be easily standardized, measured, and manualized. After all, behavioral events and behaviors can be seen, and if they can be seen they can be measured. If they can be measured, it is assumed, they can be standardized. Floersch (2002) describes this as the management of meds, money, and manners. Case managers, now equipped with newly minted management models (some now established with an evidence base), offered the many CSS stakeholders the promise of coordinating resource acquisition and social skill development. Departments of mental health at the state level, national organizations (i.e., the National Alliance for the Mentally Ill), federal policymakers, and local mental health organizations adopted one or another model (e.g., assertive community treatment, strengths, rehabilitation, clubhouse model, family psychoeducation, and medication management), and case managers were subsequently trained in the model's specialized practice language.

Next, the new theorists of case management joined with policymakers and administrators to focus management efforts on producing the conditions necessary for independent living in communities. Here, independence meant living outside the hospital. Yet it was here that both theorists and practitioners of management models confronted a puzzling question: If the goal of deinstitutionalization and community support service was to produce self-directed clients, with what aspects of the client's internal world was the manager to work? And how, in combination with the available external resources, were case managers to understand and practice in the tension between these two worlds? Management models came up short. They could not provide a clinical theory or language sufficient to account for the variations in the self-observing and self-regulating clients in thinking, feeling, and acting with managers.[5] Instead, they focused mostly on doing for in resource acquisition, and this was meant to prevent rehospitalization. Data collected for this book show that managers often found themselves besieged by day-to-day resource acquisition. And without knowing how clinical theory might be used to stimulate client self-direction, responsibility, hope, and recovery, persistent doing for became a major cause of worker burnout and turnover. This affected client well-being, and the excess of doing for affected the most significant predictor of recovery: a continuous and stable relationship with formal and informal caregivers.

By 1993, growing numbers of policymakers, activists, and practitioners had turned to the idea of recovery. And although it is a recent concept in mental health services, it has received widespread recognition across the disciplines (e.g., psychiatry, clinical psychology, social work, public mental health, community support services, case management). And recently the U.S. Department of Health and Human Services Substance Abuse and Mental Health Services Administration summarized the ten fundamental components of recovery: self-direction, individualized and person-centered, empowerment, holistic, nonlinear, strength-based, peer support, respect, responsibility, and hope.[6] Indeed, the idea of recovery has significantly broadened manager work to include the client's internal world. For example, from 1993 to the present, the Ohio Department of Mental Health, at the vanguard of defining and implementing recovery statewide, has engaged in a discovery process to define and construct a practice called recovery, which "is an internal, ongoing process requiring adaptation and coping skills, promoted by social supports, empowerment and some form of spirituality or philosophy that gives hope and meaning to life" (Beale and Lambric, 1995: 8). William Anthony, the executive director of the Center for Psychiatric Rehabilitation at Boston University and a leading proponent of the recovery movement, offers this understanding of the idea. It is for him "a deeply personal, unique process of changing one's attitudes, values, feelings, goals, skills and/or roles. It is a way of living a satisfying, hopeful, and contributing life even with limitations caused by the illness. Recovery involves the development of new meaning and purpose in one's life as one grows beyond the catastrophic effects of mental illness" (Anthony, 1993:15).

Note that these definitions mark a significant conceptual shift in case management toward the identification of client self-direction. For Anthony and many others, the recovery philosophy describes a process that is personal and unique. It is embedded with meaning, responsibility, and respect. Thus, various stakeholder groups— clients, policymakers, family members, researchers, and practitioners—have adopted the idea and philosophy of recovery to organize community work by interconnecting stakeholder objectives with client recovery goals of empowerment, self-direction, respect, hope, and living beyond the disability.

The Relational Method: Implications for Recovery

In this section we turn our attention to a central tension in helping and recovery relationships. This tension—between dependence and independence—is present in all human relationships, at many levels: between partners and friends, between parents and children, between family members, between employers and employees, between teachers and students, between doctors and patients. This tension also exists between nations and between species. In short, we live in a complexly and abundantly interdependent world. Nature depends on us. We depend on nature. Our beloved animals depend on us, and we depend on them.

Our family and ethnic cultures also provide a backdrop against which dependency needs are at first felt and then evaluated. For example, some family cultures and members suffer no negative consequence from feelings related to dependency. Others find the feeling intolerable. And these feelings may be expressed in action (or behavior) in myriad ways, both positively and negatively. Take, for example, the feeling of dependency in our culture that comes with physical and psychological decline in old age; as old age approaches, many feel dependency on children (or anyone for that matter) as intolerable. In other cultures (see Greenfield et al., 2003), dependency needs and feelings are easily felt, negotiated, and met through both family and community practices and institutions. Moreover, throughout life our dependency needs change. From birth to death, we find ourselves at varying levels of dependency: We begin life in a mostly dependent state, and we may end life similarly. Moreover, it is not uncommon for our dependency needs and feelings to fluctuate moment to moment; this was certainly true for Marilyn.

We may also think about having many forms or states of dependency. For example, what does "healthy" dependency look like? How do we know when someone has become too dependent? And are there not times in all relationships (interpersonal, familial, cultural) when we do things to encourage dependency, in both the actions we undertake and the feelings we produce? There are no easy answers to these questions, and they depend on local practices, family and ethnic cultures, and a host of related factors. This brings us back to case management and the recovery movement. The shift from the mental hospital to community-based care and case management was more than a simple reorientation of mental health practice. It was a fundamental change in our relationships (for practitioner and client) to time and space. It was a cultural change. It required our use of self to produce a proper balance between dependency and independence, as we negotiated each day our needs and wants. Let's take Marilyn, for example. In her recovery process, Marilyn moved in her relationship with case managers (and others in the recovery network) in a creative tension between various states, dependent and independent ones, as she defined, sought, and achieved needs and wants. There was an ongoing negotiation of work: the work of doing for, the work of doing with, the work of letting go, and the work of standing by to admire. Each of these, in turn, produced different feelings. Sometimes, though not always, doing for Marilyn was a necessary step toward recovering an independent sense of self, even during the course of a single day. At other times, doing for Marilyn served the needs of the case manager (e.g., just to get things done) or the agency, or complex systems of reimbursement (the agency may depend on case manager doing for activity as the central means of finance). One might even speculate that doing with may be too expensive; in short, the work of doing for will always involve, in action and feeling (for case managers and clients), varying states and forms of dependency.

In this book we have described the work of doing for and dependency in a recovery language. First, we have shown how the manager and client may use the doing-for relationship as an opportunity to move toward recovery. Doing for is a phase, or moment, in all our lives, and we must increase awareness of our own tendencies to do for others; or we may stay joined forever in dependent states. Second, dependence on a case manager may represent an essential background feeling of safety and may therefore become essential to learning. How does this happen? With Marilyn, it happened through the purposeful use of the relationship: the process of transforming the case manager's external work of doing for into an internal emotional and cognitive capacity (e.g., scaffolding) for self-direction. In short, the relationship (doing-for work) formed an internal scaffold used to construct a sense of pride and recovery.

Our study of case management has shown that when we (clients, supervisors, agencies) turn to the case manager for the work of doing for, it evokes a variety of responses, all important to consider in the daily work of engagement and intervention. First, as you saw with Marilyn, it may produce a feeling of shame. This is true for most helping relationships. Think of it this way, always: Whenever you cross the threshold into someone's home as a helper, it is very likely that they will feel you are there to help a damaged and flawed person. You can't make this feeling go away. You can only keep this in mind and when appropriate, acknowledge the feeling. Second, the recipients of case management services may feel anxiety. They may experience your work as manipulation and control. Third, there are times when those engaged with case managers doing for them may experience frightening feelings of dependency; they may fear an engulfing type of dependence. Fourth, because of meager services and the resulting lack of respect, many may not perceive or experience the helping relationship as safe, nor will they feel hope that a measured and purposeful dependence on doing for will produce a movement toward interdependence or independence. Moreover, hope and trust are integrally connected. Feelings of trust can mitigate the perceived external threat of the case manager (too much doing-for activity) or the service world by creating a background feeling of safety, and a potentially conflictual relationship is thereby transformed into one based on caring and recovery. We speculate that the relationship language of doing for, doing with, standing by to admire, and letting go can be understood by everyone in a recovery network, including those who give help and those who receive help: clients, caregivers, service professionals, family members, and agency supervisors.

Implementing the Relational Case Management Method: The Client System

When moving into her apartment, Marilyn, like other clients, lacked the language to name feeling states and associated social relations that ultimately produce helping relationships. In this book we have shown how Marilyn found it empowering to name and ask for specific types of problem-solving activity. At present, the case management system lacks a practice language accessible enough to empower clients to direct the work of recovery. Moreover, problem solving does not take the same form in all domains of life; for example, Marilyn realized (i.e., planned, implemented, accomplished) much of her desire for leisure and intimate relationships without the help of case management or the public mental health system. Because our relationship language and method is experienced near (i.e., it remains very close to the case manager and client experience, understanding, knowledge, and feeling), the method offers a structure for organizing manager and client interactions (i.e., doing for and doing with). Moreover, we have shown in this study that when this method is adopted, the result is the establishment or strengthening of the therapeutic alliance or partnership (Angell and Mahoney, 2007). And in the absence of an alliance, no model of case management (e.g., strengths, ACT) will be effective and may in fact promote varying forms of dependency. Finally, because the method and language are useful across the various divides of class, culture, ethnicity, gender, and context and are grounded in everyday needs, desires, and relationships, they may be applied to all; in sum, they are inclusive and respect the diversity of human experience.

Implementing the Relational Case Management Method: The Formal (Providers) and Informal (Family, Peers, Friends) Caregiver System

With a purposeful use of relational language, providers, family, peer, and other caregivers can help recipients of case management internalize the mental schema necessary for constructive relationships, enabling them to achieve recovery goals. With relapse, for example, the need for doing for reasserts itself. This is true for most of us; when we're in trouble, when we're terribly anxious, when we're sick, we turn to those around us for help. However, doing-for activities must be observed, named, and understood by all involved in the management relationship. This book offers a method to make us aware of this kind of relating. Likewise, when we have recovered confidence, doing-for-oneself activities should be noted and send a signal to all involved in the caregiving networks: Listen and observe these activities, pull back, and support independence.

It would be helpful, too, if practitioners use this language in the recording of progress notes and in what we call a work progress journal. For example, in the progress note, consider the following. How much of your day, week, or hour was dedicated to a kind of doing for that created dependency? List those activities in one column. Next to them, ask a series of questions. First, what necessitated these activities: the client's mental state, a crisis, your anxiety? Imagine the many things you might list here. When do you find yourself doing for? When you're getting near the end of the day or week or when you're frustrated or angry with your client? Who required these activities? Your agency, your supervisor, regulatory or reporting requirements, or funding requirements? Or you might discover that you are psychologically disposed not to do with someone but to do for them. Perhaps this was how it was done in your family culture. How do you engage in this form of relating? By taking control or by encouraging your client to observe with you how, when, and why doing for seems necessary. Do you find yourself doing for in this domain (thinking, feeling, action) over and over again, or does it occur only on occasion? If it occurs with frequency, you may want to seek supervision so that you can inquire further into the repetition. Remember, always, doing for is not a bad thing. Often, doing for is a necessary step in the recovery process (see appendix 2 for progress note grid).

In your daily journal, it might be helpful to observe the nature and extent of each activity: doing for, doing with, standing by, letting go, and the feelings attached to each. Also, the method and language can by used by family members and others in the case management relationship. Relational caregiving is aimed at helping all participants mobilize the power of relationships to internalize the doing-for, doing-with, self-esteem, and self-directed action. Moreover, agencies and case managers may find the language useful in psychoeducation. For example, as you work with families and caregiving social networks, you may want to talk about the relational method to help them get oriented to the recovery process. In a number of ways we might also engage and make more effective the wider caregiving network. First, the method might be used to help caregivers establish relationship boundaries. For example, there may be times when the caregiving network works against the case management relationship to undermine the work of creating independence through too much doing for or through too much admiring and not enough doing for. Second, by working with caregivers we might offer a relationship structure crucial to all case management models (e.g., ACT, strengths).

Implementing the Relational Case Management Method: The Supervisory System

Case management, especially under pressure from managed care and fiscal (economic) crises, must address the desperate need for clinical case management supervision (Cohen, 2003; Kanter, 1987). We are confident that with the relational method, clinical supervision can be reinvigorated, perhaps even reinvented. Agencies and supervisors can use the method as an instrument to support intervention strategies and to encourage the professional use of self. Such a development would reintroduce appropriate and badly needed clinical theories (Floersch and Longhofer, 2004; Kanter, 1995, 1996). In our broader qualitative study of case management we observed an important outcome of case manager and caregiver overuse of doing for: burnout. A relational method and language provide an opportunity for supervisors to examine the ongoing relationships between frontline practitioners and clients to identify the causes of burnout. There is no doubt that the causes of case manager burnout are numerous and complex. However, with the relational method, we are confident that we can at least begin to ask the right questions. First, case managers may easily feel overwhelmed if they are unnecessarily doing for when they should be letting go or doing with. This can be addressed only with careful and thoughtful clinical supervision in an ongoing relationship between the manager and the supervisor. For example, the case manager and supervisor may discover that doing for is in the character of the manager. Often, too, supervisors are so inclined. There are also times, no doubt, when the relational language may be used to help managers understand why, how, and when clients resist efforts to do with.

Implications for Future Recovery Research

In future research on the lived experience of recovery we must begin to pay close attention, probably using qualitative and mixed methods (qualitative and quantitative), to the less visible aspects of management and supervisory relationships. Often, when we look at the effectiveness of methods, we either avoid or simplify the effect of the nature and quality of the relationship on what we are studying. We do this because it is often terribly difficult to measure something as complex, open, elusive, and mysterious as a human relationship. In the research conducted for this book, we examined the less visible qualities and influence of relationships: close, empirical observations of doing for, doing with, standing by to admire, and letting go. Some research relies too much on observable outcomes, such as reduction in hospital visits or in incarcerations. Often this same research fails to consider how the self is used in doing the work of recovery. Although numerous researchers and client advocates have consistently argued that a trusting and continuous therapeutic alliance is fundamental to recovery (Angell and Mahoney, 2007; Bradshaw et al., 2007; Buck and Alexander, 2006; Chewning, 1997; Chinman et al., 1999; Deegan, 1996; Dubyna and Quinn, 1996; Fenton et al., 1997; Frank et al., 1995; Solomon et al., 1995; Stanhope and Solomon, 2008; Torgalsboen, 2001), it is important that we deepen our work to understand how participants in caring relationships develop a trusting therapeutic alliance or partnership.

On Being and Having a Case Manager Online

Please see our Web site (http://relationalcasemanager.com) for podcasts and additional resources on topics covered in this chapter.

SUGGESTED READINGS

Angell, B. and C. A. Mahoney. 2007. Reconceptualizing the case management relationship in intensive treatment: A study of staff perceptions and experiences. *Administration and Policy in Mental Health and Mental Health Services Research* 34:172–188.

Angell, B., C. A. Mahoney, and N. I. Martinez. 2006. Promoting treatment adherence in assertive community treatment. *Social Service Review* 80(3):485–526.

Davidson, L. 2003. *Living outside mental illness: Qualitative studies of recovery in schizophrenia.* New York: New York University Press.

Stanhope, V. and P. Solomon. 2008. Getting to the heart of recovery: Methods for studying recovery and their implications for evidence-based practice. *British Journal of Social Work* 38:885–899.

Topics for Discussion

1. It is important to learn and know how deinstitutionalization has worked in your community and how your agency or organization has experienced the process and responded to it. You might want to interview social workers, psychiatrists, or agency directors to learn more.

2. It is helpful to learn about how your local law enforcement agencies respond to those with severe mental illness. For example, what do you know about how your local jails

treat those with mental illness. Do they offer treatment? What does the release program offer?

Films

Fink, M., M. Douglas, and S. Zaentz, producers; M. Forman, director. 1975. *One flew over the cuckoo's nest* [motion picture]. Los Angeles: Warner Home Video.

Weiseman, F., director and producer. 1967. *Titicut follies* [documentary film]. Cambridge, Mass.: Zipporah Films.

Appendix 1

Funded by the Ohio Department of Mental Health (# 021150), we studied the types of relationships that facilitate recovery. In one research (client) group, three clients (i.e., one with major depression and two with schizophrenia) were followed for twenty-four months while they lived in the community and engaged informal and formal caregivers in everyday problem solving; Marilyn, the focus of this book, was one of the participants in this group. In the second (case manager) group, three case managers and their clients (i.e., two with schizophrenia and one with schizoaffective disorder) were observed for twenty-four months while they engaged in case management. Participant–observation was used to collect the data in both groups; a total of 661 management events were observed and studied (i.e., 421 events for the first group and 240 events for the second).

Recruitment

Supervisors of six mental health agencies were asked to identify case managers willing to participate. Once case managers were identified and consented (the study was approved by the Institutional Review Board of Case Western Reserve University), we asked them to identify clients willing to consent to our participation as they received help or services from them; we consistently collected data on three manager-client relationships. Through meetings at client-operated drop-in centers and at a community-based housing program, we approached clients directly without case manager introductions. These efforts resulted in consistent data collection on three people living with mental illness in the community.

Data Collection

Case managers, clients, psychiatrists, doctors, and employment specialists were observed as they engaged in relationships to negotiate the acquisition of community goods and services. We were immersed in the everyday lives of clients and managers and recorded the oral narratives of participants (for more on methods, see Floersch, 2000, 2002, 2004a). In short, we sought to observe actual case management and routine mental health service delivery. We became participant-observers. First, in the client group, we participated as case managers in transporting clients (such as Marilyn) to appointments, helping them access resources (e.g., grocery shopping), and staying in continuous contact with their experiences of everyday life; second, we observed their service providers and informal caregivers as they interacted with the clients. And third, in the manager–client group we observed managers conduct routine case management in community settings. The client group data came solely from written field notes collected in journals identifying daily interactions and activities: who did what, when, and where. We used audio recordings to collect manager-client data.

Data Analysis

In analyzing the data we used a combination of thematic and grounded theory techniques (Boeije, 2002; Braun and Clarke, 2006; Charmaz, 2006, 1990; Floersch et al., in press; Glaser, 1967). Field notes and transcribed data were read, and wherever interactions referenced a problem-solving event, it was highlighted (we used Atlas.ti software); we identified 661 distinct events. Next, we compared the problem-solving events and grouped them by shared relational characteristics. We found four categories of relational activity: doing for, doing with, standing by to admire, and doing for oneself or letting go. This coding was influenced by Floersch's (2002) previous study of case managers, where he identified a practical manager language of doing for and doing with. Finally, using grounded theory techniques of sorting the codes into higher-level abstractions and creating a conceptual framework for understanding the relational activity, we grouped the relational events by life domains of the client's everyday life: feeling, thought, and action. (The results of our analysis are explained in the Introduction.)

Codebook

Early in the analytic process, we used examples from the data to define our relational activity codes and to devise a guiding codebook. The following illustrates the code definitions that were developed from reading the field notes and transcriptions.

Doing For

CLIENT GROUP RESEARCH DATA

I (field notes) did the searching and sorting of papers in client's room. She was too overwhelmed to focus on our immediate task; I decided to limit search to finding her work termination letter, which SSA (Social Security Administration) had requested for the appointment that we were to make later in the day. This is just easier for me, much easier if I just do it. It takes less time and I can get the paperwork done before I go home. This waiting around for her to do things just gets to me, fast. To be honest, it drives me a bit crazy. I don't know how J (another case manager) deals with this. I just can't be this patient with her, not always. And I certainly feel better when it just gets done and whatever, it's so much easier for me to do it this way.

[Manager *takes over the problem-solving event*—thinking and action—to get the job done, before it was too late and they missed another appointment.]

CASE MANAGER RESEARCH DATA

Manager (transcript from recording) meets home health aide at the client's apartment to clean. Landlord says housekeeping practices place other residents in danger. Persistent problem. To avoid eviction, manager arranges for a home health worker to clean weekly.

HOME HEALTH WORKER: Good morning.

MANAGER: Good morning. Bill, this is a problem! [forceful, concern, irritation]

CLIENT: Huh? [ignoring the manager's tone, seems embarrassed, turns away]

MANAGER: This [pointing to papers stacked on a kitchen stove] is a problem.

CLIENT: It's not a problem. [gaze aversion, back turned]

MANAGER: [irritated] Yes it is. It's going to get you thrown out.

CLIENT: [long silence]

HOME HEALTH WORKER: [uncomfortable with the exchange]

[Manager *takes over the problem-solving effort*—thinking and feeling—does thinking about natural consequences for the client, feeling.]

Doing With

CLIENT GROUP RESEARCH DATA

Client & I (field notes) spent 1–2 hours (before her SSA appt.) searching room for required SSA documents; She seemed okay looking for the papers. I don't know why I felt so different today just being with her. She was more relaxed or something. She found the papers. I just hung around. I was like amazed today. Sometimes it seems so hard to just not, you know, like, take it all over. I guess it's just me, maybe, perhaps that's how I get it done in my own life. Sometimes I get mad at these people this way, like "get a job or something, get over it."

[Manager does not take over problem-solving effort—thinking and action; takes additional time to do with the client in achieving task.]

CASE MANAGER RESEARCH DATA

CLIENT: I need a set of shelves. We can buy it at Home Depot, a set of metal shelves. A whole bunch, I need shelves, close together, maybe six inches clearance, maybe a dozen shelves, so I can put stuff on every shelf.

MANAGER: I don't have a problem with that as long as you keep the stuff off the stove.

CLIENT: Okay, I only put it on the stove because there's no place else to lay it except floor and bed. I put stuff on the bed and the aide come and mop floor and dust. When she go, stove like shelf, I use for shelf. I no cook nothing, I use stove for shelf. I put papers on stove.

MANAGER: So what's holding you back from getting the shelves or from getting something?

CLIENT: Every time somebody dies or someone moves out of the apartment they have apartment sale. A couple months ago they had a whole building sale back by the garage, way in the back by the railroad, they never have anything I need, they have all kinds of stuff.

MANAGER: You just told me you've already seen shelves down at Home Depot.

CLIENT: I assume they have them. I've not seen them. I go down there, carry them on my back I guess. I send Flower [Flower is a delusional spouse of the client] out, she's good at carrying things; she carried a big fan from DrugMart.

MANAGER: And my other concern is where would you keep them, where would you put them in your apartment?" [manager says calmly, quietly, with understanding]

CLIENT: Right in the middle of the floor.

MANAGER: That sounds good, how about at the foot of your bed next to the window?

CLIENT: Okay.

[Manager works with the client in problem-solving effort—thinking, feeling, and action—to keep papers off the stove.]

Doing for Oneself

CLIENT GROUP RESEARCH DATA

Client (field notes) decided it would probably be more practical to call for a copy of her work termination letter; she placed call before we left. She found the number, called, found the right person to talk with. It was amazing to listen to her. I hadn't seen that in her. At first, it seemed like she was mad that I was just hanging, tired, end of the week routine. Headed home in an hour. I just got bored today. That was strange, bored?

[Client takes over the problem-solving effort—thinking and acting. Places phone call without manager intervention. Manager has good feeling.]

CASE MANAGER RESEARCH DATA

Here, a manager and client discuss a savings account and the challenge of keeping the account active so additional charges will not be made against the account.

CLIENT: Yeah, they fixed it for checking account, not with savings account on card when they send it out and I have to have card back, keep same card, they're going to do something internally. I have $213 in savings account.

MANAGER: Hey, you're a rich man.

CLIENT: I not touch that, it must be year and a half. I do not do anything with that. I put $200 in there a couple of years ago.

MANAGER: Well, you do have to watch because if you go a certain period of time and there is no activity in the account, they add charges.

CLIENT: That's why I put money in there yesterday.

[Client takes charge of problem-solving activity—thinking and acting—regarding a money concern.]

Standing By to Admire

CASE MANAGER RESEARCH DATA

MANAGER: You seem really happy about all this. I've never seen you getting so much done. This is really cool. What's up, man? You seem so ready to go with getting this all done. You're really, really, organized today. Rocks. It makes it easier, doesn't it, much easier? I can't wait to tell M [supervisor] about this. What do you think? [communicated with understanding, listened, observed]

CLIENT: Rocks?

[Manager observes and admires the client's problem-solving efforts: thinking, feeling, and action.]

CASE MANAGER RESEARCH DATA

CLIENT: That's why I put money in there yesterday.

MANAGER: That was a wise move.

CLIENT: $10.

MANAGER: Yeah, that's activity. Actually it doesn't matter, if you just take the money out and go back a day later and put it back in, that's activity. And that prevents it from getting reclaimed and sent to Columbus. [manager feels her success]

CLIENT: Very good. [she feels really happy about this]

MANAGER: That's really cool.

CLIENT: Where? [they laugh]

[Manager compliments the client for taking charge of a money management activity— thinking, feeling, and action.]

Our thematic coding focused attention on and identified the elements of case management relationships. We then applied grounded theory techniques and related the emergent problem-solving categories and themes to each other, creating a conceptual framework for understanding how case management relationships unfolded. For example, at times the data suggested that clients were overwhelmed by their disabilities and felt helpless and therefore dependent on providers and caregivers. At other times, they struggled with disabilities, trying to prevent themselves from slipping into helplessness and dependence. At other moments, they lived with their disabilities and managed symptoms. Just as internal (emotional) experiences fluctuated, so did the social relations of problem-solving activities; at times, clients were dependent on professionals and caregivers, who would do tasks for them. However, some were less dependent on helpers and could do tasks with them. Still, at other times, as they regained self-confidence, they needed helpers only to stand by and admire emerging independence, jumping in only when they wavered. And finally, sometimes clients recovered self-confidence and would do for themselves. Our case study of Marilyn is an illustration of the conceptual framework that emerged from the qualitative data analysis.

Interrater and coding reliability was assessed for the establishment of the four problem-solving and relational categories. First, two coders independently coded the data. Second, emergent differences were compared and discussed. In approximately 5 percent (20/421) of the problem-solving observations in the client group, coders disagreed on a match between the codebook definitions and the actual data; in instances of disagreement, data were discarded. Using the same method applied to the manager group data, approximately 5 percent (13/240) of the manager–client group events were discarded. After discarding these, the overall analysis included 628 management events.

Aggregate Analysis

In the client group, we analyzed 401 distinct problem-solving events. As table A.1 shows, the relations of formal and informal caregiver activity were evenly distributed between doing for ($N = 137$), doing with ($N = 130$), and doing for oneself ($N = 119$); in addition, and quite remarkably, there was little activity that could be coded as standing by to admire ($N = 15$).

TABLE A.1

CLIENT GROUP: SOCIAL RELATIONS OF PROBLEM-SOLVING

N = 401 events among 3 clients
standing by to admire N = 15
doing for oneself N = 119
doing with N = 130
doing for N = 137

In table A.2, the aggregate manager–client data are presented. Unlike the client group, where we observed formal and informal caregivers, the data in table A.2 represent only case manager and client problem-solving interactions.

TABLE A.2

CASE MANAGER AND CLIENT SOCIAL RELATIONS OF PROBLEM-SOLVING

	Doing for	Doing with	Doing for oneself	Standing by to Admire	Number of problem solving events
Case Manager 1	44	29	6	5	84
Case Manager 2	28	17	9	0	54
Case Manager 3	39	29	9	12	89
# of Problem solving events observed	111	75	24	17	N = 227

Twenty-three manager and client community-based sessions (about one hour each and audio recorded) were analyzed. These yielded 227 distinct problem-solving events; of the 227 events, 49 percent (n = 111) were doing-for activities. Managers did a great deal of doing for. Indeed, managers tended to conduct more doing for than their informal counterparts (e.g., friends and family). Still, formal or informal caregivers rarely used the problem-solving activity of standing by to admire (a mere 5 percent of the 628 events could be coded as standing by to admire).

The aggregate data, coded as doing for, doing with, doing for oneself, and standing by to admire, demonstrate that strivings for self-mastery and interdependency are common components of management relationships. However, the case manager data suggest that professionals may be doing too much doing for, which could limit outcomes for self-mastery. In short, as one tracks an individual case history (see appendix 2 for a suggested daily charting technique), one would hope to see a balance between all four types of activity. Moreover, the aggregate data show that both informal and formal caregivers do far too little standing by to admire (32 instances out of 628, or a mere 5 percent). Recognizing and appreciating clients' independent action (i.e., doing for oneself) is a recovery principle that the Ohio Department of Mental Health model highlights; our data suggest a need to focus future case manager training on the doing-for and standing-by-to-admire aspects of mental health work.

And finally, these four problem-solving activities did not occur in a linear fashion. Instead, they oscillated over time and within the same day. Figure A.1 represents Marilyn's relational activity over the course of twenty-four months. It illustrates how the relational activities oscillated in a nonlinear way.

MARILYN'S PROBLEM-SOLVING ACTIVITIES

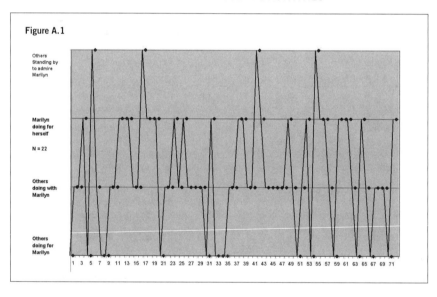

Figure A.1

Appendix 2

Relational Case Management Daily Intervention Note

_____   _____   _____

Client Name   _Date_   _Signature of Case Manager & Client_

Recovery and Billable Event(s)

[check as many boxes from both columns that apply to the interaction with the client]

Recovery Domains
[from, Townsend et al., 2000]

- ❑ Clinical Care (CC)
- ❑ Peer Support & Relationships (PSR)
- ❑ Family Support (FS)
- ❑ Work/ Meaningful Activity (W/MA)
- ❑ Power & Control (PC)
- ❑ Stigma (S)
- ❑ Community Involvement (CI)
- ❑ Access to Resources (AR)
- ❑ Education (ED)

Goal-Setting Services
[e.g., Medicaid billable services]

- ❑ Evaluation and Assessments
- ❑ Participation in development of Individual Service Plan
- ❑ Assistance and support in crisis
- ❑ Support, including education and consultation of families and significant others
- ❑ Individual interventions
- ❑ Symptom monitoring and self management
- ❑ Assist in increasing social support skills and networks
- ❑ Coordination of necessary evaluations and assessments
- ❑ Coordination of services
- ❑ Accessing resources
- ❑ Necessary follow up

Daily Relational Case Management Checklist _(check one or more boxes corresponding to the type of activity engaged in)_			
	Feeling	Thinking	Action
SBA = standing by to admire			
DF = doing for oneself			
DW = doing with			
DF = doing for			

Notes

INTRODUCTION: THE RELATIONAL METHOD FOR RECOVERY

1.   This study was approved by the Case Western Reserve Institutional Research Board. To ensure confidentiality, the names of places and all participants have been changed. The data were collected by Jerry Floersch with support from the Ohio Department of Mental Health. Jeffrey Longhofer and Lisa Oswald participated in the data collection, and Jeffrey Longhofer analyzed the data in cooperation with Jerry Floersch. See appendix 1 for a detailed discussion of the research methods.

2.   You will find at the end of this chapter a long note about how this book might be used in graduate courses on qualitative research methods and in discussions of the uses of ethnography and grounded theory in the study of practice. Also, you will find a list of suggested readings to help you deepen your understanding.

3.   Therapists, clinicians, psychiatric nurses, and psychiatrists will find this account of and method for case management useful in working with both case managers and clients. For example, the relationship method described in this and subsequent chapters could easily become the basis for developing and deepening the supervisory relationship and for organizing a consultation practice. It could also be useful as a planning tool. For example, one might learn that many practitioners are predisposed to work in the mode of "doing for," whereas others are disposed to promoting independence prematurely. "Doing for" may also become an unnecessarily expensive and wasteful use of human

capital. See appendix 2 for a schematic (figure A.2, "Relational Case Management Daily Intervention Note") useful in personal and agency planning.

4. Our title alludes to Erna Furman's book on the psychodynamics of mother–child interactions and development, *On Being and Having a Mother*.

5. We want at this early point to caution the reader about the language used to describe those who practice mental health in communities, "case managers," and the practice they engage in, "case management." We are keenly aware that these terms are loaded with meaning and potential misunderstanding. First, if there are "case managers" there must also be the "case managed." This suggests that we "manage" "cases." People are not cases. And this language is and should be troubling to us. It comes, ultimately, from the practice of law. This is not about political correctness. This is about how we think about and treat one another. We have adopted this language in the book because for now it is commonly accepted. However, as you will see in the pages that follow, we never take our terms and concepts for granted. They should always be debated, challenged, and when possible transformed. We are always and necessarily in relationship with one another, not as objects to be managed but as people in continually changing relationships. Indeed, this book is about the nature and quality of those relationships.

6. For an excellent summary and discussion of the relational paradigm in psychodynamic social work, see Borden (2000).

7. In this book we sometimes use the term *client* and at other times we use the term *consumer* to describe those with mental health symptoms who seek services. You will find that these terms have undergone change. For example, in the mental hospital, clients or consumers of mental health services are generally called patients. When our large publicly funded and managed mental hospitals were closed beginning in the 1960s, we were faced with the need to care for those with symptoms in the community. We also needed an entirely new language or conceptual vocabulary. So we turned to the language of business (*consumers*) and law (*clients*) to borrow what seemed a more familiar, everyday, and appropriate terminology. All of us are consumers, most of the time, of something. Thus, we become consumers of mental health services. Many of us at sometime will become a client in the legal system. And those who manage our services eventually became known as case managers. Clients and consumers, then, became a function of managers. Managers were charged with, among many other things, the management of symptoms in the community. Still today, in hospitals,

one does not often hear the terms *consumer* or *client*. Only upon discharge do people shed their identity as patients to become once again consumers or clients of the mental health system, subject to case management. See Floersch (2002) for a history and discussion of these issues and debates. Much is at stake with this change in language. It's not just a subtle shift in meaning. It has much to do with the nature of power in relationships. And although we'll never find a perfect language for those who receive our mental health services, we should forever strive to remain sensitive to how our "clients," "consumers," or "patients" want to be addressed and, more importantly, understood.

8. It is important to know the distinction between positive and negative symptoms. Psychosis, for example, manifests in many ways and differently affects thoughts, feelings, and behaviors. Thus symptoms of psychosis are often separated into positive and negative categories. They are positive when thoughts, feelings, and behavior are added onto how a person usually thinks and feels (e.g., delusions, hallucinations, and tangential or incoherent speech). They are negative when something is taken away (e.g., motivation, range and intensity of emotional expression, fluency and productivity of thought and speech, or goal-directed behavior).

9. Peter Fonagy, Mary Target, and Linda Mayes have conducted research and written widely on this subject. See "Suggested Readings" for recent work on this subject. See Allen et al. (2008) for a very nice application of these ideas. They also discuss how mentalization relates to ideas in cognitive psychology and the more recent literature (cited throughout this book) on mindfulness.

10. See appendix 2, figure A.2, "Relational Case Management Daily Intervention Note," for a discussion of how to use the matrix in your daily work with a client.

11. It is a good idea to be familiar with the codes of ethics and standards of practice in your profession or organization. See the end-of-chapter resources and discussion topics for an exercise on this and related topics.

12. See Arnd-Caddigan and Pozzuto (2008) for a very important discussion of a relational approach to the use of the self.

13. Some have argued that we should actively engage clients with our accumulated knowledge and awareness of who we are (i.e., our personality, personal beliefs) and with what we know from our professional training. See Edwards and Bess (1998) for helpful suggestions about the professional use of self. They talk specifically about inventory of self, development of self-knowledge, and acceptance of risks.

1. CULINARY ARTS

1. See the end of chapter for suggested readings, especially chapter 6 of Greenberg and Paivio (1997:104–131).

2. See especially chapter 3 of Germer et al. (2005) for a discussion of mindful attention.

3. At the end of this chapter, you will find an exercise related to this topic.

4. Again, at the end of this chapter, you will find a useful exercise on this topic.

5. Case manager safety has become an important issue in our current mental health system. A 2002 survey, among 800 social workers, found that 19 percent had been victims of violence, and 63 percent had been threatened. In a 2006 national study of the licensed social work labor force, 44 percent of 5,000 respondents reported facing safety problems. It is our responsibility to know when we are in danger and to be prepared and to always seek supervision when we are in doubt. See your agency protocol for safety management. Know the protocol. Follow it. Also, see the safety guidelines of the Boston National Association of Social Workers at http://www.socialworkers.org/profession/centennial/violence.htm.

6. See Newhill (2003).

7. We all do reality testing, moment to moment, in two ways. We test to know what is inside us and what is outside us. We test also to know the difference between what is inside and what is outside. Why is this important?

8. To learn more about empowerment, consider adding to your reading list Robert Adams, *Social Work and Empowerment* (2003). In this book, Adams offers a succinct discussion of empowerment along with an overview of theories, models, and methods related to empowerment. He covers self-empowerment and empowering work with individuals, groups, communities, and organizations, including examples of work with children, families, and adults. Also, Peterson and colleagues have written important essays, empirical and conceptual, on community empowerment: what it means, how it is to be studied, and a method for producing empowerment (Peterson and Hughey, 2004; Peterson and Zimmerman, 2004).

9. Salman Akhtar (1999:132–133) argues that we have a need for identity, recognition, and affirmation.

10. For an excellent discussion on knowing and not knowing, see Fulton (2005).

11. See Faust (2008), an especially important article on the role of the social worker as advocate.

12. Anthropologists Douglas Hollan and C. Jason Throop argue, convincingly, that we can easily and mistakenly assume that empathy is always and everywhere a desired goal (Hollan, 2008; Hollan and Throop, 2008).

2. AN APARTMENT OF HER OWN

1. Turnover is very costly, not only to our clients but also to the mental health system; see Gitter (2005).

2. See "Topics for Discussion" at the end of this chapter for an exercise on the treatment alliance.

3. DISAPPEARANCE

1. Jay Neugeboren has written a wonderful book, *Imagining Robert* (2003), about his brother's long struggle with schizophrenia. If you work with people with severe mental illness, please add this book to your reading list, along with Elyn Saks's *The Center Cannot Hold: My Journey Through Madness* (2008). Neugeboren (2008:49) writes, "We all need and cherish the feeling of safety that comes from knowing someone who knows us and cares about us. For most mental patients, however, such a relationship is the rarest of commodities. Even when community centers, mental hospitals, and residences try their best, they are usually compromised by inadequate budgets in which pills—the ultimate downsizing of care—become the primary, and often the sole, form of treatment. Consider: in one six-month period, my brother had seven different social workers assigned to him."

2. Agencies can develop management strategies to reduce costs and improve efficiency by helping managers and supervisors use the relational method—doing for, doing with, standing by, and letting go—to allocate effort across these areas in the case management of money. For example, if you find that some managers have allocated too much effort to doing for in money management, you may want to pay closer attention to their working relationship. You might find that the manager has too many clients in his

or her caseload for whom doing for is necessary. There may need to be a reallocation of effort so the manager is working with fewer clients in this category. Or you might find that the manager also struggles with money management, so it is very difficult to do with. You might also find that some managers should be doing for in the management of money when they are letting go. This, too, would suggest a need to look again at the management relationship so that manager and agency effort can be more efficiently and meaningfully reallocated.

4. REALIZING THE PROMISE OF CASE MANAGEMENT

1. Social scientists across the disciplines were involved in the early critique of state mental hospitals. For example, Thomas Szasz (1961), a psychiatrist argued that mental illness was a myth, invented or socially constructed by psychiatry. See Cresswell (2008) for a recent review and discussion of the debate initiated by Szasz. In a very controversial study (something that could never be done today, ironically, because it would not pass most institutional review boards), sociologist David Rosenhan (1973) placed healthy "pseudopatients," in twelve mental hospitals; they simulated auditory hallucinations to gain admission. The psychiatric staff was then asked to detect the patients feigning mental illness. In one hospital they failed to detect a single pseudopatient. In another they falsely identified large numbers of legitimate patients. The study is still widely cited in the criticism of psychiatric treatment and diagnosis.

2. Sociologist Erving Goffman (1961) studied what he called "total institutions." In one of his well-known books he describes the mental hospital in these terms: Daily life in all its aspects is under total institutional control; people must submit to and are dependent on the authorities of the organization.

3. In 1967, Frederick Wiseman produced and directed a documentary film, *Titicut Follies,* about the Massachusetts Correctional Institution at Bridgewater, a prison hospital for the criminally insane. The film, banned by the Massachusetts Supreme Court, looked into the most private lives and horrors of a prison for the insane.

4. Indeed, many adopted a "deficit model" as a kind of unreflective mantra. With this dismissive talk, one could imagine, among other things, that the self is taken care of once material needs have been met.

5. See Joseph Walsh (2000) and Joel Kanter (1987) for their work on clinical case management.

6. See the National Consensus Statement on Mental Health Recovery at http://mental health.samhsa.gov/publications/allpubs/sma05-4129.

APPENDIX 1: RESEARCH METHODS

1. The research methods used in this study have been further developed and are the subject of a forthcoming book for Oxford University Press by Jeffrey Longhofer, Jerry Floersch, and Janet Hoy, *Qualitative Research for Practice*.

References

Abramsky, S. and J. Fellner. 2003. *Ill-equipped: U.S. prisons and offenders with mental illness.* New York: Human Rights Watch.

Adams, R. 2003. *Social work and empowerment.* New York: Palgrave.

Akhtar, S. 1999. The distinction between needs and wishes: Implications for psychoanalytic theory and technique. *Journal of the American Psychoanalytic Association* 47:113–151.

Allen, J. G. and P. Fonagy. 2006. *Handbook of mentalization-based treatment.* Hoboken, N.J.: Wiley.

Allen, J. G., P. Fonagy, and A. W. Bateman. 2008. *Mentalizing in clinical practice.* Washington, D.C.: American Psychiatric Publishing.

Angell, B. and C. A. Mahoney. 2007. Reconceptualizing the case management relationship in intensive treatment: A study of staff perceptions and experiences. *Administrative Policy in Mental Health and Mental Health Services Research* 34:172–188.

Angell, B., C. A. Mahoney, and N. I. Martinez. 2006. Promoting treatment adherence in assertive community treatment. *Social Service Review* 80(3):485–526.

Anthony, W. A. 1993. Recovery from mental illness; the guiding vision of the mental health system in the 1990s. *Psychosocial Rehabilitation Journal* 16(4):11–23.

Arlow, J. A. 1995. Stilted listening: Psychoanalysis as discourse. *Psychoanalytic Quarterly* 64:215–233.

Arnd-Caddigan, M. and R. Pozzuto. 2008. Use of self in relational clinical social work. *Clinical Social Work Journal* 36:235–243.

Bateman, A. and P. Fonagy. 2006. *Mentalization-based treatment for borderline personality disorder: A practical guide*. Oxford: Oxford University Press.

Bauman, Z. 2007. *Consuming life*. Cambridge: Polity.

Beale, V. and T. Lambric. 1995. *The recovery concept: Implementation in the mental health system*. Columbus, Ohio: Community Support Program Advisory Committee.

Berlin, S. 2005. The value of acceptance in social work direct practice: A historical and contemporary view. *Social Service Review* 79(3):482–510.

Boeije, H. 2002. A purposeful approach to the constant comparative method in the analysis of qualitative interviews. *Quality and Quantity* 36(4):391–409.

Borden, W. 2000. The relational paradigm in contemporary psychoanalysis: Toward a psychodynamically informed social work perspective. *Social Service Review* 74(3):352–379.

Bordin, E. J. 1979. The generalizability of the psychoanalytic concept of the working alliance. *Psychotherapy: Theory, Research and Practice* 16:252–260.

Bradshaw, W., M. P. Armour, and D. Roseborough. 2007. Finding a place in the world: The experience of recovery from severe mental illness. *Qualitative Social Work: Research and Practice* 6(1):27–47.

Braun, V. and V. Clarke. 2006. Using thematic analysis in psychology. *Qualitative Research in Psychology* 3:77–101.

Buck, P. W. and L. B. Alexander. 2006. Neglected voices: Consumers with serious mental illness speak about intensive case management. *Administration and Policy in Mental Health and Mental Health Services Research* 33(4):470–481.

Charmaz, K. 2006. *Constructing grounded theory. A practical guide through qualitative analysis*. Thousand Oaks, Calif.: Sage.

Chewning, B. 1997. Patient involvement in pharmaceutical care: A conceptual framework. *American Journal of Pharmaceutical Education* 61(4):394–401.

Chinman, M., M. Allende, P. Bailey, J. Maust, and L. Davidson. 1999. Therapeutic agents of assertive community treatment. *Psychiatric Quarterly* 70(2):137–162.

The cities: The price of optimism. (1969, August 1). *Time* 94:5, 41–44.

Cohen, J. A. 2003. Managed care and the evolving role of the clinical social worker in mental health. *Social Work* 48(1):34–43.

Corrigan, P. W. 2007. How clinical diagnosis might exacerbate the stigma of mental illness. *Social Work* 52(1):31–39.

Creswell, M. 2008. Szasz and his interlocutors: Reconsidering Thomas Szasz's "myth of mental illness" thesis. *Journal of the Theory of Social Behavior* 38(1):23–44.

Damasio, A. R. 1994. *Descartes' error: Emotion, reason, and the human brain.* New York: G.P. Putnam.

Deegan, P. 1988. Recovery: The lived experience of rehabilitation. *Psychosocial Rehabilitation Journal* 11(4):11.

Deegan, P. 1996. Recovery as a journey of the heart. *Psychiatric Rehabilitation Journal* 19(3): 91–97.

Drake, R. E. and G. R. Bond. 2008. The future of supported employment for people with severe mental illness. *Psychiatric Rehabilitation Journal* 31(4):367–376.

Dubyna, J. and C. Quinn. 1996. The self-management of psychiatric medications: A pilot study. *Journal of Psychiatric Mental Health Nursing* 3(5):297–302.

Edwards, J. K. B. and J. M. Bess. 1998. Developing effectiveness in the therapeutic use of self. *Clinical Social Work Journal* 26(1):89–105.

Faust, J. R. 2008. Clinical social worker as patient advocate in a community mental health center. *Clinical Social Work Journal* 36(3):293–300.

Fenton, W. S., C. R. Blyler, and R. K. Heinssen. 1997. Determinants of medication compliance in schizophrenia: Empirical and clinical findings. *Schizophrenia Bulletin* 23(4):637–651.

Floersch, J. 2000. Reading the case record: The oral and written narratives of social workers. *Social Service Review* 74(2):169–192.

Floersch, J. 2002. *Meds, money and manners: The case management of severe mental illness.* New York: Columbia University Press.

Floersch, J. 2004a. A method for investigating practitioner use of theory in practice. *Qualitative Social Work* 3(2):161–177.

Floersch, J. 2004b. Practice ethnography: A case study of invented clinical knowledge. In *The qualitative research experience,* ed. D. K. Padgett, 76–96. Stamford, Conn.: Wadsworth/International Thomson.

Floersch, J., J. Longhofer, D. Kranke, and L. Townsend. In press. Integrating thematic, grounded theory, and narrative analysis: A case study of adolescent psychotropic treatment. *Qualitative Social Work.*

Floersch, J. and J. Longhofer. 2004. Psychodynamic case management. In *Psychodynamic social work,* ed. J. Brandell, 350–369. New York: Columbia University Press.

Floersch, J., J. Longhofer, and M. Nordquest-Schwallie. 2009. Ethnography. In *Thinking about social work: Theories and methods for practice*, ed. M. Gray, 152–160. New York: Oxford University Press.

Fonagy, P. 2002. *Affect regulation, mentalization, and the development of the self.* New York: Other Press.

Foucault, M. 2006. *History of madness.* London: Routledge.

Frank, E., D. J. Kupfer, and L. R. Siegel. 1995. Alliance not compliance: A philosophy of outpatient care. *Journal of Clinical Psychiatry* 56(1):11–17.

Freedberg, S. 2007. Re-examining empathy: A relational–feminist point of view. *Social Work* 52(3):251–259.

Fuller-Torrey, E. and J. Miller. 2002. *The invisible plague: The rise of mental illness from 1750 to the present.* New Brunswick, N.J.: Rutgers University Press.

Fulton, P. 2005. Mindfulness and psychotherapy. Mindfulness as clinical training. In *Mindfulness and psychotherapy*, ed. C. K. Germer, R. D. Siegel, and P. R. Fulton, 70–73. New York: Guilford.

Furman, E. 2001. *On having and being a mother.* Madison, Conn.: International Universities Press.

Germer, C. K., R. D. Siegel, and P. R. Fulton. 2005. *Mindfulness in psychotherapy.* New York: Guilford.

Gitter, R. J. 2005, March. The cost to employers of case manager turnover in Ohio's mental health system. *New Research in Mental Health* 16:170–174.

Glaser, B. and A. Strauss. 1967. *Discovery of grounded theory. Strategies for qualitative research.* Mill Valley, Calif.: Sociology Press.

Goffman, I. 1961. *Asylums: Essays on the social situation of mental patients and other inmates.* New York: Doubleday.

Greenberg, L. and S. Paivio. 1997. *Working with emotions in psychotherapy.* New York: Guilford.

Greenfield, P. M., H. Keller, A. Fuligni, and A. Maynard. 2003. Cultural pathways through universal development. *Annual Review of Psychology* 54:461–490.

Grob, G. 1995. *The mad among us: A history of the care of America's mentally ill.* Cambridge, Mass.: Harvard University Press.

Halpern, J. 2001. *From detached concern to empathy: Humanizing medical practice.* New York: Oxford University Press.

Hinshaw, S. P. 2007. *The mark of shame: Stigma of mental illness and an agenda for change.* Oxford: Oxford University Press.

Hollan, D. 2008. Being there: On the imaginative aspects of understanding others and being understood. *Ethos* 36(4):475–489.

Hollan, D. and C. J. Throop. 2008. Whatever happened to empathy?: Introduction. *Ethos* 36(4):385–401.

Kandel, E. R. 2005. *Psychiatry, psychoanalysis, and the new biology of mind.* Washington, D.C.: American Psychiatric Publishing.

Kanter, J. S. 1987. Mental health case management: A professional domain? *Social Work* 32(5):461–462.

Kanter, J., ed. 1995. *Clinical studies in case management.* San Francisco: Jossey-Bass.

Kanter, J. 1996. Case management with longterm patients: A comprehensive approach. In *Handbook for the treatment of the seriously mentally ill,* ed. S. M. Soreff, 257. Seattle: Hogrefe & Huber.

Leff, J. 2001. Why is care in the community perceived as a failure? *British Journal of Psychiatry* 179:381–383.

Longhofer, J. and J. Floersch. 2004. The phenomenological practice gap: The role of qualitative research in studies of practice guidelines, evaluation, and clinical judgment. *Qualitative Social Work* 3(4):483–486.

Longhofer, J., J. Floersch, and J. Jenkins. 2003. The social grid of community medication management. *American Journal of Orthopsychiatry* 73(1):24–34.

MacLaren, C. 2008. Use of self in cognitive behavioral therapy. *Clinical Social Work Journal* 36(3):245–253.

Mowbray, C. T. and M. C. Holter. 2002. Mental health and mental illness: Out of the closet? *Social Service Review* 76(1):135–179.

Neugeboren, J. 2003. *Imagining Robert: My brother, madness, and survival.* New Brunswick, N.J.: Rutgers University Press.

Neugeboren, J. 2008. *New York Review of Books,* 50, 49.

Newhill, C. 2003. *Client violence in social work practice: Prevention, intervention and research.* New York: Guilford.

Peterson, A. and J. Hughey. 2004. Social cohesion and intrapersonal empowerment: Gender as moderator. *Health Education Research* 19(5):533–542.

Peterson., A. and M. Zimmerman. 2004. Beyond the individual: Toward a nomological network of organizational empowerment. *American Journal of Community Psychology* 34(1–2):129–145.

Reid, W. 2002. Knowledge for direct social work practice: An analysis of trends. *Social Service Review* 76(1):6–33.

Rosenhan, D. L. 1973. On being sane in insane places. *Science* 179(70):250–258.

Roth, A. and P. Fonagy. 2005. *What works for whom?: A critical review of psychotherapy research.* New York: Guilford.

Saks, E. R. 2008. *The center cannot hold: My journey through madness.* New York: Hyperion.

Siegel, D. J. 1999. *The developing mind: Toward a neurobiology of interpersonal experience.* New York: Guilford.

Simpson, A., C. Miller, and L. Bowers. 2003. Case management models and the care programme approach: How to make the CPA effective and affordable. *Journal of Psychiatric and Mental Health Nursing* 10(4):472–483.

Solomon, P., J. Draine, and M. A. Delaney. 1995. The working alliance and consumer case management. *Journal of Mental Health Administration* 22(2):126–134.

Specht, H. and M. E. Courtney. 1993. *Unfaithful angels: How social work has abandoned its mission.* New York: Free Press.

Stanhope, V. and P. Solomon. 2008. Getting to the heart of recovery: Methods for studying recovery and their implications for evidence-based practice. *British Journal of Social Work* 38:885–899.

Strauss, A. and J. Corbin. 1990. *Basics of qualitative research: Grounded theory procedures and techniques.* Newbury Park, Calif.: Sage.

Szasz, T. 1961. *The myth of mental illness: Foundations of a theory of personal conduct.* New York: Harper and Row.

Torgalsboen, A. K. 2001. Consumer satisfaction and attributions of improvement among fully recovered schizophrenics. *Scandinavian Journal of Psychology* 42(1):33–40.

Townsend, W., S. Boyd, G. Griffin, and P. L. Hicks. 2000. *Emerging best practices in mental health recovery.* Columbus: Ohio Department of Mental Health.

Walsh, J. 2000. *Clinical case management with persons having mental illnesses: A relationship-based perspective.* Pacific Grove, Calif.: Brooks/Cole.

Walsh, J. and J. Corcoran. 2006. *Clinical assessment and diagnosis in social work practice.* New York: Oxford University Press.

Wurtzel, E. 1995. *Prozac nation: Young and depressed in America.* New York: Riverhead.

Index